Criticizing Ben Franklin

Quips, Quotes and Quandaries

GTC Press
Indianapolis, IN USA
Ken Omar Eldib

Criticizing Ben Franklin

Quips, Quotes and Quandaries

Table Of Contents

Introduction	1
Adam and Eve-n	2
Advice	3
Aging	4
America	9
Authority	11
Banksters	12
Battle of the Sexes	14
Bees and Ants…	17
Beauty	19
Ben Franklin	19
Bias	22
Bird World	23
Britain	25
Bugs	26
Business	28
Capitalism	33
Children (young and old)	34
Climate Change	40
Competition	42
Conflict and War	43
Conforming	48
Conspicuous consumption	49
Cryonics	52
Debt	54
Democracy	56
Diversity?	58
Dogs (Man's Beast Friend!)	60
Dreams	64
Driving	66
Drugs (and Alcohol)	69
Economy	73
Elites	77
Environment	77
Experience	79

<u>**Table Of Contents**</u>

Family and Relatives	**80**
Food and Drink	**82**
Freedom and Free Speech	**85**
Freedom of Association	**87**
Friends and Neighbors	**88**
Genius and Stupidity	**92**
Generation Gap	**94**
God and Religion	**95**
Government	**105**
Greed	**106**
Green Acres!	**107**
Group Think	**109**
Handyman Stuff	**109**
Haters, Sickos and Sociopaths	**112**
Healing and health	**113**
Heaven	**115**
Heroes	**116**
History	**118**
Holidays	**120**
Home Improvement	**121**
Human Nature	**122**
Humility	**125**
Hypocrisy	**126**
Karma	**127**
Language, Buzzwords and "New speak"	**127**
Law and Order	**129**
Leaders	**129**
Loyalty and trust	**130**
Machismo	**132**
Marriage, Women and Wives	**133**
Meek Shall Inherit the Earth…	**141**
Military Industrial complex	**141**
Moderation, Willpower and Delayed Gratification	**143**
Money and wealth…	**145**
Mother Nature	**149**
Music	**153**
Nukes	**154**
Obligations	**156**
Oil	**158**

Table Of Contents

Order or Chaos?	**159**
Patriotism	**161**
Peace	**161**
Peer Pressure	**163**
Police	**167**
Politics	**167**
Poverty	**169**
Power	**172**
Presidents of the United States	**173**
Quips	**175**
Regrets	**179**
Renting	**180**
Respect	**181**
Rome	**182**
Secrets	**183**
Sitting on the Fence	**184**
Smoking	**185**
Society	**187**
Soldiers	**188**
Space Case	**190**
Sports and Extra-cise	**192**
Success (Failure)	**194**
Surveillance Nation	**199**
Think Tanks	**200**
Time	**201**
Torture	**201**
Tradition	**202**
Tribes and Natives	**203**
Truth, Lies and Videotape	**205**
TV, Media and Movies	**208**
Violence	**211**
Voting	**211**
WWW	**212**
Weeds and Gardens…	**213**
Winter Take All!	**215**
Wisdom	**218**
Work	**219**
Writing	**222**
About the Author	**225**

Introduction

Quips, criticism, observations, common sense or nonsense… you decide! My desire is to encourage independent thought instead of automatically agreeing with or taking the word of *anyone*.

When I set out to critique Ben Franklin I thought it would be a lonely task, he's a giant of history and one of our most *sacred cows*. It didn't take long to find that Ben has been criticized for a long time… it also wasn't long before I realized that Mr. Franklin was indeed a great man!

Chapters begin and end with quotes I've come across related to that chapters' content. The rest are my thoughts, based on my years of life.

This book is for you if you're interested in an atypical view about; the sexes, race, space, war, religion, business, politics and other perplexing subjects.

I've tried to write in a humorous, distinctive style and present a unique perspective due to my background and experiences. I've been married for 26 years, raised a family, been a business owner for over 20 years and seen a fair amount of the country and world.

Dedicated to Ben Franklin and Mark Twain…

Adam and Eve-n

"I see that I was mistaken about Eve… it's better to live outside the Garden with her, than inside it without her" … Mark Twain

God *gave* Adam a wonderful gift, but he also may have been playing tricks. Eve was *made* to be irresistible so procreation would work, but Adam and Eve found it nearly impossible to get along. Our needs and biological imperatives overlap, but we're more like different species than different genders.

Men sometimes find women somewhat *ridiculous*, but we're drawn to them like moths to a flame… okay, *maybe* we're the ridiculous ones, but we're still like moths to the flame… I think you know why.

I suppose I could do some research into the origin of the word woman, but it's more fun to speculate. .. woman = wee-man, womb-man, woe(to)-man, woah(nelly)-man!

Have you ever noticed there's at least one good-looking waitress in every restaurant... or at least a *best looking* one to whom everyone's eyes are drawn!

How can a middle-aged man, think some young beauty should replace his wife? Shouldn't we value our wives more than that? Unfortunately men *and* women get a little crazy over time and follow their baser instincts, hormones etc.

How many times have we said, "If she were just five years older… or twenty years younger." Dreaming and fantasizing… we do a lot of that.

Women do their best to look young and fertile… this attracts men, who woo such women with gifts and compliments. The gals eventually succumb to these overtures and the cycle continues, but not without incident. The *system* - though effective for procreation and continuation of the species is far from perfect.

Is it inconsistent to love and respect women, but believe men should not be ruled by them? For that matter, ideally men and women should not be ruled by anyone, but there must be some laws... but being governed is different than being ruled.

Like an orgasm, shedding tears is a *release*... maybe that's why women cry more than men. Since women have more difficulty climaxing, crying may be a way to compensate. Reportedly, crying, climaxing, laughing and even pleasant conversation release endorphins. They say laughter is the best medicine, but I cast my vote for climaxing and place crying a distant third... certainly stewing is the worst pill to take.

Shoes are nice and men notice them... not as much as your girlfriends, but we notice. First however, we notice your face and the figure, regrettably brains and personality rank no higher than shoes on most guys' list.

"God's little gift is on the rag, poster girl posing in a fashion mag...Canine, feline, Jekyll and Hyde"... Cheryl Crow.

Advice

"Advice is what we ask for when we already know the answer but wish we didn't"... Erica Jong

If you seek advice from idiots, you'll get idiotic advice. They'll do their best to convince you the world is unfair. Like everyone, they want their world view *validated,* and dragging other people down works fine for them.

The wise man is often unavailable to dispense advice, as he's busy learning new things... the fool is always available, because he already *knows* everything!

No one is a *nobody*, we're all unique... we are all *somebody*!

When a successful person gives you advice, it's not *just* from them... they've received it from other successful people. In the end, you're benefiting from generations of good advice, when you listen to them. The theory's the same

regarding advice from knuckle heads, they're giving you the same *wrong* advice that was given to them.

When you're advised to *do one thing right every day*, it really means -- do more things right than wrong, that way your day will be net positive. You'll have had a good day, when the plus side outweighs the negative.

The fool doesn't *always* give poor advice, but you usually get what you pay for! In fact, a fools free advice is worth only a fraction of its cost... it usually does more harm than good.

Like most people, I'm *full of it...* advice I mean, but it must be lousy because no one listens, much less heeds!

Successful people aren't so much *right*, as they're followers of good advice... so called *losers* aren't so much wrong, as they're followers of bad advice. That doesn't change their feelings about each other, the loser still resents the winner. There are so many people setting good examples, that I must ask... why don't we listen to them, instead of the bone heads?

Have you ever noticed how many second string football players become coaches, and how few *first stringers* do?

You'll meet lots of people who want to *have* things, only occasionally do you meet somebody who wants to *change* things.

People are always offering me free advice -- especially when I don't want it. On the other hand, if there's something I really want to know, they clam up!

If it's true that dummies touch a hot stove more than once, why is it that repeat the mistake, in the form of hot utensils, plates etc? I don't *just* mean getting burned by something hot, it also applies to mistakes of judgment.

Aging

"A person's memory has no more sense than his conscience"... Mark Twain.

Oh, to be 18 again and not blow it this time!

What *am* I anyway? This crumbling body, or this faltering mind?

Life is so short that we can't comprehend our insignificance, it's still as worth living as ever and you don't find people standing in line for the alternative.

Don't write lists, or voice record everything you're trying to remember... instead of artificial memory, use your brain… if you don't use it, won't you loose it? However, when it comes to life and death matters have a backup system. I've lost my "list" so I have lost my mind... I need to find my list!

What is *instinct*, other than collectively remembering something *that works*. Whether an ant or a human, we have memories and some are so ingrained as to be instincts.

The human body is like Humpty Dumpty... when things break, they can never be put together *as good as new* - so take care of yourself!

Funny…turning 51 wasn't nearly as traumatic as 50… by then the damage was done! That darned 50th birthday was rough, but probably more fun than sixty or 70 might be. On the plus side, fifty has advantages, now I can *legitimately* avoid things like tubing and skiing … all I have to do is mention my advanced age.

Will life's *tribulations* make me stronger or just give me more gray hair? Father time and Mother Nature still reign …they always will!

"We may not understand the meaning of our life until we're forty"… unknown. Most people are trying to understand it long before then, but when we're forty we may be too *invested* in our world view to change. By then, we've been spouting the same lines for decades and don't want to *lose face* by jumping ship... that doesn't mean we shouldn't, or that it's impossible! Actually, it's a victory not a capitulation to change some of our views… we should consider the possibilities!

I know I'm getting old because I'm older than; the president and virtually all athletes, not to mention many of the trees and buildings around here!

As we age, the last things to go are our strongest instincts. In a nursing home, old men still have a roving eye and old ladies love babies and shoes.

Ben said, "two things in life are certain... death and taxes", and you might add to that list *never ending* bills. Regardless of what lifestyle we choose, the bills roll in and the struggle continues. As we age, we look forward to *checking out* and moving on to something better… or to at least getting a long rest. The ideal life is doing something you like, paying the bills and growing old gracefully, or excitingly if you prefer!

It's not unusual for the *proud and haughty* to become the *mean and nasty* as they age and realize they haven't accomplished what they set out to. Those who are humble earlier on, may not turn nasty, since things were never so great in the first place!

Looking in the mirror after the business trip he thought, "dang, I did some damage." Five days later, he still hadn't ventured onto the scales… he did his breast, not his best… the result is, man boobs, frick'n man boobs...

For the most part, we're sucked through the intake and spit out the exhaust… fuel for the Earth's as it circles the sun… the most we can hope for is a good run and maybe a small role in this passion play.

Young people say "don't trust anyone over thirty." People in their seventies often don't trust people under sixty, people in their sixties don't trust people in their fifties and so on… hmmm.

What is this "sleep" that everyone talks about? The only thing I'm experiening is deprivation of that dreamy state.

***If* there's anything "good" about losing your memory, it's the exercise you get hustling from room to room trying to remember what your there for.**

Regarding loss of memory, impotence, dry box etc., its possible to slow them down but impossible to curtail the… so come to terms with it!

How long does it take to forget something? It depends… a year's sufficient for most things, such as bad investment decisions and the like. That's why we keep falling for the same scams over and over.

Our butts get flat as we age… do they look even worse because our bellies never stop growing?

When's the last time you went up the stairs two or three at a time? It's been a while, but occasionally I'm still good for two at a time.

There seem to be some years that are developmentally "important" and others that we rarely hear about. Four, ten, thirteen, eighteen and twenty-one, seem like milestones, but the intervening years are seldom discussed.

Is heart bypass much different than rebuilding your car's engine, and isn't a transplant a lot like installing a rebuilt engine in your car?

If we are slowly dying *anyway*, does smoking, drinking and eating junk...just mean we're speeding up the process?

Maybe the brain is *equipped* to help us as we approach the end. For years, we snicker and think, "I still have a few good years left." Later, when the good years are behind us, the brain slowly shuts down, leaving us incapable of comprehending our plight…

Just as ADD serves a purpose, so does forgetting… would you want *to* remember every face you see, and everything you hear?

By the time you start "celebrating" the fact that so-and-so is bald and you're not, you're too old to *enjoy* it!

I used to have a pretty good arm, now, I throw like a girl… darn thing just doesn't work the way it used to.

Our neighborhood's graying… the men who were in their prime when we moved in, are now on waiting lists for transplants, or sadder still - they're dead.

Too bad we can't throw people in the dryer for a few minutes to get rid of the wrinkles!

Time doesn't really pass faster for adults than it does for children. We're just more cognizant that the sand is running out of the hourglass.

It's always something, but that's a good thing, if we weren't constantly *dealing* with things, we'd be dead! Like aches and pains… sometimes, they're the only way you know you're alive. In fact, feeling like you're dying makes you appreciate living like nothing else!

Funny how we rationalize things, I'm north of 50, but keep telling myself I might have 20 or 30 good years left. If I make it to 70, I'll be saying the same thing… we just keep pushing back the day of reckoning!

I feel for beautiful women, as they age, they fall much further than the rest of us. They continue to be judged by their appearance, which even in the best case scenario is a loosing proposition. Eventually, they become invisible like the rest of us -- welcome to the club ladies, it's really not that bad!

I thought life was supposed to get less complicated as we got a little older, with the kids moving on. So far, exactly the opposite has occurred… maybe it's in "old age" that things will get less complicated, but looking at my parents lives, I doubt that too.

The "expert" said that with medical breakthroughs, some baby boomers could live to be 150 and new babies might live to be 1,000… tell that to Methuselah.

My body's like that old truck in the barn… if I can *keep it running*, it might keep going for a long time, but once it rusts out, it's impossible to restart. The same can be said of our bodies… if we get too run down, forget about it! Maybe there'll be cheap, reliable replacement parts for us eventually, but that day seems very far away!

As we age, we're still *recognizable,* but as we approach the end, we become mere shadows of our selves, *fortunately* by then we're may neither know, or care.

When we finish our life's work, we're "called home", so why hurry? Whether it's your yard, job or whatever, take your time! Don't admit that you're finished and maybe the good Lord will allow you another season of work.

They say you see a lot more old drunks than old doctors... is that true, or do drunks just look old, sooner than doctors?

Are you better off than having a long memory so you never forget slights, or having a short memory so that you quickly forget them? You tell me!

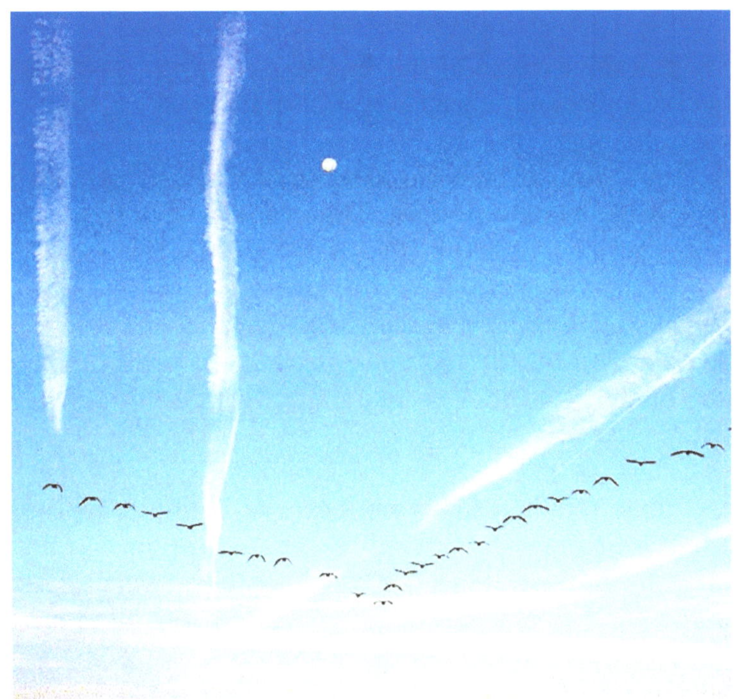

America

"What the American public doesn't know, is what makes it the American public"... Mark Twain

I wonder... if the earth was ever attacked by aliens, would Earthlings join together and stand united against them? Or just as we have divided and conquered our foes, would the aliens use the same strategy successfully on us?

There's got to be something in the water... people in different parts of the country all seem to; look, talk, and act a little different.

America is a great country, our border guards give illegal immigrants water when they have been abandoned in the desert by their Coyote guides… this wouldn't happen in some countries.

When America started, its founders had dreams of freedom and opportunity for most of its citizens, but our country was terribly flawed by slavery and Indian Wars. America's virtuousness has been as chartable as the stock market… there've been booms, busts and a depression or two.

I hope the U.S. can solve its problems, but we're discouraged from discussing exactly *why* we're in the shape we're in, and that doesn't help!

We're told we're Americans, not hyphenated Americans, and that we must stand together for the common cause. The problem with this is it requires abandoning ones heritage in favor of a common cause that benefits certain people over others... in my case, the *common cause* may be detrimental to my relatives in the Middle East. I'd rather work for a just and peaceful solution in the Middle East than for the *solution* promoted by various special interest groups. Unfortunately for me, I'm told to go with that flow, or I'm not a *true* American.

Yes, I'm grateful my father, and my mother's ancestors came to this great country, but that gratitude is tempered by the realization that my relatives overseas seem to be doing quite well. Over here, we're very small fish in a very large pond… in the "old countries" my relatives seem to have greater opportunity to effect their society than we do here.

We're reminded we should be grateful to the army, in the *old days*, we were told we should be "grateful to the king." Humans are social beings and do better when part of a group, so cooperation is essential and reasonable gratitude is good. However, those harping that we should be grateful to them have an ulterior motive…its called lust for power.

Funny how we complain so much about the French, who helped us win our independence, and complain much less about the British who were our overlords.

Have you ever noticed that Americans say "counterclockwise and Brit's say "anti-clockwise"… peculiar folks those limeys!

We have purges here too… but in our case, you don't end up in Siberia, you end up as a Washington lobbyists. It's a strength of our system that we don't have violent purges, but a weakness that such rogues remain in the power structure at all.

This *is* a great nation, so instead of resting on our laurels and bragging, we should work even harder to improve our society... it can be done!

Thanks for the Teddy Roosevelt quote, about how everybody being if they assimilate… I agree only in part. What values are we expected to embrace… would we have to believe in *splendid little wars* like he did?

It's great to see Americans doing good things around the world… it is also great to see people from any country doing good things around the world - I applaud them all!

It's an oversimplification, but I think I've met two types of Canadians... those who want to be like Americans and those who don't…I respect the latter more.

I believe we are possibly the greatest country in the world, but there are other great nations and we're not so far above them that we should be the masters of the universe.

Authority

"We are not taught to think, we are taught to agree"… unknown.

If by treachery, elections or the *kindness of your heart*, you allow someone excessive authority, you can be sure they'll use it against you!

I feel like I live in a nation of brainwashed people… not everyone, but there are millions who seem that way. The people we're at war with are also brainwashed… it doesn't make for a very hopeful situation. It's always the same, you're supposed to feel like this, believe that and most of all do as you're told!

"When the people fear their government, there is tyranny; when the government fears the people, there is liberty"… Thomas Jefferson

Banksters

"Banking institutions are more dangerous to our liberties than standing armies"... Thomas Jefferson

The banksters herd us like cattle down the long narrow chute, and we barely resist!

We have given trillions to the Wall Street gangsters, and what will we get for it? Probably just our children's and grandchildren's generations further enslaved via the national debt. Jefferson and Franklin would be proud of us if we overthrew these tyrants.

As you drive your "beater" down the street, think of the bankster, in his mansion, or yacht and remember... your hard work made it possible! The mortgages they hold on our houses, bodies and souls allows our *masters* to rule us like a herd of sheep.

If I had to choose between bailing out banks or auto companies, I would choose the auto companies. They make world-class products, while Wall Street is the menace our founding fathers warned us against. We are addicted to credit, and genuflect to the banksters when they warn that we can't get along without them. If they were defanged, we would get along fine, by utilizing contracts without usurious interest rates and the courts would adjudicate disagreements.

The transition from debt slavery to freedom will be difficult, we won't be able to buy all the toys we crave, but in the long run we'll be much better off. If we continue conspicuous consumption and incurring massive debt, we'll suffer graver consequences than any recession.

CEOs and bankers should not make hundreds, or thousands of times more than ordinary workers. Even *if* they're maximizing returns for their shareholders, the system is out of whack when workers are "axed" and their jobs sent overseas (to be performed by virtual slaves), all in the name of enriching investors. Most Americans are at least small investors, through 401k or pension plans, but that doesn't justify the greed and avarice of the bankers and CEOs.

There's nothing wrong with investing in companies through stocks, but it's unnecessary and ridiculous to reward management and Wall Street so handsomely for their roles. This is especially true when we consider that through lobbying and graft, they have altered and manipulated the system solely for their own gain. These crooks should loose their yachts, instead of "Joe" loosing his row boat. There's something wrong with a system where people make millions manipulating markets, via keystrokes on the computer, while those breaking their backs, or wracking their brains to produce something of real value make a relative pittance. The system needn't be scrapped, but if it isn't reformed, the eventual outcome will be chaos or collapse… and we don't need that!

"Let me control a nation's money supply, and I care NOT who makes it laws." -Mayer Amshel Rothschild, Founder of the Rothschild banking dynasty.

Other than psychotic dictators, banksters are the most dangerous people in the world. As Mayer Rothschild implied, control of the a nations money supply is the key to controlling the nation. With that control, comes the ability to finance and wage wars for ones own nefarious purposes… though I digress.

When you can print the money to pay the army, bribe the politicians and enslave the populace, you pretty much run the show! While the hard working tax payers are pinching pennies, banksters receive record bonuses and reward themselves with mansions and private islands.

To those who say banks simply play the game according to rules laid out by congress, I suggest the bankers had their lobbyists deliver said rules to congress, which obediently passed them into law for their masters.

By giving banksters a trillion dollars, we have enabled them to arm themselves with the financial bullets to hold us hostage for another fifty years!

If **great fortunes are not based on great crimes, as Balzac said, are they not at least based on exploitation of others?**

The pundit is defending hedge funds by claiming they are already highly regulated. "They can only work with registered investors, they can only have 99 clients in total and can only accept investments of $1 million or more."

That sounds more like collusion than regulation to me... they only work for the richest of the rich!

Unlike the nuclear bomb genie, the "to big to fail" bank genie can still be put back in the bottle... let's roll!

"If the American people only understood the rank injustice of our money and banking system, there would be a revolution before morning"...Andrew Jackson

Battle of the Sexes

"No one will ever win the battle of the sexes; there's too much fraternizing with the enemy" ... Henry Kissinger

We should realize that women eventually won't need us at all... an egg can be fertilized without sperm and implanted in the uterus. We'd better behave! On the other hand, if things ever go that far, then men might want to *make* Stepford wives after all... If it ever comes to that, then this battle of the sexes has been lost by both sides.

Women shave their bodies, paint their faces, hide their wrinkles, enhance every aspect of their fleeting beauty and then criticize us for judging the book by the cover? It may seem necessary for them to do this, just as men think its necessary to do what we do. There are deceptions on both sides and *my* how we fall for them! I suppose nature, society and the drive to succeed reproductively or otherwise is what leads to all this.

We know that supermodels are unrealistically tall and thin, but here at the mall I see many tall, stately blondes who are actually brunettes of average height!

If 30% of women are blondes and 90% of blondes are brunettes... what percentage of women are brunettes? The answer is 97% according to my daughter who helped me with the math. In any case, I guess *product packaging* is important in the mating game!

On TV, they're showing the Bunny Ranch in Las Vegas and the seemingly happy "working girls." I doubt that orgasms are the only things they fake, I'll bet there're a lot of tears *back at the ranch.*

The experts say both men and women speak 16,000 words a day on the average. If that's true can we "install" word counters and penalize people who exceed their limit?

I have to admit, I wouldn't mind "having" a bevy of beauties… with all due respect, what man wouldn't?

Most guys dream about ravaging the bad girls… but we're even more interested in ravaging the good ones!

Gals with "factory air" are cool, but too much can means they're anorexic.

Neither men, nor women are content for very long… men eventually want more sex while women *must have* new shoes.

Suspicion on the part of women towards men is hardwired and may be necessary for the survival of her and their children... why else would it be so prevalent?

What's worse, knowing somebody married you for your looks, or knowing they married you for your money?

I hear the old song, "Do You Want to Know a Secret" and it reminds me that every one likes hearing secrets, but no one can keep them. Correct me if I'm wrong, but women in particular to like secrets and use them as a form of currency. While men are not opposed to *using secrets*, they're more likely to employ violence to get their way... women also commit murder occasionally, but usually by different means… arsenic and old lace and all that.

It's ironic, beautiful women who are the most ogled, eventually become the least looked at… it's the law of averages and one of the sad realities of life.

The song says, "girls just want to have fun"... the corollary is "guys just want to have sex!"

God surely designed the female body… I'm just wondering if he had a little help from the devil?

Among mammals, the human female is one of the very few that can be sexually receptive almost all the time. This gives her the ability to drive men crazy all the time, not just during *the season!*

I believe men should consider the counsel and advice of women, but not be under their thumb... that is not natural.

Its 5:30, my wife and daughter have been gone for three hours... I pour myself a glass of wine... they have left me unsupervised for too long. Left to my own devices, my primitive instincts have a tendency to take over.

Bachelor night was fun -- I smoked a cigar, ate fried calamari, drank martinis, and later built a fire for me and the dogs. Later that night I woke up in pain, with stomach acid burning a hole in my throat. Running to the porcelain altar I tried to purge my sins, but there was nothing. The next morning I made the bed *bachelor style...* it took 10 seconds instead of the usual three minutes my wife and I spend most mornings.

Interesting how in nature, there are few species where the male and female live together and even fewer where the sexes mate for life... we humans are beating the odds!

Why do females of so many species have synchronized periods or "seasons? Scientists say it's a way of reducing overpopulation, it may also be a tactic in the battle of the sexes, by which females attempt to impose their will on males....especially in humans. In harems, women's periods tend to naturally synchronize, but they do not achieve the effect of controlling the man's sexual urges... instead he keeps seeking new women for his "stable."

The battle of the sexes has been going on forever, with men historically using force to keep women *in line...* ideally men multiple partners, available at their beck and call. Women use everything at their disposal to counter mans attempt to treat them like a herd, intrinsically understanding they are far more valuable than men suppose.

<u>Bees and Ants…</u>

"The ant is knowing and wise, but he doesn't know enough to take a vacation" … Clarence Day

I wonder… other than the Queen, are there any other "celebrities" in the hive?

The big city bank is a *bee hive of activity* with each worker performing a specific role. When their performance is in unison, they make money, when they don't, they loose customers.

Society has always operated like a beehive, historically there were countless; cities, states and countries each run by its own *bosses.* Now our leaders seem intent on creating only one gigantic hive. The people engineering our fate *may* have good intentions, but that's beside the point. The problem is, independent-minded people will have no place to go… at least until outer space becomes an option.

I enjoyed people watching at the *beer garden...* so many different shapes, sizes and interesting faces. The next morning I see an Ant on the counter and wonder, do Ants look each other in the face, or just touch antennae?

If human societies are little more than glorified ant colonies, then who's to say that a America is better than Russian, China or Iran? Maybe America is better, but if it's like an ant colony, how much better could it be and should we impose it on others?

Infrastructure is vital to human civilization... it takes an enormous effort to tunnel a highway through a mountain, but think of the benefits of the endeavor. Once completed and with regular maintenance, that tunnel could last thousands of years… I'd like to see Ants do that!

Look at how human society and construction has evolved in complexity! Compare a termite mound to an ancient mud brick structure and you'll see they look somewhat similar… fast forward to a modern skyscraper and the similarities largely disappear. A major difference between termites and humans, is the size of our brains and how the workers are treated… unfortunately we don't necessarily treat our workers better than termites do.

I'm not saying women are like worker bees and men are like drones, but I think there are a few common traits. Is our behavior *as* programmed as that of the lesser beasts? I think not... nor is it as different as we'd like to think!

Do you hear that buzzing sound coming from the hive... I think the girls are all talking at once... I'm kidding... kidding, kidding!

Like bees in a hive, we are taught to, *want what's best for the society.* Secretly however, we want what's best for ourselves, and when possible we act accordingly. That's separates us from Bees, although even in the hive, there may be a few rebels... undoubtedly they're dealt with harshly!

Other than through a police state, how can huge numbers of self-centered people be controlled? Society is a bee hive of activity, where the rich get richer and the poor get enough to keep them from rioting. Gals love to shop and guys like to watch sports etc. our masters know and allow this. These activities along with *happy meals* are all that's necessary to keep us in line. If you get rowdy the local SWAT shows up at your door, and if a country gets out of line the *alliance* pays them a visit. It's not all bad, and certainly not all good... it's just the most efficient way to manage this thundering herd called humanity!

Factory workers, salesman, construction workers, secretaries and executives... we're all part of a gigantic human ant farm. We may be at the apex of evolution on our planet, but in the greater scheme of things, are our lives that much different than an ants?

If you want to get some idea about the future of American society, study China, where the government "manages" over a billion people. China reminds me of the proverbial Ant farm, and America is taking major steps in that direction. With our restless and growing population, our leaders will hold increasing power and exert greater control.... those who don't like it will have little recourse other than to submit.

Beauty

"A frail gift is beauty, which grows less as time draws on, and is devoured by its own years" … Ovid

I don't know if this is a snafu or catch 22, but men look for beautiful wives, while women often select less attractive men who they think are better providers. The problem is that both sexes are fooled… men ignore brains and personality, for fleeting beauty and too often women beguiled by all kinds of rogues!

Looking in the mirror at his saggy face, *how much is that doggie in the window*, came to mind. They say beauty is only skin deep... but how many people *really* believe that? Aren't most of us just paying lip service?

What is the connection between the words "ravishing beauty" and "ravage a beauty?" One describes beauty, the other alludes to destroying it… tragically they often come together.

Walking around Manhattan, I see hundreds of beautiful women and wonder *how* there can be so many? I suppose you're bound to pass a hundred beauties when you've passed ten thousand people in a day!

Ben Franklin

"I disapprove of what you say, but I will defend to the death your right to say it"… Evelyn Beatrice Hall

I was surprised that the above quote which I thought was attributable to Ben Franklin apparently is attributable to Evelyn Beatrice Hall. She reportedly penned it to describe how the philosopher Voltaire felt about the subject. Voltaire it seems, was an acquaintance of Ben Franklin… so using the principle of six degrees of separation, I somehow attributed that quote to old Ben.

The closest Ben Franklin quote I can find to the above is, "those who would trade freedom for security, in the end, get and deserve neither"... and this one I like!

Why you ask, would anyone criticize Ben? It's because he deserves a bit of criticism and because I think he can take it! Ben was a bit more like most of us, than Washington or Jefferson... they seemed more like marble statues than human beings. Surprisingly, the more I learn about Ben, the more I respect him... I can't say the same for some of our other *founding fathers.*

Ben seemed less pompous than George Washington and the others, yet just as brilliant. Like George and the rest of the *gang*, Ben was far from perfect... these men were not superheroes!

I've never read about Ben fighting in a battle, but he did risk being hung as a traitor for his revolutionary activities, which included lobbying France for weapons and naval support. Franklin also romanced the ladies of France this while his wife was alone in Philadelphia! I'd have to give Ben a "B", for his walk and an "A" for his talk... of course I'm an easy grader.

***Oddly* enough, while Ben was whooping it up with the ladies of France, George and Tom may have been *having their way* with women they held as slaves!**

By protecting the rights of the weak, and disposed, we're protecting everyone's rights. The more of an "outsider" one is, the better chance he has of surviving the whims of the "insiders", *if* a policy of protecting everyone's rights is guaranteed. On the other hand, if someone's speech is insidious and may cause harm to others... why aid or abet them? Even if it's in the name of protecting "free speech", we shouldn't help those who if given power, would curtail the freedom of others!

Ben is one of our favorite founding fathers, but it's difficult to idolize this roly-poly dumpling of a man. Unlike the stately Washington, Lincoln and Jefferson, old Ben just doesn't fit the mold of an idol. Which leads me to ask, was Franklin the most perfect of the founding fathers, or simply the least imperfect?

I was shocked to learn that a thousand human body parts were found under the house Ben Franklin occupied during his years in London. *Allegedly*, he, or a friend was involved in facilitating the procurement of human body parts

for doctors and professors of medicine. Apparently the idea of donating one's body to science hadn't caught on yet in Franklin's day!

The government's job should be to guarantee free speech, by preventing the majority, or other groups from persecuting people with different views… however, *defending to the death* those whose speech you disapprove of, should be a personal decision.

Ben Franklin patented the Franklin stove, invented bifocals and lightning rods, "discovered" electricity, charted the Gulf Stream and was indeed a genius! On the other hand… he also invented the "Glass Armonica", one of the most bizarre musical instruments ever!

Ben Franklin's, "Old Mistresses Apologue" is a classic! In it, he advises a friend, "that in all your Amours you should prefer old Women to young ones" and goes on to enumerate the reasons why… very interesting!

The government says we must protect everyone's freedom of speech... but there seems to be certain speech, that is "more equal" than others and worthy of greater protection under the law… and that disturbingly sounds like Orwell's Animal Farm to me.

Beatrice Hall's statement on freedom of speech, is almost universally admired, but rarely practiced … so what's wrong with criticizing it? If everyone had the right to decide what causes they would fight for, the elite might find it more difficult to field armies!

Ben Franklin was a Freemason, as was George Washington, Paul Revere and many of the founding fathers. That's interesting, but I wonder how many of our current leaders are Freemasons? It's more likely they're members of the CFR, Trilateral Commission, Bilderberg Group, Skull and Bones, or other reincarnation of the secret societies of the past?

In elections, some people win and some people loose… though an imperfect system, its okay, unless the same people always win. When that happens, it reminds me of Franklins definition of insanity, "doing the same thing over and over and expecting a different result!"

Okay already… if you're thinking "he's beaten this horse enough", you're right, enough already!

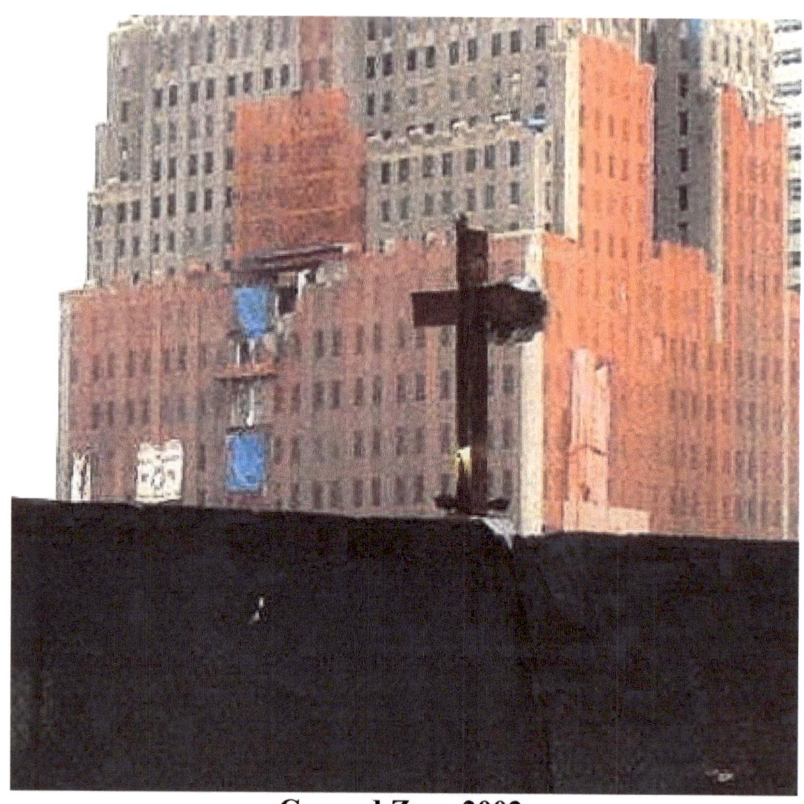

Ground Zero 2002

Bias

I've got opinions, and admit they are biased if not stupid. With that in mind, the less I say, the better and when drinking, I'd better say nothing!

How can anybody have an unbiased perspective? Here we are, right smack in the middle of our own culture, and our own lives. Until you leave your city or country, and look at things from the point of view of others, walk in somebody else's Moccasins, so to speak, it's impossible to be objective about your own society… or anything else!

I'm reminded that the military protects my freedom and the right to speak my mind. In the next breath I'm advised to be careful what I say… isn't there something strange about that? Society encourages us to unconditionally praise the military, but that's something quite different from freedom of speech. Our leaders and peers tell us what to be grateful for… but shouldn't we figure that out for ourselves. We're spoon fed the truth by

the powerful who are as biased as anyone else… not surprisingly, their motives usually revolve around profit, ideology or religion.

"Bias and prejudice are attitudes to be kept in hand, not attitudes to be avoided."
… Charles Curtis

Bird World

"It is the beautiful bird which gets caged" … Chinese Proverb

High in our old Cottonwood tree, sits a Crow, atop the neighbors tree is another one. Spread across the hood like sentries, they scan for food and predators. They in turn are under scrutiny of numerous Grackles… which are in turn surveilled by Sparrows *and so on.*

A dozen Grackles harass a hawk and I'd like a picture of the drama, but as usual I don't have my camera when I need it!

Watching a hawk and a goose I wonder, if you looked back 10,000 years, would our ancestors have shared a similar scene? If we went back millions of years, would the sky be filled with dinosaurs?

Once in a blue moon (why aren't there more blue moons?), I see a hawk from my hot tub. Usually it's being harassed by the smaller birds, but occasionally it has the advantage and goes on the attack. I guess Mother Nature designed it so the hawk can't out fly all the birds all time, just some of the birds some of the time.

I hear a flutter of wings and a Mourning Dove flies from our deck... I don't know where it's living, I just know where it's pooping, and I don't like it one bit!

Even the birds are on welfare, cardinals and finches come to the hot tub and pester me for a hand out... they're bad as our dogs!

A brilliant Cardinal is hopping around in the Pear tree… he looks at me and seems to ask, "why don't you fill the bird feeder anymore?"

The bird world is easier to observe than the world of fish. You can look up and see birds, they're usually all around. To observe fish, you have to find water, locate the fish, hope for clarity and probably get all wet.

It's too windy to see many birds, and the one I see, is struggling greatly, blown sideways, it makes no progress at all!

"A bird in the hand is better than two in the bush", and "killing two birds with one stone", are self explanatory … the second expression indicates a lucky shot, or a very strong arm!

On top of the house, I see a Robin and a Dove perched 10 feet apart. They look in opposite directions and seem to ignore the other. Perhaps they're lookouts and their relationship is symbiotic.

Once again I see the hawk perched on the neighbor's roof. I don't know how he can hunt, there are so many eyes watching him! Robins, Doves, Crows, Grackles and Sparrows shriek when he moves … even the Rabbits and Squirrels benefit from the early warning system.

Can you imagine what the birds see in their travels… if they only knew the wonder of it!

Despite their beauty and sweet songs, I'm just about sick of birds… they poop everywhere, and are presently making a mess of our roof. I think I'll go with butterflies, they're also beautiful, twice as rare and soil nothing with their waste…I just wish we could hear them sing.

I see a lone goose flying towards the lake were the flock landed a couple minutes ago. It seems nervous, almost panicky – surely it seeks the security of its "gaggle."

"A small bird will drop frozen dead from a bough without ever having felt sorry for itself" … D.H. Lawrence

Britain

"Britain's most useful role is somewhere between bee and dinosaur"... Harold Macmillan quotes

Not long ago a Brazilian mining company paid $ 98 billion for a British mining company, and India's Tata motors purchased Jaguar and Land Rover for a mere $ 2.8 billion. This tells me a couple of things, one is that we're in a "commodity bull" markets and second, until recently, who would have expected Indian and Brazilian companies to be buying up the Brits?

When dealing with the Brits, I am amazed at their intelligence and business savvy. That doesn't mean they should be running the world, or that anyone else should... the great powers have always been motivated primarily by self interest. Not to mention the powerful screw up and someone else usually pays the price. When I discuss the Brits, guess I'm really commenting on; Celts, Picts, Normans, Angles, Saxons, Romans and God knows who else!

How did English end up with the letter "W?" Did somebody show up one day hung over and decide that the task of coming up with a letter to follow "U", would simply be too much?

We're told our military protects us from countries that would destroy us if they could. No one's tried to do that since 1812, and then it was our good friends the Brits!

You've got to hand it to the British, they're no longer a super power, yet they manage to keep up with them when it comes to influence peddling and geopolitical meddling.

The caller to the radio said we should accept new government powers that may infringe on our personal liberties, unless we have *something to hide.* So, exactly what were our ancestors *hiding* from the British", when the Redcoats trampled on their freedoms?

The British are incredible... but I give them only a "C." They might disagree, but *they've* been the principal beneficiaries of all the so-called "good things" they've done for their colonies...

The Brits have a world class military even if they aren't a super power, *and* they have nukes. As the Spanish Armada, Nazis and most recently Argentina found out, the Brits are not to be trifled with.

Bugs

"One thing the inventors can't seem to get the bugs out of, is fresh paint"... Unknown.

I dropped a peanut and while picking it up noticed a bug, half the size of an ant scurrying away. It had almost been beaned ... can you imagine being killed by a peanut!

I'll have to accept that God made bugs for a reason and take no joy in killing them... I guess they're just here to bug us.

There's nothing like living in a farmhouse for acquiring a dislike for bugs. Aside from their pooping all over the porch, they also like to die in the bath tub. For a real treat, take a walk by the creek – if you're not saturated with bug spray they'll eat you alive!

I was walking through the backyard whistling a tune, when a bug flew right in my mouth... now that rascal had good aim! Another time, a huge bug committed suicide on my eyeball... I hate that!

Have you ever noticed that when you squish a spider its legs curl up?

I can't stand flies... can't they at least wait till we're dead to bug us? The "biting ones" seem especially intent on tormenting me, especially when I'm on a ladder and don't dare swat at them.

The experts say that fish, like "structure", things like sunken trees and reefs attract them. Insects, also seem to like structure – as I take a walk, my face is the *structure* they're attracted to.

The conventional answer to "what goes on inside an ants head", is *nothing*! But we could be wrong... they demonstrate a high degree of "intelligence"

for having such tiny brains, suggesting that instinct is an extremely powerful force.

Another thing I wouldn't want to be is a Ladybug, I just squashed one with a piece of dryer lint… what a way to go! In the fall, we're infested by the imported variety of these bugs…

"Don't be a spider", he warned the creepy thing that was on the box… turned out, it was plastic pine needles from a Christmas wreath.

It's amazing how agile the ants are when I try to squash them on our kitchen counter. When I turn on the light they scurry for cover with the skill of a pro running back... wow! Their skill should come as no surprise, when you're that small, you'd better be good at running in circles and hiding under things. Despite their relative success eluding me, our kitchen counter is still a dangerous place for an Ant to be!

I was stung two or three times today by Wasps whose nest I accidentally disturbed. If insects are that territorial, why are we surprised that humans will defend for their land till the very end?

After working in the yard, I come in to wash up and squeeze some liquid soap onto my hands. Several aunts scurrying for cover, but I scoop them up and add them to the soap, producing my own abrasive cleaner… it works well, but smells like acid!

It's Autumn and the yellow jackets seem almost tame, as they hang around the picnic table like dogs waiting for scraps. They're unlikely to sting unless we do something foolish in their direction... which my flyswatter often does!

"Nothing personal", he said as he squashed the bug, "but you're a bug and this is my house."

Funny how when on a ladder, the flies bite and harass me. They know that people on ladders can't swat… so much for insects being dumb! I'm also amazed at how patient, the wasps have been, they crawl out of the attic and watch I paint the eaves. The line up in formation and *eyeball me* like the offensive line of the an NFL team! Eyes are trained on me, they're ready to penalize me with venom if I move "off sides."

It's 80° and a fly is trying to get in my car window... he looks like the biting variety and would surely drive me crazy. Out of boredom I play chicken, raising and lowering the window, offering it a chance to dart in and pester me -- "Street fighting Man" is on the radio.

Have you ever had a Firefly hit your window while driving 80 miles an hour? This one glowed for 30 seconds then became a mere smudge. Reminds me what they say, "sometimes you're the windshield and sometimes you're the bug."

Flies... in the end they get most of us and if they don't, the worms do! Starting in September *our flies* become lethargic and are more tolerable. That's precisely when the Yellow Jackets acquire a taste for *people* food and I become nostalgic for the flies!

Years ago, the kids wanted an ant farm, but I didn't buy it. We now have one in the wall and its inhabitants make regular forays onto the kitchen counter. I feed them poison every day hoping they'll feed it to the queen and her "babies" as the instructions claim. Unfortunately, new generations keep visiting us like clock work... they actually seem to thrive on the poison!

Business

"To open a shop is easy, to keep it open is an art"... Chinese Proverb

When you're trying to make sales, there's nothing wrong with just *going through the motions,* especially if you put a little emotion in the motions. The key is, show up, give the presentation and the more emotion you can muster, the better!

"We're too ugly to be cheerleaders for the market" Say the Fellas from "Fast Money." I don't know about that, but they certainly have some good lines... dead cat bounce pushing on a string, fat finger mistake, best looking horse in the glue factory, wall of worry, skin in the game, bear trap, catching a falling knife, a skinny puppy is a sick puppy. None of them agree on anything, and no one knows what the heck is going on, maybe that's why they turn to comedians for material!

Just as I'm getting quite sick of the Michael Jackson death investigation /celebration coverage, a certain business show comes on and I realize the Jackson coverage wasn't so bad after all!

Business, busy, "busy man" -- businessman… hmmm.

I'm ashamed to admit I've lied to obtain market information and to make sales. On the flip side, if there is one, is that the money spends just fine and everyone wants to help!

The client commented that the figures in my report *seem skewed,* which was a nice way for him to put it! Heck, I'm writing a market report, not painting the Sistine Chapel, I just need to get the darn thing done! It's like flipping burgers, my goal is to offer a reasonably good value and not make anyone sick… hopefully they'll come back for more!

Every now and then I make a completely unexpected sale… these are like the proverbial manna from Heaven!

After 10 years, the ribbon on my electric typewriter has finally worn out... there's a spare on the shelf, which I bought 10 years ago. Since I hardly ever use an actual typewriter anymore, I'm hoping this ribbon lasts till retirement!

Amazing how many experts claim they were the first to warn about the economic disaster… of course they make the claim well after the fact!

Business is good... I've got prospects and work -- but I can't become complacent or rest on my measly laurels… history shows things can turn sour in an instant!

With five reports due before our 25th anniversary trip, it seemed there'd be no way to finish them all. Rightfully or not, the clients with the *squeakiest wheels* got the oil, and their reports!

It's ironic that Britain and the US forced forced China and Japan to open their markets to international trade and now we have negative trade balances of hundreds of billions a year. Of course Wal-Mart stockholders might think that's okay, after all, they've made out very well!

The Dow, S&P 500, NASDAQ and Wilshire aren't really good indicators of the overall economy, they tell how things are going for investors, but indicate much less about how things are *trickling down* to Joe and Jane six pack.

Regarding the high price of oil, the pundit suggested raising margin requirements, as that would drive the *smaller* speculators out of the business... yeah, that's what we need, leave the whole thing to the largest speculators!

The cheerleaders keep talking up the market… after all, they say it's *largely psychological.* So is a Ponzi scheme – does that mean it should go unchallenged?

I drive by the house that I almost bought and see a young real estate investor outside, he's cutting his teeth on this old money pit… good luck buddy whoever you are!

Globalization? If nothing else, it's made rivals more dependent on each other; U.S.A., Russia, China, Japan, Germany and France and the UK… we're less likely to dump bombs, or bonds for that matter, when we're so financially interdependent. Globalization also makes for cheap labor, and greater mobility for money… all told it's great for the rich!

The wealthy are masters at relocating their businesses, homes and money where they get the best terms and protection from their workers. Ironic how the latest havens are former communist enemies like China and Vietnam. Of course their poor are still waiting for the benefits to "trickle down" to their mud huts and squalid tenements… patience my friends.

When a man tells you "my word is my bond" or, "my handshake is all you need"... it usually means he's a shyster and doesn't want to put things on paper, legitimate businessmen put things in writing!

Business has picked up, and I find myself in the usual dilemma of busting my butt to get the work done. That way I can make more money, pay more taxes and satisfy all the other money *requests*. Instead of getting off the treadmill, the speedometer is speeding up!

A new business channel was launched because the owner thought a friendlier view of business should be offered to the American people. My question is,

how much friendlier can it be than the other corporate owned business channels?

I stink at math, but use a *spread sheet* that allows me to calculate faster than "Rain Man"... and it's a program any ten year old can learn... brains are becoming as much a commodity as strong backs!

Certain acquaintances insist that *the deck is stacked against them* and only manual labor, is *honest* work. If they would put down their beer and cigarettes and use their brains, instead of their backs, they could escape the paycheck to paycheck existence they complain about!

By using one's head, instead of one's hands, or learning some skills, you can get ahead, but be prepared to be criticized by those who are too lazy to learn anything new... there're a boatload of people like that.

He's trying to sell water filtration systems... but the leads they give him are ridiculous. Some of the people are on welfare and only interested in the free coupons you get for listening to the pitch. He'll have to make a few sales the hard way before he gets the *good leads,* the sales manager only cares about results! He has mouths, (or addictions) to feed and naturally give his best leads to the proven salesmen... that my friend is survival!

Microsoft was making a big deal about protecting its users website search histories because they were so concerned about our privacy. What a bunch of baloney, every new operating system they come out with is more intrusive than the one before. It's all about Mr. Gates making a few billion more than he already has!

"Drive thy business, let not that drive thee" ... Benjamin Franklin

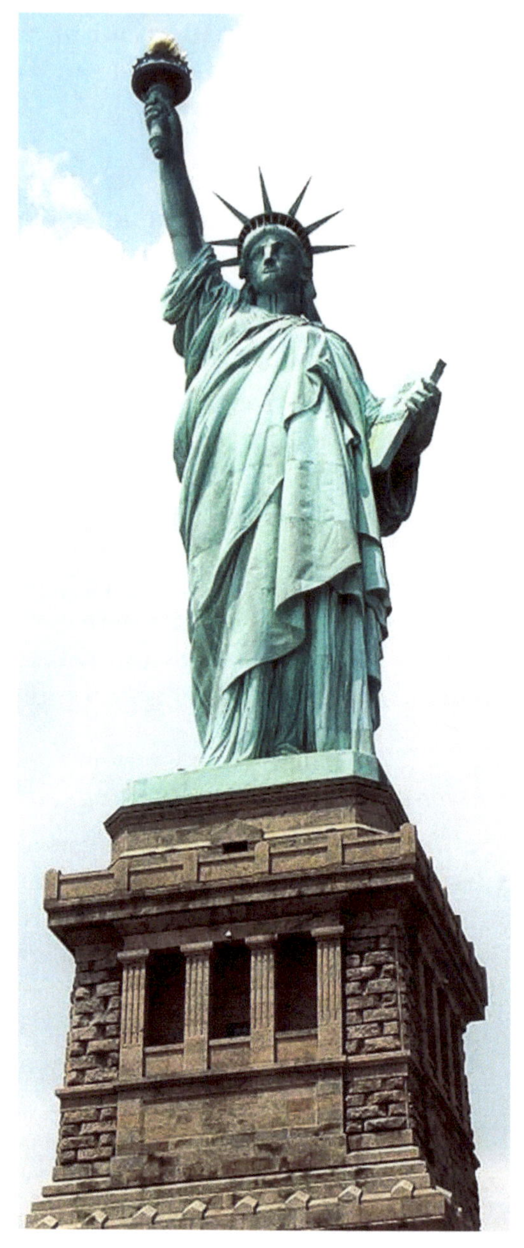

Capitalism

"The inherent vice of capitalism is the unequal sharing of blessings; the inherent virtue of socialism is the equal sharing of miseries." ...Winston Churchill

With capitalism, *if* you use your head you can get ahead, with communism, few get ahead, except party members. Under both systems lots of people are resentful of others... with capitalism you have the chance to turn that feeling into something *positive*... or at least get rich trying.

I don't see class warfare (yet), as much as I see antagonism towards those who are doing a little better than we are. Americans, it seems, want unbridled capitalism, thinking that someday they'll *benefit*, or at least their children will...

I'm not against capitalism, but society needs to protect the average Joe from those who massively profit from things like the subprime mess. On the other extreme, there are unbridled moochers! Just as there are principled capitalists, there are principled freegans, and there unmitigated scoundrels in both camps. Regardless of one's place in society, some contribute, some prey on others and most are somewhere in between... but we're not necessarily where we think we are.

From day one, capitalism was set up by the wealthier to help them preserve their wealth... the only changes have been to allow them to become even wealthier. On the bright side, capitalism allows those who are willing to work hard join the ranks of the ownership class, and anyone can participate to some degree. Those who never get anywhere, are usually people who would rather not apply themselves, or who think that crime pays.

"Capitalism is the astounding belief that the most wickedest of men will do the most wickedest of things for the greatest good of everyone." ... John Maynard Keynes

Children (young and old)

"Children have never been very good at listening to their elders, but they have never failed to imitate them" ... James Arthur Baldwin

We seek gold and jewels, but the real treasure is our children!

I love my relatives, but don't want to be held hostage by them, or for that matter by my ancestors. Admittedly one of my priorities is the continuation of my humble blood line, not just for me, but for those who came before me. This idea is frequently scoffed at, but for 99% of mankind's history, it was the predominant point of view. Only in the last fifty years, has the view shifted so that it's considered ridiculous, if not hateful and antisocial... this because the social engineers have *reformed* most of us!

I will always love my family, I will never give up on them, but I will not always *support* them... so, let's talk about this last point. It has to do in part with the question of how far must a family go, if certain members can't seem to make their way in the world? It also has to do with basic world views of family members... when *worlds collide* it leads to problems, but neither party should feel compelled to capitulate. It also is related to love, respect and admiration, I will always love you, but respect and admiration may ebb and flow... do you feel that way too? When family members are addicts or mentally ill, it complicates things even more... perhaps society's resources should be redirected to help our afflicted, instead of meddling in the lives of people half way around the world.

On a related note, how can our children learn from experience, if they're not accountable for mistakes? This applies to adults as well, but it's a major cause of children going astray.

Kids... it's nice that you want to make us proud of you, but I hope you aspire to more than that.

When you walk through the *woods* of life, don't count on the person in front of you to hold the branches. Be prepared and your walk should be pleasant, be unprepared and you may not finish.

I want to be a good husband, but I don't want *that* to be my legacy... like the kids, I want to do "big things!"

Every family has a prodigal son or daughter... or in some cases, prodigal parent, sibling or cousin. The prodigal is simply the one that needs more help than the others... he or she is loved no less, but often spoiled the most!

So what's worse... growing up to be a worker bee, or an army ant? In both cases, you're a tool, a dollar, to be used and expended.

If my children are opposed to my beliefs, what should I do? I suggest we allow some leeway and agree to respectfully disagree. Now in there twenties, the kids are still my top priority, but I don't subscribe to the *wisdom* that they have to be a parents ultimate and sole priority... at least not when they're grown.

Our kids decided they wanted to do something worthwhile when they became young adults. Sonny wanted to be a Navy Seal and our daughter concentrated on missionary work... both were influenced by the world around them in their decisions... but as far as I can tell, not by me.

Relationships between fathers and sons are often strained, as either may think the other doesn't respects him. Sometimes it's true, sometimes it's false... hopefully it's not insurmountable.

Son, there will be fights enough without picking any... watch your back, and as much as possible, be a man of peace!

The kids were home for one of their friend's weddings and it reminded me of the cycle of life. They are now at the marriage and kids stage, like my wife and I were 25 years ago. We may be grandparents in the near future and our parents are now "enjoying" their golden years...

I joked that our kids are "Mamas kids", after all she's the one they call most often and have the longest conversations with. She disagreed, but I think she was being nice and knows better! I shouldn't complain though, she's earned her *position*, she's kept up with their activities better and of course carried them for nine months. I've have had the opportunity to try and make them closer to me, but I've often floundered. Despite having a case of "Mama envy", I'm grateful for the relationships we have and pray it can get even better.

If you're going to question authorities, such as government, or religion, do it while you're young... otherwise, they'll just call you a grumpy old man!

I tend to smile easily and not as genuinely as I should, but today the kids put real smiles on my face. Sonny's had graduated and my daughter's text messages did the trick too!

They were talking about Sargent Shriver the other day, and it made me wonder... why is it that boys are named; Sargent and Major, but never hire or lower ranks -- what gives? Michael Jackson however named his boys "Prince" and there's an artist, famous for being formerly known as Prince.

I can only *conditionally* recommended marriage to a young man, as it's the only game in town. For women, it wouldn't matter what I recommend, and I think they invented marriage anyway. I could compile a list of pros and cons but as mentioned... it is the only game in town! Personally, there *may* be other *systems* I wouldn't mind exploring. The bottom line though, is being responsible for the children you parent, and be a good man to the women in your life.

"The 18-year-old girl had made a religion out of flirting", said the author, and I wondered how short of wearing a *burqa* she could do otherwise? Beautiful girls are flirts without even trying! Perhaps they're hardwired to *show their wares*, just as young men show off theirs.

My kids tease me for telling so many "precautionary tales"… don't do that, or bad things will happen. They may not realize that unlike some guys, I haven't planted my seeds far and wide. Those guys, including the ones that depend on other tax payers to pay for their numerous offspring, may have it right. They're cool and they don't have to keep a sharp eye on their kids… after all, they're there trying to make new ones all the time!

There's no good excuse for lying... forget about "putting food on the table", or other rationales. Our kids look at our *walk* and our *talk*, and if they don't see a match, we lose their respect, and worse than that, they might imitate our behavior. Blame me if you want to for being a bad example, I deserve that, but please don't use that as an excuse for making similar mistakes!

As you walk through this concrete jungle, bring pepper spray... there are lions and tigers and bears… oh my!

Next time you're ready to blame your teenager for loosing something, look some more. Then you won't appear foolish when it's discovered you're the one who lost it in the first place!

My kids don't listen to anything I say… should I try reverse psychology, or just save my breath altogether?

Young people prefer hanging around people who don't *lecture* them, they seldom realize those people are doing their very best to influence them anyway!

You think young people should *enlist* in order to learn discipline and respect for authority… on the contrary, I think they should learn to question authority, and certainly not to automatically submit to it.

My kids are annoyed when I *point things out*, but I'm only doing what my parents did, and what my kids will eventually do too. Admittedly, it's better to let them discover as much as possible on their own, but there is nothing wrong with discouraging them from re-inventing the wheel. At least parents are nicer about it, which is more than you can say about the school of hard knocks!

If you want your children to learn how to solve problems, don't explain the obvious to them… figuring out easy things is the first step towards figuring out difficult things… let them do it themselves!

Children make the most honest observations... in fact, they seem to be born with Tourette's, only their upbringing *cures them.*

When talking to my kids (they call it lecturing), I never say the right thing, or what I mean to say... even when on the right track, I tend to screw up the message!

Raising the kids I've made mistakes... lots of them. Fortunately they're resilient enough for me to be optimistic! On a related note, there are things we need to learn, and things we need to *unlearn*…this certainly applies to things I've taught my kids.

We have spoiled our kids a bit and now wonder if they'll be able to function in society. Another guy *fathered* ten children with various women and

walked away. His will survive with the taxpayers help…in evolutionary terms, he's kicked my ass!

If you want to be *compensated* like an adult, perform like one... that's life!

When you disregard your parents advice, it's not *just* their advice you're disregarding, it's also the advice of many who came before them. Don't join the ranks of those who insist on learning everything the hard way!

Everyday is a chance to *do one thing right…* a chance to "upset" the balance, in favor of improving your life… but part of youthful discretion, is to automatically disregard parental advice.

The kids and I are alike in some ways and different in others… one difference, is that I can't sleep and they can… boy can they sleep!

Most families have a prodigal son or daughter, who receives extra attention and assistance. Other siblings are likely to be a bit jealous, but from the parents point of view the ultimate goal is to successfully send all their children into the world prepared to support themselves and a family.

Parents find it unfortunate, but sometimes necessary to give more support to the prodigal son or daughter. This is not so different than society's willingness to provide "special assistance" to members of society who have difficulty *making it* on their own. In both cases, the extra attention isn't a bad idea unless it is carried to extremes... which it often is!

Young people can't help but be pleased, when they're touted as "the future of our country." Don't forget you'll only be recognized as the *nations future* for a while so make the best of it. There's already a new generation nipping at your heels, and blaming you for any predicaments they may find themselves in.

"What is happening to our young people? They disrespect their elders, they disobey their parents. They ignore the law. They riot in the streets inflamed with wild notions. Their morals are decaying. What is to become of them?"… Plato (2,400 years ago)

Looking at my daughter's, straightening and curling irons, I can't but think they look more like instruments of medieval torture, than beautification devices.

It was New Year's Eve and the teenage girls and boys were outside in the hot tub. We looked in from time to time, as we didn't want there to be any hanky-panky. This despite rumors that the boys were "harmless." Regardless, you never know when someone might want to *try out their equipment*... even if they already know how it works.

The morning after our daughter's *open house*, I had to re-hang the huge "Congratulations" banner on the garage door. Forgetting to photograph the banner would be a major failure on my part, it was important to all for me to document this memorable day. I wonder though.. how many years will it be before anyone looks at that photo?

I'm showered, shaved and combed in ten minutes, since long ago I've reached the age where spending more time doesn't make me look better! My wife and daughter spend an hour accomplishing the same, their definition of *diminishing returns* is different than mine, and their results are far more pleasing!

According to our daughter, I have a; dino-phone, dino-cam and muffin top... of course none of these are anything to be proud of!

"I'll have to let my pudding chill", said my daughter. This from the same young lady I overheard talking to someone on the phone about strawberries! How do words like pudding and strawberry come up, in normal phone conversation?

We dropped our daughter off at college today... she'll be a freshman, and tomorrow our son leaves for Florida. As empty-nesters, will our lives revolve around things like watching the grass grow and keeping the plants alive through the long hot summer?

Fathers and sons - now that's a loaded relationship, filled with love, envy, jealousy, anger and other complicated emotions. What am I to do, give my son and my father money, or advice? Is it even possible for me to lead them to water, while I'm still *looking for the bridge*?

Climate Change

There's weather and there's climate…like the stock market, the trend is your friend, or your adversary.

I'm enjoying the heck out of this year's "global warming" winter -- but there could be heck to pay in the spring when the hurricanes hit.

To reduce the effect of global warming and sea level rises... maybe we can figure out a way to move the ice caps into northern Canada and Siberia... created enormous freshwater lakes in those relatively unpopulated regions of the world. Those freshwater reservoirs would be a cash cow for the people of that area, as it could be piped anywhere in the world, specifically to desert regions that are lacking water. The trick would be figuring how to get it from the ice caps to the dry land of Canada and Siberia and how to contain it there in giant inland lakes.

If glaciers typically run through valleys, why can't those valleys he dammed? They don't have to be concrete dams, but why can't our "explosives experts" use their knowledge constructively? Of course it won't make a difference if Antarctica melts!

I believe that man-made climate change is happening, and that the trend is towards warming. As dire as global warming may be, it wouldn't be as catastrophic as a new Ice Age. Unfortunately according to some scientists that is what global warming could rapidly deliver.

Some say global warming is a religion and its adherents will consider you a heretic if you call it a fallacy. The same can be said of many things, including of course religion.

By insisting we have overpowered vehicles that consume twice the amount of gas as vehicles used in most other countries, and having no mass transit in 90% of the country, we are setting ourselves up for potential disaster. If you need a big truck, fine, if you don't, think twice before *investing* in one.

It seems many people would prefer to pass on the problem of climate change to their grandchildren. Let them deal with rising sea levels seems to be their attitude after all driving gas guzzlers is "fun!"

Some say global warming is part of God's plan... after all *some* will benefit from it!

I think it's likely that human activities have caused climate change. Will global warming lead to horrible problems such as inundation of coastal areas, or will it lead to changes in ocean currents causing an even more devastating ice age. The effects are likely to be far reaching, most pronounced in certain regions, and guess who will be impacted the most… that's right, the poor.

Should we continue raping our planet to make room for another billion humans? I love people, but if you've seen one human you've seen them all… just kidding. Meanwhile, there's only one Earth, most of us have seen very little of it, and soon that might be impossible.

"Whiskeys for drinking, waters for flight and over"...Mark Twain. This in light of news that areas close to San Francisco, may face serious water shortages in the future due to global warming. As precipitation falls in the mountains as water instead of snow, there may be flooding instead of a gradually melting snow pack that has historically filled the reservoirs... but don't worry folks, Rupert says climate change is a myth. If however climate change becomes *obvious*, the network will change its tune, but don't expect them to admit their mistake… the spin will be quite different!

Its likely climate change is occurring and people are the cause, *however* if the accuracy of hurricane predicting experts is any indication, the climate scientists could be wrong too!

It's not surprising wealthy Americans tend to be skeptical about global warming. Not only do the own the smoke stacks, they also expect their money to insulate them from any problems, and can't they always head for the hills if they have to?

The farther one lives from the ocean, the less likely he is to believe in climate change… even many coastal dwellers could care less, after all, any major problems are unlikely to occur in their lifetimes.

Even where there is real suffering due to climate change, they tell us that humanity can; adjust, make lemonade, find a silver lining etc. Isn't that what we've always done they ask? The problem, is *that* during the past climate change periods, there were at most hundreds of millions of people

inhabiting our planet, making it tough but possible to migrate... now there are 6 billion people and those with a good real estate are more protective than ever!

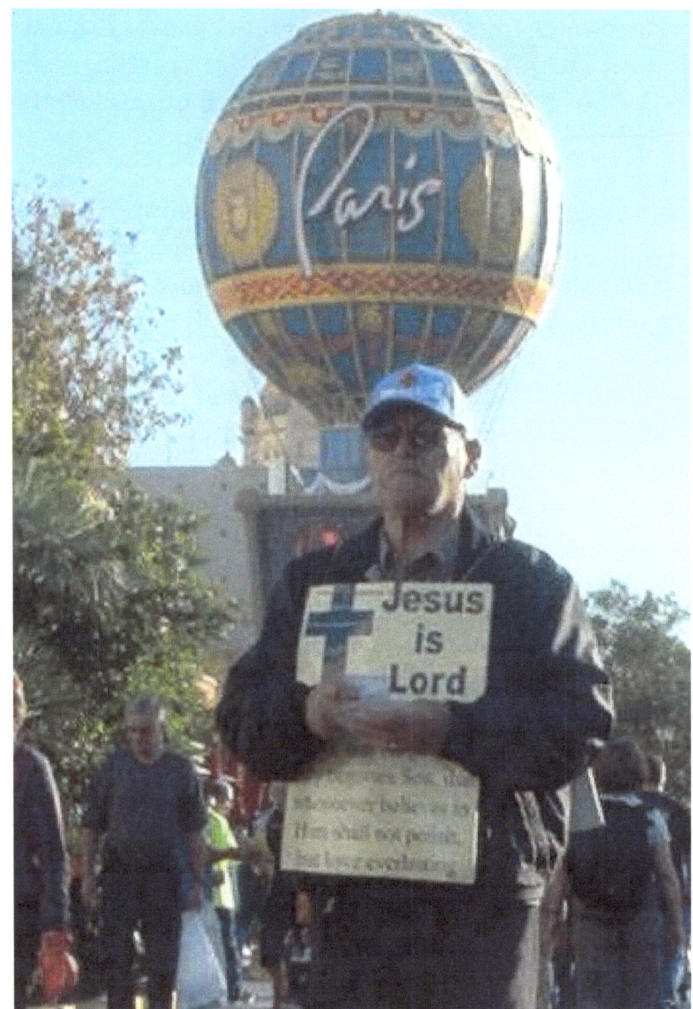

Las Vegas

Competition

"Competition is a sin" ... John D. Rockefeller

If life's a competition, then we're all "winning" relative to some, and losing relative to others. So who's the "Top dog" and which Jones' are you trying to keep up with?

The post office is facing a lot of competition from UPS, FedEx etc. That old saw about "neither rain nor Snow nor dead of night", is becoming ridiculous... our letter carrier hasn't been here in three days… another venerable institution down the drain!

Was Hendrix the greatest guitarist, Ali the greatest boxer and Laver the greatest tennis player? It's impossible to compare masters from different eras. Style, nutrition, training and other things change over time. Even if they were to compete, one might be having a bad day… wait a minute, do the great ones have bad days?

We care greatly about winning, on an individual, team and societal basis. This leads to competition which is okay, but also to conflict and violence which is not. Are we, or should we emulate ants... do they compete with each other, or with other colonies?

Conflict and War

"Conflict is inevitable, but combat is optional" … Max Lucade

It's amazing how often humans fight for turf… at its most basic, it's in an alley or street corner… at it's extreme, it escalates to unimaginable violence and atrocities.

The term "noble officer" may be related to the historic term "nobleman", a title bestowed on those willing to do the kings dirty work … some things never change! Many still believe that *murder for hire* is noble, if you're doing it to the right people, for the *right* reasons.

The president said "my job is to protect you"…so why am I more afraid of the government than anything else?

"The purpose of the military is to kill people and break things"… Unknown

I'm told that the military guarantees peace and prosperity here and abroad. If so, I'm saddened that doing so still depends on bombing people into the Stone Age. I'm told it's necessary to kill so many *of them*, that eventually they will surrender and submit to our will. If I mention that this is at odds with their religion, they tell me religion has nothing to do with it.

Ever notice that treachery often trumps brilliance… just another unfortunate fact of life.

Historically, warfare has provided the most reliable form of upward social mobility... its unfortunate that other avenues have not proven so effective!

Is war a terrible "mechanism" for controlling overpopulation? Historically, there's never enough prime real estate and too many people anxious to fight over it.

Instead of addressing root problems, we like to declare war on things. War on drugs, poverty and terror… maybe the next one will be the war on highways and bridges, after all, those are the location of many tragic deaths.

"Don't just stand there - kill something!"… Waterworld

The Vikings were ferocious warriors, but they may have exported their crazies to the rest of the world centuries ago. The Scandinavian countries are currently prosperous welfare states... is that how we will end up? As for the "Berserkers" amongst us, I think they'll continue to find new ground upon which to wreak havoc.

I've been hearing the terms *permanent war* and it reminds me of our Indian wars, which lasted hundreds of years. It makes me wonder how long will this latest unholy war between the Christianity and Islam last?

Apparently the New Guineans are just quaint primitives minding their own business… and of course they have no WMDs. There is no *outrage* at their strange customs and behavior, instead many think they are noble or funny. This despite them trading their women for baskets and pigs… but you've civilized them quite a bit, at least they no longer eat people.

Then there are the wars in the Congo, the genocide in Rwanda, etc., you decry the violence, but do nothing to save lives. Oil, resources and religion seem to be the common denominator in determining who you will liberate and who you'll ignore.

Liberation is almost always a very bloody affair with no guarantee of anything except death for some and profit for others.

You want third world countries to advance? Why not stop selling them sophisticated weapons? Aren't they likely to kill fewer of each other with stones and machetes than with bombs and missiles… although unfortunately they do an *efficient* job with those too.

"We are still cavemen…there has been no evolution"… txcup.

If we're going to spend trillions of dollars, let it be on cures for cancer, heart disease, diabetes, paralysis, etc., not on bombs and bail outs.

If you choose to be at peace with the world, does it mean surrendering… and if so, to whom?

The difference between Americans and people "across the pond", is that they know they were governed by despotic royal houses. We haven't figured out that it's the same here as it was there. The titles, lines of succession and ruling houses may differ, but everything else is the same… if not worse.

Seems that scarce resources are at the root of most wars… although, ideology, religion and at least one beautiful face has launched a thousand ships.

I'm a bit tribal, so when it comes to fighting for something, I want to be in on the decision... not just cannon fodder for some Wall Street prince, captain of industry or "decision maker-in-chief."

Microsoft has released Halo Three, a hugely successful video game… to me it just looks like another stinking war game.

The "boys" may end up having two choices… join the "home guard" (like in the Civil War) and put their neighbors in the "camps", or end up there themselves. I'm not optimistic about the choice my they'll make… after all, *a jobs a job* – isn't it?

The vets say *only they* know the "truth" about war, implying no one else should, critique, or offer an opinion on the subject, but I respectfully disagree. It's somewhat analogous to *not having to be hit by a bus to know you don't want to be*, and I won't hesitate to state that war is *way* overused.

If you demand unconditional surrender from others, be prepared for a taste of your own medicine. If you impose your will on others, be prepared to fall

from your lofty perch… you are not so perfect as to determine such weighty things! Standing up for your rights and values should not include destruction on the scale in which you have inflicted it.

Wouldn't it be nice if now and then a few soldiers would beat their swords into plowshares? It would be even nicer if such became a *movement.*

Time Magazine's cover, June 5, 2008 -- "the military's secret weapon... antidepressants"... hmmm?

Be it Andersonville, Guantanamo, Baghram or Abu Graif -- when one group of men is given on limited power over another, or abusive if not atrocities will occur. At the beginning, Lincoln said there were no prisoners of war in the north, just traitors…. hmm, that sounds familiar!"

I meet lots of people who say they hate war, but they love the uniforms, pomp and weapons….

Apparently humans must have armies and police, otherwise the likelihood of anarchy would be very high. Unfortunately, unlike Wolves where a rogue pack leader is capable of only limited mayhem, a rogue human leader can commit horrendous crimes.

"Military solution"… may be an oxymoron, but around here chalking up another victory is more important than solving underlying problems... we care more about the win/loss column than the number of bombs we toss column.

On one day in World War I, 20,000 French troops died trying to move the line several yards… I can't think of any way this could have been justified.

Historically people died of disease, famine and violence, and if they were traumatized by each death, they'd be unable to function. Even today, we care less about people dying outside of our immediate circle of love ones and friends.

You know there's going to be a war, when *even* the vegetarians are crying out for blood…

It's not just that we fight un-necessary wars, we also meddle so much that we find ourselves in positions where we *have to* go to war.

Regarding bombing, we seem to do it as if it were a sport. Between drones, cruise missiles, bomber jets and other ordinance, the joy stick boys love playing the violent video games they grew up on… only now their taking real people's lives.

Everyone is "encouraged" to play a role in the war effort, we need; soldiers, generals, engineer, doctors, nurses, businessmen, musicians and shoppers! As long as you fit in some where you are useful… if you do nothing, you're ostracized or worse.

We're moving 30,000 more troops into the war zone, along with thousands of "enablers." I thought you weren't supposed to enable people when they're doing things like killing people…

"It's a shame", they say, but "war *is* necessary"… but is it *as* necessary as they tell us? My friends buy video war games for the kids, vote for war and have little or no compunction about the necessity of waging it. Are we hard wired, or indoctrinated to accept violence as the only way to achieve our goals? Will people ever learn that there's more than one way to skin a cat when it comes to war?

We devise war contingencies against numerous countries, but how many have attacked us? Only Britain, Japan and Al Qaeda have done so, yet we have bombed dozens of countries. We are reminded that American's have died defending our freedom and that of other countries, and I don't dispute that, but we have taken millions of lives in the process… apparently our *excellent kill ratio,* is immaterial, or something to be proud of. If you're going to be measuring "kill ratios" I guess its nice to have a *favorable* one, but it would be even nicer not to need such macabre benchmarks at all.

Pacifist? I wouldn't mind being one, if I thought it realistic, but up till this time in history, its rarely been a rational choice.

While putting things away, I bump my elbow on the door and my head on the shelf, which makes me think, everything around here is too small. Maybe that's why people are always fighting over land and property, it's expensive to legitimately acquire land in order to build things bigger. It's expensive to put a roof over your head and the bigger the roof, the more you have to spend… no wonder some people opt for *alternative* means of acquiring these things.

America is increasingly using drones to target its enemies, which saves American lives, but probably increases the killing of innocents on the other side. Military lawyers have decided its okay, and our people seem to have few qualms either. After all they say, its saving American lives, and these weapons will never be used against us... or will they?

What is it that makes one country invade another? Is it greed or need... and is it the greed or need of the entire country or just their ruling elite?

If war is about old men and women talking, and young men and women dying, who's responsible for the carnage... is it the old men and women who send them or the young people who are so willing to kill each other?

If we tell children to keep their hands to themselves, shouldn't the same apply to countries?

"It is my conviction that killing under the cloak of war is nothing but an act of murder." -- Albert Einstein

Conforming

"The unexamined life is not worth living"… Socrates at his trial for heresy

Do the people who love brand name athletic shoes know, or care that the shoes are made in poor countries, sometimes by veritable child slaves? Many Americans who are proud of their basket ball shoes are themselves the descendents of slaves. Do our children even care, or is conforming and looking hip all that matters?

You can conform a little, or you can conform a lot… either way there's a price to pay. If you're a great leader, others will conform to you, but that's not without cost either. Humans can exhibit robotic behavior, in the same sense that ants and bees do… it's called crowd or mob mentality. We have a million years of evolution as well as conditioning, socialization and genetics that seem impossible to completely overcome. We do what humans have always done… fight, love and anything else necessary for survival. In the end, we die… exactly like people have done since the beginning of time.

The commuter train lights went off and I saw something new … the faces of many riders were illuminated, like when you hold a flashlight under your chin. In this case, it was cell phones and Blackberries… the gamers and talkers about their business as if nothing unusual had happened!

"Become one of us, by becoming none of us"… Toyota Scion advertisement

Conspicuous consumption

"A Big Mac - the communion wafer of consumption"… John Ralston Saul

When we're not busy buying new stuff, we're busy throwing out old stuff, to make room for the new stuff *we need so bad*!

I get some satisfaction out of being frugal, *waste not, want not* and all that. Fortunately things are changing a bit, but frugality is still un-cool in our consumption based society. I wonder if attitudes will change if we run out of cheap energy and people are walking everywhere? Till then conspicuous consumption and wastefulness will remain our religion… and that's plain stupid!

Via education, tax codes, news, entertainment etc., we've all become part of the mega ship, and if it sinks, we've been *set up* to go down with it. That's why Americans will fight tooth and nail, and possibly take the rest of the world down too, in order to preserve our *wonderful* system of; debt, consumption and materialism.

Who came up with the line, "you don't own your stuff, your stuff owns you." Like the bow and arrow and fire, it's been circulating in one form or another since antiquity.

Consumerism makes us shallow and empty, even as it speeds up environmental degradation. If we can slow the rate of population growth, and mindless consumption, we'll be going a long way towards improving the lives of future generations. Without advocating zero population growth, I'm saying we should not be consumption maniacs. The flip side is that those in poor countries should think twice before having numerous children, unless they plan on supporting them…

My daughter's wearing a T-shirt that says "what you wear matters." So… some genius is getting free advertising, and teaching her what's *important* in life! Madison Avenue's marketers, and social engineers are guiding us toward the outcome they desire and we're falling for it hook, line and sinker!

I wouldn't be entirely against social engineering if it was beneficial to all… but I suspect such an outcome would be impossible for anyone to orchestrate.

I did my best at the high end outlet store to be; pleasant, attentive and involved. We left after 15 or 20 minutes and my wife said, "that didn't take very long did it?" It really didn't, but I had a knot in my stomach that persisted till we reached the parking lot. Inside, Christmas music played in fast tempo and it seemed to fuel a shopping frenzy… like chumming the water does for sharks!

I have nothing against "stuff", but I'm getting tired of feeling like a Hamster on a treadmill... if others want "stuff" let *them* work for it!

Black Friday, is the day after Thanksgiving, when the retailers hope to go *in the black* for the year. Through commercials, they tell us what we need to buy in order to be "happy." When and how did this shopping religion get started? Is it as old as time, or something more recent?

I cruise through the mall like someone on a sociological field trip… the women are amazing. Shopping seems to be as engrained in their DNA, as girl watching is in ours! Enjoying the sights I walk past the cookie, pretzel and chocolate stores, but *score* no free samples… I have to remember, this isn't Costco. Have no fear however… the food court is sure to offer a sample or two! I proceed to the Chinese counter and sure enough Orange Chicken and other treats are available on a toothpick.

I try not to look like a *sample hog*, or stare too much, and I don't mean at the chicken… but the usual *distractions* are everywhere. I ask for a sample at the first counter then move on to the competition for a taste of Bourbon Chicken. Without warning, a chair crashes to the floor, piloted by a little boy… his mother tenderly picks him up soothes his aching body… aren't these gals incredible!

Too much of our energy is spent figuring out how to buy stuff that will be next year's garbage. If we retool our minds, we can spend our energy on things other than a vicious cycle of production and consumption. We can

work on getting along with each other, identifying similarities, instead of differences and learn to build bridges, instead of blowing them up.

How you take care of your "things", determines if your ownership will merely be taxing, or if it will break you. *Things* can be a burden, or a benefit, just like phones can be useful, or royal pains in the neck.

As far as people being "overly" materialistic, I suppose that's a basic human character trait. Unless you're extremely *spiritual,* or hoping to accomplish something great, the goal in life for many people is simply to enjoy life while they can. I find that hard to criticize… who am I to judge thousands of years of such a successful strategy?

Spring has spring and conspicuous consumption is manifested by tons of mulch trucked in and spread around our neighborhood. Those who spread the most mulch *win,* and they watch with glee as their neighbors feverishly try to keep up but fail. We don't have to play this game, but there's peer pressure to... after all mulch keeps down the weeds -- right!

I don't propose living like hermits, but conspicuous consumption, presidential "orders" to shop and overemphasis on materialism is unhealthy. It's likely to lead to shortages and extinctions… our grand kids may never have the opportunity to see a Tiger or enjoy a California Roll made from real crab… heck that's already rare!

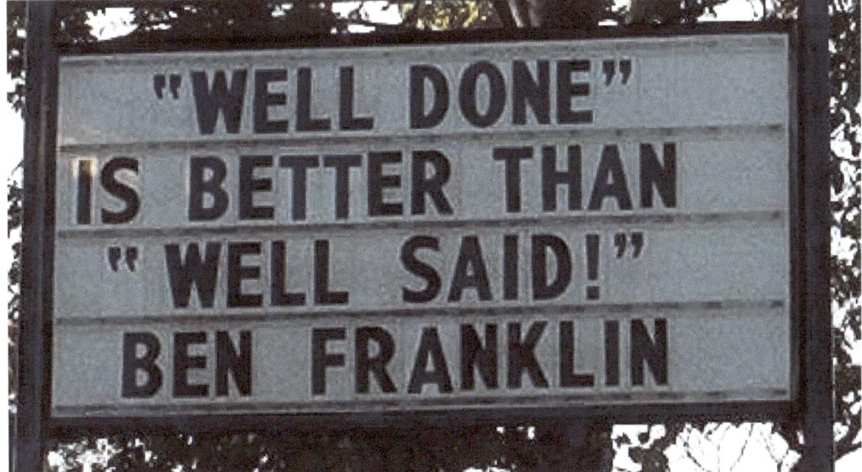

Cryonics

"It ain't no crime to be glad you're alive"... Bruce Springsteen.

If someone has a brain transplant, would you say - the body is a person with a new brain, or the brain is a person with a new body?

If one is suspended and reanimated hundreds of years later, will the brain synapses be intact? Will the patients be zombies, or could providing photos and memory files allow them to be the people they once were?

For cryonics to work, they'll have to map brain synapses while people are alive and well, which could make it possible to re-create the synapse when people are revived. Otherwise the patient may be revived in a zombie like state. Some say, be concerned with this life because it's the only one you have, others say live the way *they* tell you to, so that you will have ever lasting life in heaven. Only a few believe cryonics will offer humans a "second chance" and the *procedure* is frowned upon, considered ridiculous or worse. I'm told it's selfish and unnatural... but respectfully suggest there are two sides to the argument.

In the future, the laws of nature will be stretched in regards to what is the normal lifespan of a human being. With medical discoveries and cryonics, people may "be around" for hundreds of years, but will they be a burden on society? Earth's resources are already stretched thin, so pioneers will take cryonically suspended heads with them into space? When the time is right they will reanimate these brains, and engineer real or mechatronic bodies. Meanwhile, the brains only need liquid nitrogen to *survive.* I'm not suggesting we can fool her, but maybe Mother nature will no longer feel compelled to limit our lives to 70 or 100 *brief* years.

One nice thing about just having your head frozen... if you're revived, I guess you can eat all you want!

I don't want to tempt fate, nor offend God, but if I have the chance to be cryonically suspended, I'll take it... meanwhile I'm just, sitting here resting my bones.

Cryonics is wrong you say? Aren't embryos kept frozen in liquid nitrogen? That's another indicator that cryonics is not ridiculous.

Cryonic science needs "repair molecules", which by the way have already been found to occur naturally in the human body. There are DNA chains that correct mistakes during the billions of cell replications that take place regularly… we will have to learn how to make them do more things.

How wise might a person become, if he or she lived to be 1,000 and didn't loose the youthfulness of his brain cells? How about a Chimpanzee… would it continue to learn and become as intelligent as a human if it lived to 1,000? It's a bit scary in both cases!

It's been said that, everything on earth has, or will go through a worm. That's probably true, and if anyone escapes the worm, they'll probably go up in smoke instead.

Heard a report they're experimentally placing wounded soldiers in a state of suspended animation until they can get them to the best hospital for their type of wound… geez, what's next… cryonics? I'm just enough of a science fiction buff to think its possible.

What will the news be on the day each of us dies? There's always something going on, and we all want to be around for the second coming, or whatever… for the most part however we're disappointed. There're a lot of things that won't happen in our lifetimes, and a lot of things that will... things that grandpa was either looking forward to, or could never imagine!

Some are against cryonics which may be the ultimate anti-aging measure, but they're for using everything short of it, to look and feel better. There position is not wrong, but it's not the only reasonable one.

Experts say our earliest memories are most likely to survive in the brains of Alzheimer's patients... does that mean that if somebody is revived after being "suspended" for 100 years those earliest memories would be the most likely to survive?

"Torpor", which means depressed body temperature, and hibernating are both related to suspending animation, although the techniques are different. During torpor, (an extreme form of hibernation), the Thirteen Line Ground Squirrel's body temperature drops to 38 degrees F… the same temperature selected for the shipment of transplant organs.

I choose cryonics because I have no more faith in theologians than in politicians. I don't think either tells the truth, my faith in God has little to do with these *salesmen*, so I don't mind taking chances on this emerging technology.

"On the day that Curtis died nobody came to pray... preacher just said some words and they chucked him in the clay"... Lynard Skynyrd.
You say it's wrong to want to live more than the 70 or so years the Bible prescribes, but the Bible says; Methuselah lived to be 969, Jared 962, Noah 950 and Adam 930 years… and that's just the tip of the Biblical iceberg when it comes to longevity!

If humans eventually colonize space, there will be fewer of them *over populating* the earth. I'd rather take cryonics' one chance in 1 million, than assuredly go through the worm, although I don't question that *in the long run* we're all dead. As far as what happens to one's soul during cryonic suspension, I don't know, nor is it likely that anyone else does either!

The fact that frogs which freeze solidly for months thaw out with no ill effects is an indication that cryonics may work. Frogs are a long way from humans, but this and other examples, such as the Thirteen Line Ground Squirrel, are indications that cryonics is not impossible.

Some criticize cryonics, insisting we must enjoy life now and not obsess over living longer. That's quite fine, but there's nothing wrong with hoping to extend ones life a few years, or a few hundred years. It reminds me of the ancient Egyptians… they loved life so much that they wanted it to continue even after death. Although their mummification efforts were ineffective, there was nothing wrong with their intentions!

"Better dig a hole for him..." -- Humphrey Bogart

Debt

"Debt is the slavery of the free" … Publilius Syrus

The more people there are with "nothing to lose" - huge debts, no confidence in social security, sub-prime mortgages, beater cars and dead end jobs… the more society is at risk!

The downside of *good* credit, is the temptation to accumulate more debt…

Some people need credit like they need a hole in the head… those with the worst credit ratings, are given the highest interest rates, setting them up for failure and a serious spanking! The banksters extend credit to people who can't handle a savings account, much less a credit card... they're constantly looking for new victims.

He doesn't need credit, and says he can always "live like a Mexican." I don't disagree, but think he should be careful about which "Mexicans" he emulates. Many are smart, industrious and *getting ahead*, others aren't and they're suffering the consequences… so choose wisely!

He's concerned about his credit, and the bank is calling 3 or 4 times a day to harass him, so I said "tell them to take a hike." They'll be knocking on your door again in no time, after all their job is to extend credit, even to the over extended… they need you more than you need them!

The Russians warn they'll have to respond to what they call an arms race initiated by the West. The US has spent 10 times more than any other nation on its military for years... largely funded with credit extended by the Chinese, one of the countries we're preparing to fight. The Russians couldn't match our spending, but oil profits will allow them to increase spending, this at a time when the US may be running low on easy "credit." Will the rest of the world continue to buy our debt forever, or will the bill soon come due?

The debt market allows people to buy things they can't afford, makes a few people filthy rich and allows the nations that control the banking system to finance wars more *efficiently* than nations that are under the yoke of the bankers… is this sadly ironic, or just sad?

"He that dies pays all debts" … William Shakespeare

Democracy

"A democracy is nothing more than mob rule, where fifty-one percent of the people may take away the rights of the other forty-nine" … Thomas Jefferson quotes

Democracy? I like the idea, but not necessarily the reality of it. People are squeezed for their rights and for the fruits of their labor. Eventually in any human conceived system, the majority and the rich impose their will on the rest of society. Is it possible that the *means* is not as important as the *end…* with that being the preservations of our right to; life, liberty and the pursuit of happiness. The founding fathers got a few things wrong, but these inalienable rights are not among their mistakes.

I read that the founding fathers were for liberty, *not* for democracy… hmmm.

We should have constitutionally guaranteed human, civil and economic rights…not entitlements. Whatever form of government can best guarantee and protect those rights, is what I'm for. If it's a democracy fine, if it's something else, then so be it .

Our democracy appears to be less grass-roots, lobbyist inspired and special interest controlled. Democracy at its best is an excellent if not superior form of government, but in practice it rarely is excellent and never is perfect.

Democrats *tax-and-spend*, Republicans *borrow and spend...* neither bodes well for our grandchildren.

As far as democracy being superior, didn't Hitler use it in his rise to power? After his failed attempt to take over the government by force, didn't he run for office and win enough seats in the German government to eventually become *der Führer*? Didn't the democratic process actually position this mad man to rule Germany?

Reportedly, there are sixteen clandestine *intelligence agencies* in the U.S. some of which have the power and *authority* to permanently take out *troublemakers*! Their powers of surveillance, through the IRS, cameras and God knows what else would make Joseph Stalin green with envy!

Democracy may be the best system of government, but it's still administered and controlled by people, so its imperfect and getting more so all the time! Admittedly or not, we keep voting in favor of our own self interest and against that of our rivals. We know that if we get enough people behind us, we can make our lives more comfortable, by taking from others, and borrowing from our grandchildren!

If there are not irrevocable guarantees of individual freedom and rights, then what good is democracy? If the majority, can usurp the minority's rights, then what's the use? In the final analysis, the weak are always susceptible to tyranny by the more numerous and by the powerful.

If and when the barbarians arrive at our gates, our "liberal democracy" may take a sharp turn to the right. That's when the powerful, will *spend* us like dollars and use the populace for canon fodder. They know it takes force to keep the common man *in line*, so be prepared to see our constitutional guarantees sprout wings and fly away.

Democracy is not nonsense, it's wonderful unless it's corrupted by banksters, corporations, or anyone else, the problem is, that's what's happening… again!

I prefer democracy, but like anything else, it should not be above criticism, because it's certainly not above reproach. Democracy is imperfect and at times, a *strongman* is preferable to a democracy controlled by special interests.

I respect democracy but don't trust politicians to manage our daily lives anymore than I trust organized religion to secure our salvation.

Who in their right mind would turn over control of their lives via the "democratic process" to other people? If you are one of the outnumbered minority – it's natural to struggle for control of your life. It may be "proper" to respect the majority's will -- but if doing so means surrendering your constitutional/natural rights -- ye must resist!

Since I'm in the minority, I try to fly below the radar and stay out of the crosshairs of the majority!

It's been said before, the majority is not always right... in fact it may be wrong most of the time!

We have a great political system in theory, but in practice democracies tend to self destruct. The various factions elect politicians who's goals are to be reelected, and who will grant the electorate all the largesse and benefits they can to achieve that. Eventually the tax base erodes to the point where the nation's very survival is at risk!

Why should anyone be surprise that our democracy is in danger of failing… they usually do, and we aren't doing *anything different* than those free societies that failed in the past.

"Democracy... while it lasts is more bloody than either [aristocracy or monarchy]. Remember, democracy never lasts long. It soon wastes, exhausts, and murders itself. There is never a democracy that did not commit suicide" …
John Adams (Second president of the U.S.A.)

Diversity?

"Variety is the spice of life"… American Proverb

The definition of diversity is a moving target, controlled by opinion makers and social engineers. What is the ideal goal of *diversity?* Is it best exemplified by people of different ethnicities living together, or by all these *peoples* blending together to make a single race? We are encouraged to prefer the latter, but once that's achieved, will there be any *diversity* left?

We're encouraged to believe that if we eventually look more alike, society will be more peaceful. Unfortunately, one need only look as far as Rwanda or Cambodia, to see that people who look alike, can still be quite keen on killing each other.

Guess I'm a bit tribe or clan oriented and that puts me at odds with the current trend of favoring the "global village."

If it comes down to my DNA disappearing completely, or surviving minimally inside another populations gene pool, I'd have to say, that's better than nothing… but it wouldn't be my first choice by any stretch! That's a case of *if you can't beat them join them.*

I no more believe in master races than in chosen people... we're all born equal and hopefully every blood line has equal value in the eyes of God. That being said, it's up to each *blood line* to preserve it self... or perish. I don't want mine to take over the world… I just want it to survive! Every bloodline is unique and worthy, but if its members make no effort to preserve it, (consciously or otherwise) then ultimately it may fail. This is a disaster for the blood line, but of no interest whatsoever to the competition!

Personally, I like the diversity I see at this market, which includes beautiful children of many races, as well as mixed races. I hope the remaining human populations are preserved, which doesn't mean mixed race people shouldn't thrive as well…there's room for everyone!

The government should not have an agenda regarding race, other than promoting peace and prosperity. If it is determined to racially re-engineer society, it is exceeding its authority.

If a group of people is being out-competed and feels threatened with extinction, they're unlikely to *play fair*. Those who are *loosing* may consider the stakes too high to be *good sports*, it will become a case of all is fair in love and war.

Not that it matters to most people, but we are not all one *race*... we are all one *species*. At this point in time however, it's politically incorrect to mention this fact.

Why are there so many people with last names like; brown black and green, but so few named after the primary colors; red yellow and blue?

There are *saints* and *mad dogs* among any ethnic group, no group stands out… the problem is when our saints are *mad dogs* too!

I need to balance my desire to *keep my genes in the pool*, with appreciation of the fact that the world will be just fine without them!

Consciously, or otherwise, most men want to spread their ideas, and their seed... in the first case laziness prevents our success, in the second, laws and customs prevent it… often for the better!

Hearing someone's accent, even someone from a different region of the US, "tells us something" about that person… unfortunately more often than not it also tends to separates "us" from "them."

<u>Dogs (Mans Beast Friend!)</u>

"Whoever said you can't buy happiness forgot little puppies"… Gene Hill

Our Boston Terrier is a perfect example of why you should not buy a dog just for its markings. Our little buddy has little going for him other than his looks… and exhibits none of the outstanding traits our previous Boston had. That one was great, so the law of averages must have predicted that this one would be a *whack job.* It doesn't mean I won't be a good owner… I just want to take that responsibility to the ends of the earth. Actually, I like him more all the time and some day he'll probably surprise me to the upside.

"Want a friend, get a dog", rings truer all the time… at least with a dog you have half a chance. All the dog wants is a bone and a good scratch. If you want an even truer friend, rescue a stray dog. Our dogs *seem* to be my friend, at least they wag their tails, and have no control over me… at least not as much as some people do!

Fall's here, leaves are changing color, the temperature's dropping and I marvel at the beauty. Meanwhile, our Boston Terrier sits there and shivers... he has no idea that the Earth's farther from the sun in winter… all he knows is it's cold and that sucks!

It is nice to have a smart dog, unless it uses its brain to drive you crazy… that's when I prefer a dumb one.

So who's the *Pavlov's dog* around here anyway, me or the terrier? When he hears me putting on shoes, he flips over… it's time for a tummy toe rub. I'm obviously more "conditioned" than him.

"In dog years I'm dead." - Unknown

The dogs are hungry and following me around… we go outside, I put dog chow in their bowl but they ignore it. I go back in the house and they follow me… what are they expecting, Filet Mignon?

Most people consider it a crime to put down a nuisance dog, but *nuisance* people are often bombed into oblivion. I guess it's harder to find new homes for *bad* people than bad dogs… just pray they never put you on their list!

"You can't teach an old dog new tricks and you can't teach a dumb dog anything"… unknown.

I'd like to put the darn Cottontails out of business… they're eating more dog food than the dogs! Our automatic feeder is visited nightly by every cottontail in the hood, resulting in fat bunnies, and a doubling of our dog food bill. Leave it the dogs to figure out a solution… they started eating the rabbits!

Last month it was Cottonwood fluff, this month it's the Chow's fur messing up the deck. Despite repeated sweepings, fluff remains in nooks and crannies as if these spots were carefully sought out. The Chow fur also avoids the broom, seeking and sticking to splinters, wicker furniture and plastic chairs.

The *experts*, including veterinarians and dog food companies, advise us not to give leftovers to our dogs. What do you expect, they both want to sell us dog food! What better way to spice up our dogs lives than give them tasty leftovers?

All you have to do is watch an episode of America's favorite home videos to see that dogs are born comedians!

Pavlov's discovery, that dogs are predictable *should* give us the edge in training them, but they have an advantage… dogs have time on their side, after few of them work for living!

Why do they call it fixing a dog when you remove its gonads? It seems to me the poor things been broken, not fixed. On the other hand maybe they call it "fixing", because historically a dog that needed "fixing" probably wasn't much good to begin with!

Its weird, but I think my dog winks … but he does it with two eyes, not one.

My dog has won every battle we've had... I'm about to move into the dog house and give her the bed, she'll settle for nothing less!

Humans are lucky to have this symbiotic relationship with the dog. They deserve some credit for helping us get to where we are today... at least to the good places.

For thousands of years, dogs were primarily bred to *work* and the fact that they made good companions was a fringe benefit. Now however, if you expect your dog to do something useful instead of just being a pet (often a neurotic one), you're considered cruel -- what's up with that?

If we could ask, I think our dogs would tell us they want their remains properly "disposed of." When alive, dogs also deserve a little respect… shouldn't we treat people at least as well?

Just wondering… does having a drink with your dog qualify as - not *drinking alone*?

We have real and implied contracts with customers, family, friends and even dogs. If we take care of them, they'll take care of us… theoretically that is.

Why are male dogs always horny? If you're around dogs enough, you see lots of hank panky. It's usually males haunching females, but you see the opposite occasionally. Funny, you rarely see cats doing it, at least I never have. Maybe that's why we have expressions like "horn dog" and "doggy style" instead of cat analogies.

I brought the riblets home in a doggy bag, but instead of dumping them in front of the dogs, I hurled them across the yard. There were about 30 of them and they spread in a wide arc... it's the closest thing to an Easter egg hunt the dogs will ever experience!

These dogs are no dummies, they have an exquisite sense of timing. Five minutes after I leave the house, our Boston Terrier pulls a cushion off the couch and makes himself comfortable. I think he waits just long enough to feel confident we won't be coming back any time soon.

I take a letter out to the mailbox, the dog follows... and pees on the bush, mailbox and tree. Marking his territory is the most important things he'll do all day!

Even the dog ignores my commands…when I say "heel", she wanders off, when I finally give up and release her, she heels nicely. Maybe there's something wrong with my "delivery."

It's part of a dog's nature to probe for weaknesses. My dog was present when I removed the chicken wire protecting the Cedar spindles from her... two days later she started chewing on them to get on to the deck… she saw the weakness and took advantage of the opportunity!

Our dogs respond better to grunts and other guttural sounds than to spoken commands. After all, the lead Wolf doesn't speak the Queen's English… when I growl, they don't need an interpreter!

Took the dog for a walk off her leash the other day and the results were typical…she pooped one neighbor's lawn and rolled in what was left of a dead possum… yuck!

The experts say if humans disappeared, dogs would end up being something's lunch, and cats would fare much better. I wonder if the "expert" realizes that dogs form packs and cats would end up on the plate as often as dogs? Eventually dogs would adapt themselves to their environment, lose many of the useless traits we've bred into them with and probably do quite nicely. Instead of loosing out to them, I think cats would be a major part of their diet!

I barely missed running over a three-legged dog in the blind spot as I rounded a curve. A week or so later I saw him in the same spot... if Pavlov's theory is right, this dog will eventually learn… or run out of legs!

I thought his pot roast farts were bad, but they're nothing compared to the fumes emitted when I fed him Deer meat. It stunk worse than Newark, NJ circa 1966…doggie, you're killing me!

Dogs are easy to please… all you have to do is let them in, or out for them to feel like they're on vacation.

It's raining outside and I could use a Collie to herd my dogs outside-- in bad weather they won't go out unless they're forced to!

“The dog is a gentleman; I hope to go to his heaven, not man's”… Mark Twain

"If dogs could talk it would take a lot of the fun out of owning one." - Andy Rooney

Dreams

“I woke up in between, memory and a dream…” – Tom Petty

As I age, life is more about memories…it used to be about hopes and dreams.

The words dreaming and scheming, not only do they rhyme… there may be a more serious connection.

“Dream no small dreams for they have no power to move the hearts of men” … Goethe

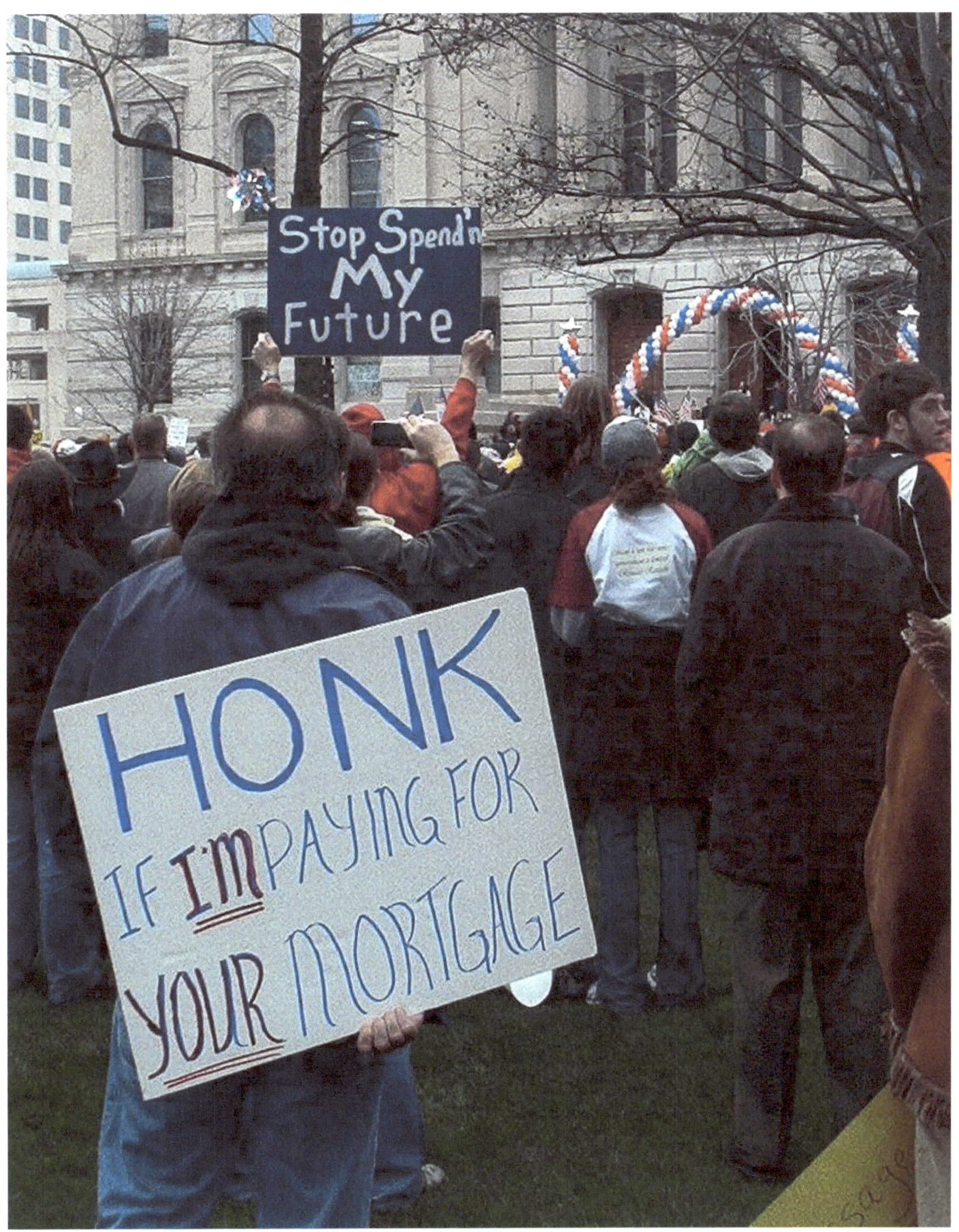

Tea Party Indianapolis

Driving

"Have you ever noticed that anybody driving slower than you is an idiot, and anyone going faster than you is a maniac?"... George Carlin

***Way back when*, a friend stated that if gas ever got too expensive for him, no one would be driving. I still think of that when fuel prices are on the rise... it was cocky and I wonder how he's doing now? Chances are he's still driving something big!**

Pulling out of the lot I notice the ballet of cars and pedestrians moving as if choreographed. When everyone plays their part correctly, traffic moves like clock work... even the Geese are learning the advantages of hustling across the road! When everyone obeys the rules and drives considerately, things go quite smoothly. Unfortunately, that's rarely the case... therefore we need traffic laws to cope.

It's rush hour and a vicious circle, someone pulls out in front of me, I honk and mutter and expletive. Moments later I'm *forced* to cut off another driver... I wonder if their response was any kinder than mine!

Cars whiz by, trying to beat the red light... reminding me of Zebras trying to cross the Zambezi before the Crocs grab them. At least here, *almost* everyone makes it home...there're a few fender benders, but even slow pokes avoid being eaten!

Visiting my *home* town, I see luxury cars, Chocolate Labs that retrieve nothing but treats and overpriced real estate only stockbrokers can afford. Having forgotten the local etiquette, I don't yield in time when a Land Rover approaches, and almost get run over by a particularly harried driver, after all this is a high adrenalin town!

It started out innocently enough and turned into one of the worst traffic jams I'd ever been in. The cause of all the frustration, was a few cones forcing three lanes into two, in the middle of the Chicago rush hour!

Coming out of nowhere, the car blew by me in the right hand lane, only to have to come to a screeching halt at a red light. Ha, I thought, hurry up and wait sucker! Then it occurred that he probably didn't mind the abrupt stop.

His satisfaction comes not just from getting somewhere in a hurry, but also in blowing past people and taking off from the red light like a race car driver.

Ah, the feel of smooth asphalt on the highway instead of the bone jarring concrete that lasts forever but drives miserably, especially when you're pulling a trailer.

You never get a red light when you need to look for *that something* you dropped, but when you don't want them, every light turns red!

My wife washes her car regularly, while I usually wait for a heavy rain. We were just wondering what gets bathed more often, my car, or our dog… I think it's a tie.

Having been pulled over repeatedly, I know how the Zebra feels when it's ambushed by lions... on the plus side, I don't have to worry about being eaten.

A car pulls up on my right intending to pass before his lane ends... I slow down a bit and let him whiz by. I'd rather have him in front than tailgating… once he's out of my hair, so to speak, we'll both be a lot happier!

Driving home on the Kennedy a sign reports it's 46 minutes to downtown, and I wonder, *why don't they just leave us alone*? It's bad enough were in bumper to bumper traffic, they're just rubbing it in! On the other hand, a "positive" thing about the recession is bumper to bumper traffic isn't as bad as it used to be… instead of going three miles an hour, now we're doing 10!

Some people leave early, some people leave late -- that explains tailgating and road rage. We play the part of *tailgater* when we're running late, and the *tailgated* when we leave early.

Funny, we all think we're pretty good drivers and we're critical of everyone else… except maybe our favorite NASCAR driver.

We live in a fantasy world... whether its the guy in the BMW, the guy on a Harley, or the MAN in Air Force One, we all have grandiose dreams, … it's what separates us from the apes!

Is the center console in your car like the junk drawer in your kitchen? Mine has everything you could possibly imagine... of course I can never find what I'm looking for!

Looking up at the approaching storm, I smile and think, "I'm going to make it", but Mother Nature has something different in mind! The only good thing about driving through storms, is leaving them behind... although you never know how long that will last.

It's a shame that people live in fear of being pulled over... many can spot a cop car in their rearview mirror a mile away. The Zebras are swift, but no match for the Lions lying in ambush, radar and tickets in hand!

We're masters at rationalizing... if someone's on my tail I complain loudly, but when *I* tailgate the other guy must be driving too slow!

As gasoline prices rise, I notice more people running red lights, guess the less time spent idling, the less gas you burn!

There's something in our psyche that wants to be "better" than other people. When I drive my old Hyundai... everyone acts like they deserve the right of way... after all, I'm in the cheap car!

When you're behind a slowpoke there's usually a good reason for it. Usually it's an oldster or a youngster behind the wheel... that should put the onus on the rest of us not to be jerks. The problem is they're *just driving*, while we're in a hurry to get somewhere -- it's a basic conflict of interest.

I'm running late, it's foggy and I'm driving too fast. I don't want my epitaph to be, "he was on time for his appointments... except the last one."

Chill out... the car tailgating you might be doing it because he's being pressured by an even bigger jerk.

Another example of hierarchy and dominance, is *the action* at four way stops. When arriving simultaneously, men often *take the initiative* and whiz past women. Chivalry be damned, guys must feel they have more important things to do! When two people of the same sex arrive at the stop simultaneously, the one with the faster or more expensive car feels entitled to go first.

I'm still getting used to my new car, haven't figured out where to put things and my phone keeps flying through the air! Dashboard controls should be standardized, it would be safer if you could get in any car and know where to find the; lights, cruise control, stereo and wipers. Imagine if steering, brakes and gas pedals were placed as randomly as these!

I pass the possum that was run over last week… it's kind of like an old friend, as I've seen it twenty times. Come on crows, do your job and clean up this mess! By now, the poor Possum baby that crawled out of her pouch is just a smudge next to momma… if I had a shovel I'd clean them up myself.

I saw a bumper sticker the other day that said "I hope that God isn't too picky"... now that's one I like! In fact I think it's much cooler than the one that says "in case of rapture this car will be unoccupied"... I consider that a tad presumptuous.

Wait in line at the four way stop on the way to drop the kids off at school, I see frazzled parents, kids combing their hair, CD holders on sun visors and babies in child seats… it's a veritable microcosm of society!

"You never really learn to swear until you learn to drive"… Author Unknown

Drugs (and Alcohol)

"An intelligent man is sometimes forced to be drunk to spend time with his fools"… Ernest Hemingway

Most of us are exposed to drugs and alcohol and we're influenced by the people that use them. Is it controversial to say there will be negative consequences, if you're influenced by the *wrong* people? If you swallow the line that "real men" get drunk and act stupid, you are likely to get in trouble… so please don't ask society to bail you out when it happens.

I've met alcoholics who're in denial, because they don't drink alone. They forget to mention that you can always find someone to drink with, just go to a bar! Actually, they'll drink alone if they have to, but since misery loves company, they work very hard to get others drunk too!

That pot which you say sets you free, is more likely to make you its prisoner. If you've smoked pot, you've already accrued any possible *benefits*... all that's left are; damaged lungs, memory loss and lack of motivation!

Thanks for the invitation, but getting wasted is counterproductive, not just for young people, but also for people with more "serious" responsibilities... find reasons not to get wasted, not the other way around.

Often, an addiction simply has to run its course… with time alone revealing whether the addict recovers. Meanwhile life consists of wasted years or decades…the turning point, if there is one, comes when the addict becomes severely ill, or realizes he won't live long enough to see his kids grow up etc.

I have nothing against having a good time, which in my opinion can include drinking. Unfortunately, at many a party, drunkenness is the host and his friend stupidity is there with bells on. When it comes to drugs, alcohol or even food, less is better!

The path of least resistance eventually leads to a tough row to hoe… so don't be a punk get off the junk!

It's okay to have friends who drink too much, unless they harass you for not overindulging with them. If they demand that you go down the same road, if their misery demands your company, its time to find new friends. They can join you in drinking less and you should encourage them, but if you can't lead them to water, ultimately it's their problem, not yours.

There are many *down sides* to excessive drinking, for example, you're shrinking brain cells and bloating fat cells!

Don't mistake misery loving company with generosity on the part of somebody offering you a drink or smoke… they're creating an obligation, in hopes that you'll buy the next round, even if you're not into it… it's a scam my friend, a scam.

Some people should never touch another drop of alcohol, because of the negative effect it has on them, and others. Other's have very little problem drinking responsibly, but there's a *poison* for everyone. When you discover your poison, never touch it again, because it's too strong and you like it too much! Despite thinking my poison was liberating and giving me *insights*, I was wrong… I wrote no more, and no better with, than without it.

The bad news is for the millions of pot smokers is it's an addiction… the good news is, it's primarily psychological not physical, making it a little easier to quit – wish I could say the same for tobacco.

Nothing would make me happier than to see boards of the tobacco companies *strung up*… what misery their poison has caused people!

The woman in your life wants to be your only intoxicant… no wonder she hates it when you smoke!

People with addictions, either chose that way of life, or have been hardwired in that direction. We can succumb to the wiring, or strive to rise above the wire.

When it comes to; drugs, alcohol, over eating etc., you can let your miscreant friends drag you down, or encourage them to follow you to higher ground… what will you do?

Even if addicts work, they will not escape the cycle of poverty, as long as they're paying black-market prices for their "fixes." Since they're jailed for *using drugs*, instead of for committing property or personal crimes, our prisons are overflowing and we're not making a dent in this vicious cycle. If we don't realize that altering one's consciousness is something humans have done since the beginning of time, and that many people always will, we will not get past this ridiculous "war on drugs."

As long as a large portion of the population, it is willing to persecute a smaller portion of the population for using "illegal" drugs, even while they use "legal" prescription drugs, we will remain in this hypocritical morass called the *war on drugs*.

Drugs…where does the tendency or propensity towards substance-abuse comes in? From a biological or evolutionary standpoint, does it serve any purpose… is it always counterproductive or can it be productive? If it's always counterproductive, why do we do it… is it a way of weeding out certain genetic "lines."

Who's in an altered state, them or me? If everyone I know is on some kind of mind altering or mood changing prescription or street drug, are they normal? Am I the one who's abnormal? Makes me think of that Jim

Morrison line, "…and all the children are insane…" If the parents are addicted to licit or illicit drugs, what does that make the kids? To add fuel to the fire, many children are medicated from early on…Ritalin, etc., etc.

The body and mind are designed to deal with a great deal of stress, but we're being sold on the premise that we should relinquish our coping skills and depend on pharmaceuticals. Of course there are cases where drugs are useful, or essential for people with chemical imbalances, or extremely stressful lives. Regardless, these wonder drugs are over-prescribed on a massive scale… all in the name of the almighty dollar!

We are surrounded by poisons (funny how the words poison and passion are similar) and these poisons are many people's passion. They include; alcohol, drugs, tobacco, sugar and fat, all of which are destructive like poisoned air or water. If we're smart, we'd eliminate as many of these poisons as possible… naturally *something* gets us in the end and we die, but why not combat what poisons we can?

Saw a sleeping pill commercial... describing it as non--narcotic, but towards the end there's a disclaimer stating that all sleeping aids have some risk of dependency... then they offer you a free seven-day trial supply!

Maybe pot's illegal, because unlike alcohol and tobacco, it's not consistent with the "American way." It generally making the user passive and questioning of authority… just the opposite of what Uncle Sam wants!

If your priority is smoking dope, you're likely to find out why they call it *dope*. If you don't eventually *grow up* and quit, that word may become your nick name.

Another obstacle to kicking the habit, is that pot tells you *everything's okay*. It whispers *there's no reason to give it up join the rat race...* it's a little bit right and a lot wrong!

Who says they can't kick in your door at 3 am? If the police believe you have pot, they can. When interviewed, a former drug cop, said he routinely stopped cars with college stickers, as well as black and Hispanic drivers, because there was a "high probability" they would have of pot. He made bets with the agents he trained, that he could put someone in jail before the day was done and claims he never lost!

When the same cop started busting children of wealthy citizens, he got in trouble. He claims 750,000 Americans are busted for marijuana possession each year… he now wishes he hadn't participated in the drug war!

"Alcohol is necessary for a man so that he can have a good opinion of himself, undisturbed be the facts"… Finley Peter Dunne

Economy

"The economy depends about as much on economists as the weather does on weather forecasters"… unknown

Those who hold the financial strings, want to increase the investor class so it will be large enough to withstand any onslaught by those that have been pushed into poverty. With wealth *and* poverty rising, guns everywhere and an economy that looks like a slow train wreck, we're indeed living in interesting times!

The Dow Jones is a measure of how the rich are doing and as usual, it shows that they're getting richer. The Wilshire, NASDAQ and S&P 500 are measures of how other segments of the investor class are doing, but none are accurate measures of how the working class are doing…

Alan Greenspan used men's underwear as an economic indicator, because when times are tough, men hang on to their briefs till there's nothing left. My economic indicators are; is OJ tracking down his memorabilia, how many credit card offers am I shredding, are the Somali pirates making money, and can people still afford to eradicate their dandelions...

Is the economy a gigantic Ponzi scheme? Don't worry, our fearless leaders always have World War III up their sleeves… it's a time tested way of *saving* the economy!

If capitalism requires occasional recessions to "clean house" does freedom need occasional wars to maintain its vitality? Conversely, if putting off the inevitable recession can lead to a depression, does putting off the war lead to genocide and cataclysm? Are freedom and the economy similar to our bodies… should we give both of them small doses of poison so they can develop anti-bodies?

I don't believe very much in trickle-down economics... the wealthy are too adapt at investing money solely for their advantage, leaving only minute scraps for others. Unfortunately, those at the bottom often squander their money … didn't Jesus say, "You will always have the poor with you."

It's the middle class, who are most likely to spend money so that some *trickles down*. As far as trickling up, that should be the least of society's concern… the rich will get their hands on it no matter what!

The numbers are staggering... we used to say, "Bill Gates could fix that with his $ 50 billion." Now that kind of money is a drop in the bucket, when you consider the multi-trillion dollar mess we are in... what comes after a trillion? It's a quadrillion and I'm wondering when that word will come into use on a regular basis.

My friends who are having a tough time are become increasingly socialist... anyone they consider prosperous, who is unwilling to "share" their good fortune is considered an enemy of the people… off with your head!

Passing the bailout was easy… all they had to do was promise the rich hundreds of billions, and scare the working class half to death.

Trickle-down economics, prosperity seeps through the cracks, but if you don't even have a pot to pee in, it's hard to catch the trickle! Kind of like a rising tide raises all boats, unless yours has a hole in it.

I'm not as concerned about our form of government, as I am about having a government that guarantees our constitutional rights and I care less about what economic system I live under, then with it being fair, maximizing opportunity and minimizing exploitation.

In the tradition of Lenin's, "taking from each according to his ability and giving to each according to their needs", they will impoverish and control us. Despite cloaking it in Robin Hood rhetoric about taking from the rich and giving to the poor, they have no right to steal from the taxpayers…obviously *power's* more important than rights.

I wonder if under socialism, even the kids become lazy, and at what age do they realize there's no reason to work hard?

I'm optimistic about the future of the USA, but not infinitely so. We may be able to solve our problems, or this could be a slow motion train wreck. If we can't solve them, then the people who don't get out of the way will be hurt. When the train comes to stop, will the dazed passengers be able to stager away and make the best of things?

If you're going to have a train wreck, the slow motion variety is the best kind to have… at least you have a chance of doing something about it, before it's too late. The nature of the wreck is also important… will we just grind to a halt, or will we go over a cliff?

As I stroll around our neighborhood, a few people look annoyed that I'm taking a walk while they're on their way to work. Shouldn't I be *buying* or *selling*, to keep the economy rolling along? They seem to think working from home doesn't count!

The economy, geopolitics … *everything* seems to be moving slowly, inexorably - like the Titanic towards the iceberg. Some people want solutions, others say let's just get it over with!

Is there a difference between an excuse and an explanation? They're both self serving, but is one less so than the other.

If, and more likely when Wall Street's run ends and the banksters finally brings down Main Street, will the shills who pushed the Ponzi scheme say they were just trying to keep the economy going, or will they say they always knew it was a house of cards? In any case, they'll probably be saying it from some "safe" haven.

If there aren't technical breakthroughs soon we could be in for a world of hurt. I'm not sure that conservation, or regulation can save us at this point, could we experience a meltdown of the environment and the economy… simultaneously?

Those who are doing lousy don't want to hear success stories from those who are doing well... keep it to yourself, anything else is seen as bragging!

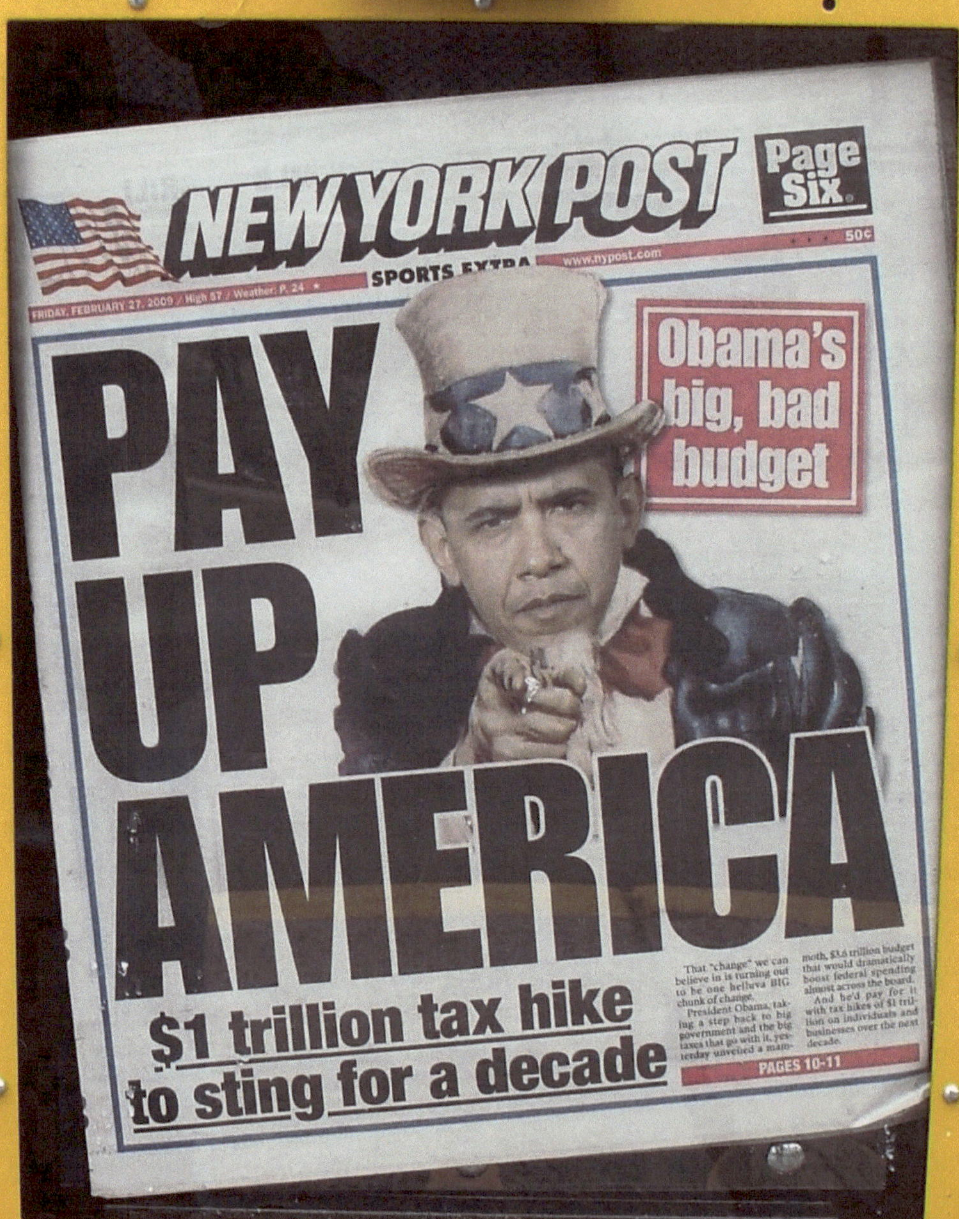

NEW YORK POST

Page Six.

FRIDAY, FEBRUARY 27, 2009 / High 57 / Weather: P. 24

SPORTS EXTRA

www.nypost.com

50¢

PAY UP AMERICA

Obama's big, bad budget

$1 trillion tax hike to sting for a decade

That "change" we can believe in is turning out to be one helluva BIG chunk of change.

President Obama, taking a step back to big government and the big taxes that go with it, yesterday unveiled a mammoth, $3.6 trillion budget that would dramatically boost federal spending almost across the board.

And he'd pay for it with tax hikes of $1 trillion on individuals and businesses over the next decade.

PAGES 10-11

Elites

"A people that values its privileges above its principles soon loses both"… Dwight David Eisenhower

Being raised to *agree* instead of to *think*, is nothing new. It's been going on since time immemorial – how else could the elite manage the masses so successfully?

I heard someone say that if voting really worked, it would be illegal and that may be accurate. The elite have no problem with the masses voting… after all, the will of the people has rarely been an obstacle to the plans of the rich.

Is it just me, or do many of the so called "rebels" out there, like rockers and rappers feed their audience pabulum while sucking on the corporate teat? They are tools of the establishment, saying nothing new and accumulating wealth, so they can *join the club.*

Nations are like cults... newcomers are supposed to assimilate, embrace its mythology, and leave their *tired old values* at the border. Nations seek to instill a *common vision* in all citizens, but it's a vision devised by those who are the wealthiest… and determined to stay that way!

Are you part of the economic elite, or part of the proletariat? It depends on who you ask… your workers will say yes and your boss will say no.

Environment

"Waste is a design flaw"… Kate Krebs. In nature, nothing is wasted.

Strange how hurricane Katrina, one of the new breed of super hurricanes, severely damaged the oil and gasoline refining infrastructure. *She* almost seemed to target the industries causing climate change… Will we heed the *warning*?

Environmental degradation is due to man's desire for sex and woman's for shoes.

I'm wondering if these *hands-free* devices waste more than they save? There is a learning curve, so eventually they should save water, paper towels and soap, but I'm not buying the statistics yet. I wave my hand in front of all three soap dispensers, that way at least one might work! It's a harder to get water though, as it's impractical to jump back and forth between three faucets!

Some people are anti-environmental, because they believe environmentalism is counter to *manifest destiny*. Our presidents champion consumption, because it creates jobs. Frugality has been made to sound unpatriotic, do you remember being told to fight terrorism by "going out and shop!"

If this planet isn't warming, I'll eat my hat - just look at the melting ice caps and our warming weather. The only hope we have, is that the climate scientists, are as imperfect as the weatherman? If the meteorologist on TV can't accurately project today's weather, then perhaps the climate scientists are inept too.

We should encourage renewable energy, recycling and energy conservation… these technologies may not be essential on earth for a hundred years, but they'll be essential in space from day one.

Society is incapable of stopping on a dime and changing course towards a green future, which according to climate scientists means we may face a catastrophe. Some say global warming will lead to a change in the Gulf Stream, which could result in an ice age instead of global warming. Wouldn't it be ironic if everything evens out in the end and things turn out all right… let's not hold our breath, it would be better to address climate with everything at our disposal.

The price of gas is "reasonable" again, at least for some, so the sales of hybrids is down and SUVs up. After all, we have the right to drive whatever we want as long as we can afford it… I don't disagree *in principle*, but wonder how much longer will this prevail?

Another reason the rich "don't think" global warming is true, is they need more time to unload their beach front properties on "greater fools."

The weatherman described the breaking of the Wilkins ice shelf in Antarctica, but was careful not to mention climate change. As an employee

of the corporate media, that would be a *mistake* – regardless of his opinion. The best he could must was, "it's a complex system, that's for sure."

Instead of government censorship, America is subject to self censorship… we've earned to keep our mouths shut about controversial subjects. Some things are better left unsaid, especially when your paycheck depends on it!

Corporations and politicians tell us we can't enact tougher environmental laws, or the economy will loose thousands of jobs. On the flip side, countries with stricter environmental laws seem to be doing quite well!

"I can remember when the air was clean and sex was dirty"… George Burns

Experience

"God will not look you over for medals, degrees or diplomas, but for scars"…Elbert Hubbard

How, will you learn from experience, if you're not accountable for your mistakes?

My kids would like for me to give money to invest in their ideas, but I would rather give them ideas and experience… you can imagine how that's being received!

You can see everything traumatic that happens as a downer, or you can learn from such experiences.

While walking the hood, a young Cottontail whizzes past me - dangerously close. I've seen him acting recklessly before, threatening his very survival. Maybe that's why rabbits have short tails -- if you're constantly chased, you don't want a long one streaming behind… deer are like that too.

If you think you've got life all figure out… you've figure wrong!

"Life is the art of drawing without an eraser" …John Gardner

<u>Family and Relatives</u>

"Families are like fudge - mostly sweet with a few nuts"... Unknown

Wonderful moments, last only as long as our memories, which themselves are like a vapor...good things should be passed along to others!

When you say something terrible, the words are impossible to take back, or to forget. On the other side of the coin, we should realize those hurtful things, are blurted out in anger and haste - so be willing to forgive.

Why do our lives sometimes... I mean *often* seem to revolve around keeping other people supplied with baubles and trinkets.

Did *we* create this mess, or was it our parents and grandparents? It's pretty hard to find anybody who blames their own generation... fact remains, we keep leaving the next one with a greater and greater mess!

When friends or relatives come to visit, my wife wants everything perfect... and such occasions *are* good opportunities for deep cleaning. On the other hand, if we make things too comfortable, we could end up with new roommates! It's nice to be gracious, but if hosting is a competition, it's one I don't want to win.

There're lots of people around here who believe in keeping ones' nose to the grindstone... especially mine!

Funny how some relatives and ancestors are held up as heroes worthy of respect, while others are pointed to as examples of *what not to do.* I doubt it's that simple... none of them were perfect, and none were total *screw ups*... were they?

Despite you protests to the contrary, I've yet to meet anyone whose world view is not based, on self serving rationalizations! On some level, life is just a great big grab... we should strive to do better.

We all have overbearing relatives... I hope I don't follow in the footsteps of the ones I know!

“No one notices what I do around here, until I stop doing it”… unknown.

I think men want grand kids as much as women, we just want them for different reasons. It has to do with women having no vested interest in the continuation of “the line” as the men are. Women don’t seem to care as much about the family name being perpetuated either… after all, in most cultures, it’s the mans name that lives on.

We should master our neuroses and not expect others to enable, or subsidize our compulsions. As families we have to help each other, and put up with a bit of neurotic behavior… but we mustn’t be held hostage! Similarly, society should extend assistance to those who need it… but tax payers must not be held hostage by gamers.

My dad didn't teach us how to play ball or fight... which caused a problem or two along the way. On the other hand, he taught us that knowledge is power and to be open minded… for these things I’m eternally grateful, if not always comfortable with the results!

Too often, I’ve pointed out the obvious to my children and that didn't help them think for themselves. I’m trying to keep my mouth shut and let them figure out the world themselves. They don't want my advice anyway, but as a parent sometimes I can't resist!

Jealousy and avarice is common among relatives and friends. Admittedly or not we’re trying to “win the contest” and end up with the most toys and largest bank account balance when we die… how silly is that!

I’ve noticed that my son and my father are similar…they both do the opposite of what I want!

Our loved ones are the most important things in our lives. They *usually* don't ask for much... and mostly just want to stay in touch. If they do ask for too much -- we have the option of saying no. We’re not responsible for making family members lives "easy", just easier.

My dad got us to this country and I’m very grateful, but supremely grateful… I don't think so. Our lives would have been quite different “over there”, but who’s to say they’d be worse? The overseas relatives I’ve visited *seem* to be doing quite well! In addition, it’s next to impossible for an average person to make an impact on American society… would it have been

different if I'd grown up in the old country? There I'd be a bigger fish in a smaller pond and might be able to make a difference!

Social Security is a *throw back…* it's a way for workers to indirectly support elderly or infirm relatives who can't work. In the old days, families directly took care of grandparents and other relatives. Now we pay a tax so the government can provide for the elderly, disabled and lazy. The able bodied and sound of mind, still pay for the security of their relatives!

Too often I say "don't blame yourself", when my loved ones have problems, they take that advice to heart… and blame me instead!

Kids... please don't expect others to "look out" for you... it won't happen. People have been messing with each other since the beginning of time... don't expect *that* to change any time soon. When you walk through the woods of life, it's up to you to catch the branches… believe me no one else will!

"Other things may change us, but we start and end with the family"… Anthony Brandt

<u>Food and Drink</u>

"Americans have more food to eat than any other people and more diets to keep them from eating it"… unknown

We like our beef, chicken and fish wrapped in plastic… no fur, feathers, scales or bones please! We don't want to think about how they got there, or about crowded farm factories.

You tell me not to eat meat and to treat the animals as equals, but if you re-engineer the Lion to lay down with the Lamb, is it still a Lion?

If it's wrong to eat meat, why do we have teeth specifically designed for that purpose? We're omnivores plain and simple, meant to eat both vegetables and meat. You say, the brain is mightier than the mouth and we should learn to feed ourselves without killing animals… that's fine for your, but I'm sticking with the teeth!

Many people disdain hunters, even as they feast on beef or poultry raised and butchered solely for our consumption. Is the quality of life better in the feed yard than in the forest? Of course not! In the wild, animals live as they always have, avoiding predators… as long as they can.

Why should I feel bad about eating fish, foul or meat ... they're part of the food chain and so are we. If they aren't eaten, they'll end up maggot and worm food… as will we. From the lowliest parasite, to the POTUS, our mortal remains share the same fate!

For thousands of years, men have brought home the bacon and women have prepared it. I think women considered it a privilege to put the food on the table. Even as men garnered sexual favors for supplying the meat, women bartered food preparation for influence and protection. In the process, men have been well fed... in many cases too well fed, "eat everything on your plate!" they say. The resulting obesity is our own fault, since no one holds a gun to anyone's head forcing them to eat every last bite.

Once again, I over did it, in fact, I way over did it, but at least I didn't way, way ,way over do it... thank goodness for small miracles.

My wife has contaminated the trail mix with almonds! I don't mean to complain, but the original trail mix was much better than this adulterated concoction. Almonds are fine with chocolate... but when added to a delicacy product like trail mix, they just water it down.

We embrace the technologies that we need… while my friends have learned to use TIVO to record their favorite TV shows, I have learned the art of thawing cake in the microwave so it's *as good as new…*of course my waistline shows it.
Didn't Marie Antoinette say, "let them eat cake?" I'm confused… isn't cake good? I wouldn't have beheaded her, I'd have voted her a second term!

Okay…I had a stupid breakfast, so I'll try to have a smart lunch.

I'm over 50 and have eaten a burger a week my entire life, that's 2,500 hamburgers… which is probably enough. I won't stop eating them, but I'll slow down a bit. Drinkers and smokers should look at things the same way… how many times have you partaken during your life, and do you really benefit from these things? Less is better!

Losing weight can be so difficult because of cravings that our body demands we satisfy. We try to "fool" our body with artificial sweeteners, diet pill's and carrots... but fat cells are smarter than brain cells. In order to lose weight, it's helpful to tap into the mind, body connection. It's not a complex equation, but it must be understood to solve the riddle… good luck!

Weight loss involves considerable challenges; portion control, calorie reduction, delayed gratification and exercise… many of us are hard wired against all these, so success requires a huge, but worthwhile effort!

Greenpeace does its best to prevent the Japanese from catching whales... but I don't see them protesting the millions of cows we slaughter. Whales are more intelligent than cows, but if they're anything like Bottle Nosed Dolphins, then they can also be very nasty. The French eat horses and many nationalities eat dogs... why doesn't Greenpeace harass them? I like whales, but don't think we should force our culinary values on others, especially if as nation we are going to eat more meat per capita than just about anyone else. As long as the Japanese manage the whale populations so they don't decline, I don't think its any of our business.

I think my wife has again hidden the Christmas cookies. She thinks she's doing me a favor, but I usually find something even worse to eat, and lots of it! Today I only looked briefly, then gave up and went on my way... this time she really did do me a favor!

I complained about the oatmeal raisin cookies our neighbor brought over, "why would anyone ruin a perfectly good cookie by putting raisins in it?" A week later when I ran out of *better* treats, the oatmeal raison cookies started tasting pretty good!

Does anybody else think that chocolate makes all nuts equal? I'd rather eat Cashews than Peanuts, but when both are dipped in chocolate, the Cashew looses its advantage!

I slice a piece of cake, put it on my plate and walk towards the couch, trying not to start eating until I sit down... if I'm not careful it will be gone before I even get there!

One of the greatest inventions of Western civilization is Coffee Mate... I'm not kidding, even though according to both my wife and mother it's terrible stuff!

There's more peanut butter floating around our kitchen than in a kindergarten class, but I'm not complaining, after all that's what my girl likes!

I'm a connoisseur, but I do like my wine bottle to have a real cork… screw tops, fake corks and boxes just don't have the same panache.

There's good coffee and there's bad, there's also cheap and expensive… and there's not a direct correlation between the two.

"Once, during Prohibition, I was forced to live for days on nothing but food and water"… W. C. Fields

I've got the luckiest stomach in the world, it gets whatever it wants!

Come on Vlasic…if I can't open your darn jar, how am I going to eat your pickles…today, you've lost out to a bag of chips!

Vegetables are a must on a diet. I suggest carrot cake, zucchini bread, and pumpkin pie. ~Jim Davis

Freedom and Free Speech

"No one is free, even the birds are chained to the sky" … Bob Dylan

Freedom of speech, comes with an asterisk… there are several points of view tolerated by society, stray beyond and you may face the ultimate repercussion.

Everyone should have a voice and use it to speak their mind… even if we can't expect to change the world, there is nothing wrong with trying.

If were going to have freedom, we're also going to have drunkenness, but what truly deserves protection is freedom, not drunkenness. Some celebrate the right to party as a cornerstone of freedom… remember the Beasties Boys song "You've got to fight for your right to party!" Alcoholism is most common where freedom of speech is not guaranteed, and booze is the one "gift" given to his *subjects* by the dictator. Drunkenness keeps people's

minds off of other things, but America was not founded to protect it. We should not confuse the freedom to get drunk with the larger meaning of free speech.

It's important not to just criticize other governments, but also our own, we must have the right to do both.

My immediate family knows my views and they're relatively tolerant – but I still walk on eggshells, especially regarding *certain* issues. The boundaries are so well-defined, that to stay on good terms I must hold my tongue … even with them!

Freedom of speech is the people's most powerful right, followed by the right to maintain it through any means necessary. That's why the powerful will not allow the people the right to bear the kinds of arms necessary to maintain their freedom. They allow ownership of weapons suitable for killing each other, but not for facing down the government.

Free people need iron clad constitutional guarantees *at least as much* as they need elections. Our rights were won by a revolution, not by an election. Elections have robbed Americans of more rights than foreign enemies ever could, we may need another one to win them back!

Should we be able to choose whose speech rights we want to defend… or must we defend the rights everyone, no matter how onerous we consider their agendas?

I don't think *this group, or that* needs to be crushed, but some may need to be resisted, so that others are not crushed instead.

I don't think this government is going to fall anytime soon, what might collapse is the concept of *liberty or death*. Our own government may do what the British could not... make up subjects, instead of citizens. Not surprisingly the lazy will be pleased, because the property of hard working people will be given to them. After taking our liberty, the government won't even have to *give us death*... the fear of prison will be sufficient to keep most of us in line.

There are influential people around, intent on forcing their views on the rest of us, so resist, think for yourself and if necessary, follow the path of resistance!

When we were young, we were told we should grow up to *speak our minds*. Later I learned it only applies if *our mind*, concur with the minds of those in charge. Like children, we are to be "seen and not heard", unless our opinions are in the acceptable range, and ideally in synch with our leaders.

You have to be willing to fight to protect your God given right to; life, liberty and the pursuit of happiness. If not, there will always be someone ready to take your precious freedoms away in the name of one damned thing or another.

On such a crowded planet, can we afford to let individuals act in their own "best interest?" I don't know, but the government seems to be making it more difficult all the time.

We have free speech, but not enough of it to say what I want to about the most powerful people. There is never completely free speech... there are mechanisms in place everywhere designed to "encourage" people not to criticize their leaders.

Freedom of speech seems strongest when society is stabile and the status quo is not threatened. The true test is retaining it when the powerful feel threatened by criticism. Eventually the First Amendment will be put to the test and we'll see if our handlers want us to be free, or bond.

"Take away the right to say "fuck" and you take away the right to say "fuck the government"... Lenny Bruce

Freedom of Association

There should be no state sponsored discrimination, but if individuals are not allowed to make decisions regarding who they can live with or among, then they have lost another fundamental right... freedom of association.

Its insane when someone else decides, who you should associate with, who's club you can join, who's you can't and who you must invite to your party.

If you want to associate with all of the people all the time – great! If you want to associate with some of the people, some of the time – great! I believe

you should have the right to do this… however "Big Brother" may beg to differ.

There are certainly many people who will not want to associate with me… and that is their God given right!

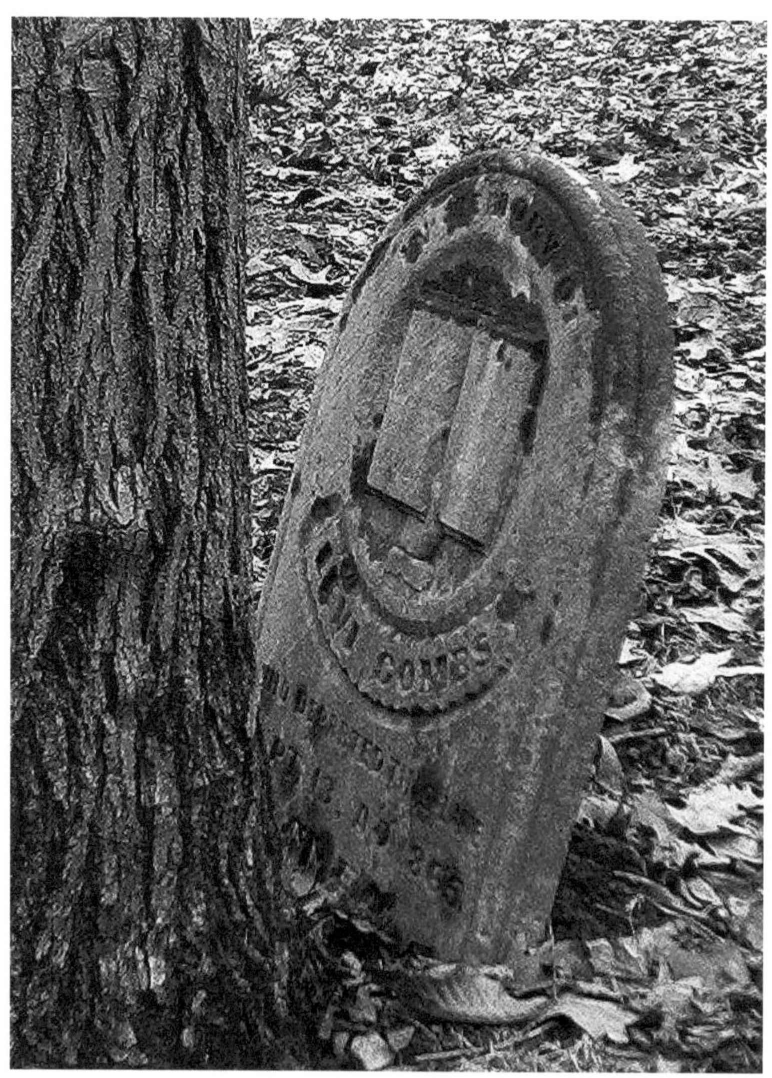

<u>Friends and Neighbors</u>

"One's friends are that part of the human race with which one can be human" … George Santayana

Friends sometimes treat you bad and vice versa, because relationships are like the weather. Occasionally friends feud, due to politics, religion or whatever, and then we end up doing rotten things. If possible, persevere... as long as the *nonsense* is an aberration and not a pattern.

The same applies to relatives, if there is a pattern of crummy treatment, then even if you can't pick your relatives, at least pick the times and places you interact. If they straighten out great, if they don't, give them just *the time of day*. After all, if you are not demanding of them, they have no right to make demands of you. Its not that we have no obligations, its just that our *actual* obligations are more limited than those that friends and relatives try to foist on you.

Sometimes I think there're only two choices when it comes to friends... lousy, or none at all! That's an exaggeration, I guess my expectations are way too high.

Some people need a lot of friends, some just need one or two... but when you find that even those are fickle, who can you turn to?

My neighbors are like neighbors anywhere -- as long as I don't rock their boat, they're unlikely to rock mine.

If you take me for a fool and treat me like a fool, does that mean that I am a fool? If I keep *letting* you treat me like one, than most likely I am.

When it comes to buddies, strike a balance between holding on to their friendship, treating them right, keeping in touch and "moving on", if they crap on you. Treat people with respect, insist on the same, do no harm, watch your backside and keep on truckin!

I backed out of the garage and stopped in the driveway to put on my gloves... meanwhile my neighbor walked back from his mailbox, a third neighbor pulled into his driveway, raised the garage door remotely and drove in. Although we get along fine, on this occasion not one of us acknowledged the others in any way. In a well coordinated orchestra, the three of us ignored each other completely! Its a busy afternoon and we have *lots to do*... regardless of friendly hello would have been a nice way to start the week!

Despite *occasional* anger, jealousy or whatever, I want my friends to prosper. Heck, that way they're happier with me, their mental health is better and since most of them are armed to the teeth, less likely to do something stupid.

"True friends stab you in the front"… Oscar Wilde

One reason we don't have very many *friends for life,* is that unlike relatives we can choose our friends. It's easier to discard friends who aren't "working out" then it is to get rid of relatives. We should however be slow in discarding friends, as they're note as easy to replace as we think. Despite their foibles, friends may be irreplaceable. Another thing about friendship, is the mystery of attraction…as with the music we like, it's a *chemical reaction.*

At this point, my wife is my best friend, followed by my children, other family members and a couple of fellows I've known a long time. She's like my good friends of old, kind, moderate and unlikely to stab me in the back. So things really aren't much different than they were 40 years ago when I had one best friend and a few other good ones.

The flip side of losing all of your friends for speaking your mind, is that you have the opportunity to make new friends who might accept you in spite of your views… good luck with that!

A friend took us out on his boat twice this weekend... another friend took us out on his twice last month, so I think I've had enough boating for a while. I'd rather *have* friends with boats than *have* one myself... there only a few things in life I require and a boat is not one of them!

Most of what my friend and I do is competitive... whether it's debating politics and religion, or playing basketball in the old days. The one non-competitive thing we did was, was smoke the *peace* pipe… and we haven't done *that* in years.

I was trying to broker a deal that could make me rich… and I wondered, should I mention it to my friends? Of course not, came the answer… that would just lead to jealousy and outstretched hands. Keep such information to yourself, it will get out soon enough anyway! It will also sound better if you're not the one spreading it, and it will result in problems regardless!

Funny how people remember *everything*… at least if it's something that can embarrass me. Anything good I do is quickly forgotten!

The problem with not having very many friends, is you have to handle the ones you have with kid gloves… and that is not a good situation.

Friends are not free... they come with a cost, although true friends usually charge less.

Friends, relatives and lovers... we've had our share of bumps in the road, and we'll continue to, although hopefully not as often as before. If we cease to hit those bumps, it would mean our relationship is over and I don't want that.

The guys called me a "woman" for not wanting to run amok at the party, my wife was disappointed I didn't "stand up to them more vigorously... I call it getting it from both sides!

It's starting to dawn on me, if you don't agree with your friends, eventually and almost inevitably, they stop being friends. This is a very sad observation, because God knows we need friends!

I don't wish ill on my friends... but have to admit occasionally hoping they don't get "ahead" of me, which by the way is selfish and counter productive. When they're "ahead" they seem to like me better, and when I'm "ahead", they're jealous! It's in our own self interest, for our friends to be doing well financially and emotionally. We're all so interdependent, that it makes no sense to hope that others fail.

Ironically, the things ruining our friendship now, are the same things that led to our friendship in the beginning. I admired my friends character and he seemed to appreciated mine. Unfortunately, during these stressful times, we resent each other for those same qualities!

Got a call from an old friend around Christmas… guess it's part of the holiday spirit to reconnect. I called him last year at about the same time. After missing his call, I jotted down a note to call him, but misspelled his name... that shows how long it's been since we've talked!

"I get by with a little help from my friends"… John Lennon

Genius and Stupidity

"Everyone has a right to be stupid; some people just abuse the privilege"... unknown

Have you ever seen the Wizard of Oz? If nothing else, a diploma is proof you've persevered, without one people take you a bit less seriously. A degree doesn't prove you're smart, it just proves you've persevered through mental trials and tribulations. It may not be fair, since rich kids have fewer obstacles to overcome in obtaining degrees, than poor kids... but life isn't remotely fair anyway.

"Rainman" can tell you the weather, or what happened on any day in history... but what good is that kind of genius? And what good was Einstein's genius if it just gave us nukes? I guess it depends on if you're the bomber or the bombee... Unlike Rainman, Einstein was apparently quite a ladies man... women seem to love successful geniuses. Einstein applied his genius to real-life *situations...* autistic geniuses like Rainman have no such capacity.

Intelligence and wisdom do not necessarily go hand-in-hand... everyone knows that.

I'm not saying you can't *talk and think* at the same time, but don't people think most effectively when their lips aren't flapping? Doesn't it follow that people who talk constantly spend less time thinking?

Ask an idiot a question and you're likely to get an idiotic answer, but even that can be enlightening... you can learn something from anyone, even if you're learning what *not* to do.

"Live and learn from fools and from sages."... Aerosmith

Geniuses who reject the knowledge of others and insist on figuring everything out themselves end up screwing up. If he'd they'd just *read the manual*, they'd benefit from the experience of its authors. Even if none of them were geniuses, their combined intellect is great! Geniuses rarely accomplish as much on their own as a few "average" people accomplish as a team.

Increasingly people believe that open-mindedness and doing their own "due diligence" is a waste of time. The *opinion makers* they listen to, are doing their best to convince them that they have all the answers and that *intellect* is a "four letter word."

Some people are *gold mines* of information and we say, it's too bad their brains can't be saved for posterity. The thing is, *magnetic* memory is a better storage medium than grey matter…if these people would just record their wisdom it wouldn't be lost.

The flipside of a bunch of normal people being able to do more than a genius, is that genius can occasionally do more than the team of normal people... at least if he or she applies himself to the full extent of his ability.

Short-term, people with *street smarts* prevail over people with higher IQs, because they *routinely* employee deception and treachery to get their way. In the long run, high IQ people prevail, as they organize and devise even greater treachery. When "geniuses" survive the initial onslaughts of thugs, they tend to wreak havoc on such predators.

The worst thing you can tell a young prodigy is that he or she's a genius… that's when they *take their foot off the gas* and start coasting. It's foolish to think that being a genius means, you have it made! The exception is telling the child they're special and then giving them the support necessary to advance their flowering.

In the UK they have knighthoods, over here we have "medals" and honorary degrees… I put no stead in either.

Don't use geniuses as role models, unless their doing something useful. We've all met highly intelligent people who seem intent on pickling their brains, instead of using them. That's not what the creator intended… win, lose or draw, try to make a difference!

I may be stupid, and a glutton for punishment, I'm just trying not to be both simultaneously.

There's a niche for "crazy people" too… we can learn from them too. After all, who was the first people to harness fire? Who *foolishly* grabbed that burning stick and realized the flames potential? Was it a genius, or a crazy person… it could have been anyone!

I simply have an inquiring mind -- *simple*, but inquiring.

The *nice* thing about people who talk too much, is that it's difficult to talk and think simultaneously. Let them blab all they want, that way they'll have less time to implement their schemes! When an idiot's lips are flapping, you can be sure they're conniving to pick your pocket, or meddle in some one else's life.

"Imagination without execution is hallucination"... Albert Einstein

Generation Gap

"It's one of nature's way that we often feel closer to distant generations than to the generation immediately preceding us"... Igor Stravinsky

Show me a grown man or woman who doesn't try to influence young people and I'll show you a dolt who's missed the boat. Every adult wants to pass their world view on to younger folks, whether they admit it, know it, or are oblivious to the fact. I'm not saying we want to take over the young minds we come in contact with, but we all have beliefs and hope to influence the next generation to move in that direction.

There's always a collision or two occurring...generations, races, sexes...someone's always clashing!

Different styles for each generation... why not? I'm watching a program on baboons and suspect their *styles* have changed very little in the last million years. Maybe that's why they haven't evolved into anything more advanced. We on the other hand keep changing... for one generation its ear rings for men, for the next its nose rings for everyone. We're a dynamic and innovative species -- squelching change leads to stagnation and less innovation.

We often complain about the "younger generation"... maybe that's why people get old and die. Eventually most of us have *had it* with young folks, but we can't seem to change them – so why hang around?

Oldsters love telling youngsters how to do things, because they learned the hard way and want to spare others that trouble. Unfortunately, the younger

generation prefers to learn the hard way… it's a family tradition! No matter how much we want to "inform" them, they just don't want our advice. Even if we briefly get their attention, they're usually immune to good advice … on the other hand, they soak up bad advice like sunlight! Maybe we should find some other way of justifying our existence.

If you find you've dug yourself a hole, it's probably because you've followed the advice of idiots and slackers. Have you joined them in ridiculing the examples of the hard-working people around you? Have you been convinced that being serious is un-cool, but being a fool is cool?! It's a shame, because the advice successful people give is not *just* their own, it's the advice of generations of successful people…

Nowadays, you don't hear many protest songs... it seems the corporate media has largely co-opted the latest generation of songwriters.

Every generation complains about those that come after them. Some of those from the great generation that fought World War II, are highly critical of the generations that succeeded them. Ironically, many of the loudest critics are the men who *did not* serve in that war, they remind me of the current crop of chicken hawks, who did not fight in Vietnam, but are the most hawkish voices of our time.

"There was no respect for youth when I was young, and now that I am old, there is no respect for age - I missed it coming and going" … J.B. Priestly

God and Religion

"You'll never win a argument over an emotional issue, using an intellectual argument"... Ed Rollins.

Ironically… religion is the first thing some people will kill for and the last thing other's would kill for.

You disparage me for questioning the *sacred beliefs*, and I admit having more questions than answers. Meanwhile, I question those who only have answers and no questions… that's a red flag. To me it makes no sense to believe a single *anything* all the time… so why would I believe a single religious point of view is always right… especially when all have tarnished track record?

Everyone I know claims to be doing a good work... frankly I just don't see it!

Funny how the *check list* of mandatory beliefs is short when you're being wooed by a religion, but it gets longer, after they've *acquired* you. Then you find out you're just a *baby*, and your arrested development can only be cured by accepting a much longer list of; beliefs, talking points and positions.

We shouldn't use God's name in vain... don't say God &#(@ it when you bump your head... its not his fault you weren't watching where you were going...if anything, maybe he was trying to knock some sense into you!

Growing up Unitarian we felt isolated, there were no rituals, no rites of passage... I was envious of the kids who had confirmations, or came to school with ashes on their foreheads. We were un-cool, no one had heard of our church and I preferred not to even talk about it, "you're a what?" they'd ask.

"Do you know where you're going when you die?", they like to ask. It drives some people crazy if you're not alarmed by their question, It's a valid question, as well as a way to scare people... if you don't react the way they want, they tend to be disappointed, or anger. My answer is called *weak kneed*, but it's fairly honest.
I'm not sure where I'll go, or if I'll go anywhere... but the near death experiences described by people of *all* religions give me hope that there's something out there and possibly it's not the exclusive domain of just one religion or another.

"I do not feel obliged to believe that the same God who has endowed us with sense, reason, and intellect has intended us to forego their use"... Galileo Galilei.
Poor Galileo... where did he get such crazy ideas! Galileo was found "vehemently suspect of heresy," he was required to "abjure, curse and detest" those opinions and then imprisoned, a sentence that was later commuted to house arrest.

Funny how in 1992, Pope John Paul II expressed regret for how the Galileo affair was handled, issued a declaration acknowledging the errors committed by the Catholic church and in 2008 the Vatican proposed to complete its rehabilitation of Galileo by erecting a statue of him inside the Vatican walls!

Condemnation without investigation is the highest form of ignorance – Albert Einstein

Did Jesus spend his *missing years* in India? There may be some evidence, although it's a divisive topic. Among other things, at the *Sermon On The Mount*, Jesus preached the Golden Rule, which perhaps Buddha and others had preached hundreds of years earlier. Confucius is quoted as saying, "never impose on others what you would not choose for yourself"... hmm.

It's too bad Jesus wasn't *around* longer... maybe he'd have clarified a few things and taught us *how* to live in peace. Christians might say *that would have been nice, but he and the Bible teach us all we need to know.* I respectfully disagree and think we've been left with the Apostle Paul *and others* to interpret and fill in the blanks for us... and that is unsatisfactory in my book.

"The world is my country, all mankind are my brethren, and to do good things is my religion" ... Thomas Paine (another slaveholder.)

My daughter was discussing religion with someone the other day, and it occurred to me that she and I had never *really* discussed it with each other. She's made a few religious remarks to me and vice versa, but of the many serious conversations we've had about religion, none of them have been with each other. I should have encouraged that conversation from the beginning, instead of falling for the premise that anything I had to say was likely to be wrong, if not *blasphemous*. That we have discussed religion so little, is not her problem, and certainly not her fault, but it is I believe a very sad thing.

Upon further reflection, I wonder if such a discussion would in any way be productive, or might it lead to a distancing between us? I hope we could agree on some things and "agree to disagree" on others. That might be the case, but *all things* considered, it would be difficult for either of us to make much *headway* vis-à-vis the other. This doesn't mean we shouldn't discuss religion, I think we should, but we should have realistic expectations regarding any changing each others views... I'll be satisfied if we can simply achieve a better understanding with each other.

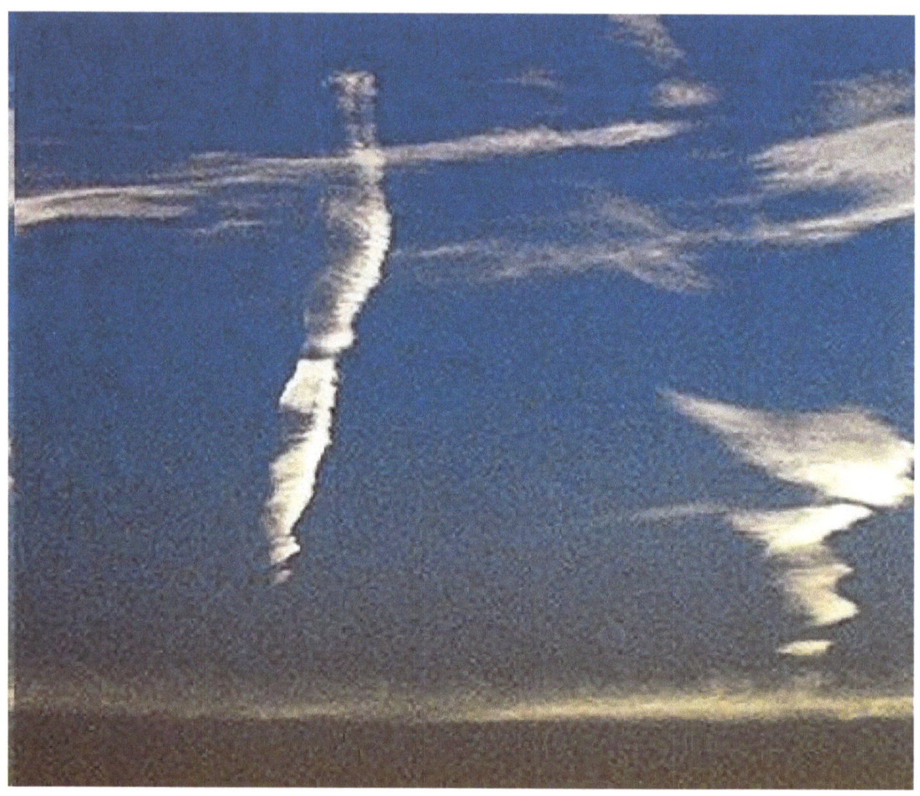

The steeple of the church represents the same thing whether it's a fundamentalist Christian church or a secular humanist Unitarian Church. In both cases the members aspire for something beyond this life, and that something is popularly believed to exist *in the heavens*. Christians have been told exactly what to look forward to, while Unitarians are taught to be seekers.

She came back from church feeling unsettled and said, "I shouldn't feel this way." Why, I wondered should she feel *any* particular way? Unless you are being brainwashed, you have the right and responsibility to feel any way you want.

What is more *subject* to Group Think, political or religious thought? I don't think it's even close, religions generally leave little room for independent thinking.

God created the Tower of Babel to confuse men's tongues because they were getting too big for their britches... maybe it's time for him to do this again!

It may be 1,000 years before people discuss religion rationally... if ever! Not only are we hardwired to want a *guaranteed afterlife*, we're also trained to strongly, even violently oppose those who challenge our beliefs.

I'm unaffiliated by choice, which doesn't mean I want to be... it just means I haven't come across a religion or political party I care to join, but someday I might.

Just as somebody will believe anything if his job depends on it, that goes double if they're convinced their salvation depends on it… and such people are likely to *do* anything their religious leaders tell them to.

Are we any freer to question the church, then we were 200 years ago? We've made strides since the Inquisition, but it's been one step forward and two steps back.

Call me naïve, but I think the most important messages in the Bible are things like, "do onto others as you would have others do unto yourself" and "beat your swords into plowshares." Instead of following the good book's teachings on *who* is good and *who* is bad, I prefer its teachings on *what* is good and *what* is bad.

I've visited a number of churches with my wife, as *she* tries to find one acceptable to both of us. Last week it was an Apostolic church, which was as satisfying as any of the other churches we've attended. I noticed only one blonde in the audience and wondered, are Apostolics unlikely to be of northern European stock? Later my wife reminded me that they rarely color their hair… so that's what the other Churches would look like if the brunettes weren't all trying to "have more fun!"

Watching the show about the famous cave paintings in France, I speculate on why Europeans are typically more secular than Americans. We have Indian artifacts, going back 12,000 years, but they're not associated with Americans of European descent. I've heard some Christians say God created the world about 10,000 years ago, which might make Euros scratch their heads… after all, there's evidence in the caves that their ancestors were living on the same ground as them 50,000 years ago.

The scholar stated, "with *evidence* of two miracles, you can be canonized as a saint by the church." Maybe that's why I find it so hard to accept the Bible as the Gospel truth, there's too many human fingerprints on the pages!

We're told that God is jealous and like a husband or wife, he'll allow no one usurp his place with his loved ones. That makes sense, even though you say *sense* is often irrelevant when it comes to God. You may be right, but that doesn't make your understanding, or Paul's, or the Council of Nicea's any more authoritative... men and councils are imperfect, if not worse.

Why was Mary Magdalene largely expunged from the Bible? I doubt it's because she was irrelevant... perhaps it's because she was too relevant.

W*hen* the rapture comes, will America, which is perhaps the *most* Christian nation on earth, be depopulated. Does that mean there will be plenty to go around for those who remain? I doubt it, since *assumably* the good; doctors, nurses, pilots, police and military will be raptured, leaving only bad ones to make a go of it...or to *go at it!* Will only bad cops, hack doctors, gang bangers and assorted *unbelievers* who didn't heed the church's call be left? That would be quite the predicament and a horrible time of tribulation indeed!

If I have doubts about parts of the Bible such as Noah's Ark etc., should that make me doubt the prophecies of; Daniel, Ezekiel, Jesus and others? Not necessarily, but it does make me more likely to consider alternative interpretations.

Another *speculative possibility* is that God is like the force in Star Wars, although I hope *He's* more personal that that. In any case, I'm content to wonder and yes, *speculate* about the nature of God... that great incomprehensible force.

We're told to think like children and that deviating from the Canon of the Bible is heresy. This has kept people in line and under the thumb of religious and princely *authorities* from day one... make that since before day one. What is this *Canon* anyway, if not artillery designed to mow people down if they dare question the *holy men*? Is Canonization just a tool to keep the herd moving down the chute... like lambs to the *you know what.*

Scientology is being attacked by the French government for defrauding the public. In the old days they'd be called heretics and burned at the stake, now their called fraudsters and their book stores are closed!

Superhuman efforts *might* save us, but only supernatural efforts *will* save us… will ancient astronauts that may have visited us and been perceived as gods soon finish their lap around the galaxy and return *in the nick of time?*

As we drove, I saw billboards with messages like, "Hell is real" and "believe in Jesus or go to hell." I know these folks think they're doing us a favor, but I wonder if they're also trying to buy redemption?

I thank God at the dinner table when it's *my turn* pray, other times its for things like the chime in the car when the headlights are left on, when I remember something important, for not twisting my ankle traversing the back forty, when I *almost* knock a glass of beer over… and most of all for the kids!

Does God use scare tactics? Why not, after all this isn't a reasonable world, why would he rely on logic? Certainly those who claim to speak for him use scare tactics after all, nothing's quite so effective!

Just out of curiosity, what happened to the souls of cavemen? Reportedly they buried their dead, adorning them with flowers and gifts. Even tens of thousands of years ago, humans believed, or at least wondered about an afterlife. Did our prehistoric ancestors have souls, and if so, what happened to them?

"Oh when the Saints come marching in!" Can you imagine a dinner party attended by; Jesus, Mohammed, Confucius, Buddha, Moses or other holy men! Would they get along, or would they clash? Would they amicably share a spot of tea or would things get heated? Would they act like gentlemen, or would they expect deference from each other? I'd like to believe they'd have a friendly exchange of *opinions*… but who knows!

"And when you asked for light, I set myself on fire"... Audioslave.

As in love and war, so it in religion - "all is fair." Religions and even denominations tend to divide the world between themselves, and others… with people in the *other* category often destined for hell. Another similarity between war and religion are the concepts of "divide and conquer", and

"with us, or against us." These are useful in defeating enemies and winning converts, but they're also a sad commentary on the level of humanitarianism of organized religion.

Religions teach that even *if* their members aren't *better* than non-believers, they're at least *better off*, which serves as a powerful recruiting tool. Reading between the lines, it seems to me they teach that their members are also *better* than the rest of humankind... and that attracts converts too!

We're reprimanded by the women for saying "oh my God", they want us to say something like "oh my word", or "oh my gosh." I'd rather have a gender worship service than conform to female conventions. Women try to constrain *everyone* and demand that we obey *tradition*... they even want our spiritual lives to be as orderly as a bee hive!

The church sign said, "worry is interest paid on problems before they happen" and it makes sense, but not perfectly. Can we really live like, the *fowls of the air*, neither sowing, reaping, or gathering into barns? If so, will our heavenly Father feed us, or will we starve? There're already too many starving people and freeloaders for that lifestyle to be encouraged! Certainly it's better not to worry *excessively*, but it's a good thing to plan for the future.

Church?...I favor the one that has no walls, I'd rather listen to a red bird singing than a red face crowing!

Funny how everyone's for freedom of religion, as long as it's *their* religion that's free... everyone else's is a bit suspect.

"Lighthouses are more useful than churches"... Ben Franklin.

They tell you to think like a child regarding religion... otherwise you're accused of *intellectualizing* spirituality. There're times to think like children, and times to think like adults *even* when it comes to religion.

Why should people of one religion "expect" those of another religion to believe their story, and abandon their own religious tradition? Almost all religions tell us to do no harm, and warn us of the punishment awaiting those who do? If organized religions can not co-exist with a degree of respect for each other, then we're in deep doo doo... the problem is, history show's they've a heck of time tolerating each other.

Lifetimes of indoctrination make it almost impossible for people to honestly consider that perhaps their religion is not 100% correct, 100% of the time…

Churches are nice places to pray, but I'm often in crawl spaces, or on ladders, when I feel the urge! Though not as dramatic as prayers from a foxhole, scary little places are where much of my praying occurs. At my wife's urging, I'm trying to pray more often for the needs of others… I wish I could say I've been more successful.

The sophisticated level of communication between human beings, has been a driving force in the advancement of religion. As the only species with thousands of years of sophisticated verbal communication under our belt, we've been able to advance complex theories on the afterlife and the other great questions of mankind. When there's a disaster, other species just try to survive, we try to make sense of it, which often means attributing it to God's wrath.

Not surprisingly, the church was upset when Copernicus and Galileo proclaimed the earth was not the center of the universe. After all, the church wanted everyone to believe the world revolves around us… or more specifically, around them. It only took a few hundred years for them to admit they were right!

Religions have been known to *misrepresent* the facts for centuries but eventually make 180 degree turns, when their versions prove to be untenable. All the while, the flock maintains its blind faith, after all, religion's still the only business selling eternal life.

Even those curious enough to question whether the Bible *is* the "gospel truth" are reluctant to do so. Why rock the boat? It's easier to go with the flow, than to ask questions that will get you in trouble. It's not just society that would ostracize you, it's also family and friends.

All those people out there working for the return of Jesus, or the return of the Mahdi both of which apparently will be preceded by the apocalypse, may get their wish... after all they're working extremely hard for it!

Does God listen to the prayers of madmen and mass murderers? Can such people have a personal relationship with God? I'm told he does and they can… this thing gets curiouser and curiouser all the time.

Are we as individuals and as nations certain to reap what we sow? On one hand I hope we do, on the other hand I hope we don't… I think we must, yet I pray we won't.

The Pope has declared two new sins, polluting the earth and being obscenely wealthy… right on! Just don't expect everyone to agree!

Hopefully, extremism and "final solutions" are prohibited by God… maybe that's why grand alliances like the Allies in WWII often come together in the worst of times, to "save the day." Will it happen one more time, multiple times, or never?

It's funny…we're told not to feel sorry for ourselves, cause there's always some poor bugger worse off than us. Even folks in the most dire straights are told that, and almost everyone can think of some one in worse shape than themselves. When such people die, we're told not to feel too sorry because if they were *right with God* they've gone to a better place. Makes me think there's always hope, or at least the chance of something better to look forward to.

No one is great… when you think of the sum of the wisdom of everyone who ever lived, as being *the human knowledge base*, then each individual holds but a tiny fraction of that information. The fact that God lets us die and take what we know to the grave, is an indication the universe probably doesn't need our *knowledge*.

Does God hear the agnostic's or theist's prayer? He's omnipotent, so surely, he hears it, but does he answer them? I hope he answers some of them… if and when they pray. Prayer, meditation, contemplation and hope… maybe they're intertwined anyway.

"There's a fine line between salvation and drinking poison in the jungle"… unknown.

Government

"I don't make jokes. I just watch the government and report the facts" …Will Rogers

I care less about the form of government, than about having our God given and constitutional rights preserved. The problem is, we can't even agree on what *those rights* should be!

I don't think the government can solve all our problems, but if it can't rein in Wall Street and protect us from street thugs, then what good are they?

As an independent, I see government as a "racket" and a necessary evil, not a benefactor to the people… that being said, anarchy is almost always worse.

If I can change the world for the better, great! If not, I'd like to just survive another *administration.*

It's bad enough when the government wants to dominate its own people, but when it tries dominating the entire world, something's really wrong! Does our government really know what's best for us, much less what's best for the entire world?

The ninth amendment states that rights not given specifically to the government are reserved for the individual, I like that… unfortunately big brother doesn't!

Dot your "I's" and cross your "T's" when dealing with the government… they make life difficult enough when you do, and impossible when you don't.

I don't think this government is going to fall anytime soon, what might collapse is the concept of liberty. The American super state will do what the British and King George were unable to do... turn us into subjects instead of citizens. Remarkably, many will be pleased with the outcome, because income from hard working people will be given to them. After taking away our liberty, the government won't even have to *give us death...* the fear of prison will be sufficient to keep most of us in line.

"The more corrupt the state, the more it legislates." - Tacitus

Greed

"Earth provides enough to satisfy every man's need, but not every man's greed"... Gandhi

Just wondering... who's greedier, the rich who act like glutens at their own expense, or the bum who does so at yours?

People are different from the beasts, because our hands and brains, allow us to impose ourselves on both nature and humanity. One powerful human being can make millions feel the effects of their; wrath, greed, malice, *or*... their good will.

Envy, greed, jealousy and other negative traits seem hard wired into the reptilian part of our brains. It's difficult for the more advanced frontal lobe and it's *reasoning*, to override the decisions of the reptilian parts. Our reptilian brain stem knows what has worked, for millions of years and is unlikely to defer to the *well intentioned* frontal lobe.

We are utterly self centered, and virtually everything we do for others, is upon examination, actually done for ourselves... but I digress.

Nature's way is cutthroat competition and for thousands of years that was also humankinds way. Starting in ancient times and sputtering along until now, enlightened people have sought to create benevolent societies. This is wonderful, but usually undermined by greed among virtually everyone in the populace. From the lazy who want a free ride, to the rich want to be even richer, everyone throws their wrench into the works.

Maybe there's a reason that the words need and greed rhyme.

Despite being treated like little gods, doctors are among the biggest liars in the world! After each surgery I've had, the doctor has said "it went perfectly, it couldn't have gone better." Each time however the result was far from perfect... I think they're worse than auto mechanics, and can only imagine what they've left inside.

The day is by no means over, but enough of it has passed that I have to ask myself "where has the day gone and what have I accomplished?" Then, it occurs... why should I be so concerned about "accomplishing" something

every day? Why can't we live like the birds and the deer... isn't there enough abundance to satisfy our needs as long as we're not greedy? *Actually…* if we try living like the birds and the deer I expect we will end up like the birds and the deer - eaten by predators or smudges on the side of the road.

As the slow motion train wreck proceeds and our economy possibly implodes, it occurs to me that the brilliant minds of Wall Street with their astronomical IQs, have very little wisdom, common sense or compassion. Superior intellect seems to have no correlation to doing good. The mega brains who invented; sub prime mortgages, hedge funds, derivatives and predatory lending are simply white collar criminals.

"There are many things that we would throw away if we were not afraid that others might pick them up"… Oscar Wilde

Green Acres!

Tromping around the farmyard collecting the branches that fall after every storm, I wonder… shouldn't I be writing a book instead?

So often, life involves a battle over turf… whether it's fighting over Jerusalem, or me and the Daddy Long Legers fighting over our porch, everybody wants prime real estate. Our farmhouse is beautiful but it's also habitat for competitors like spiders, flies and wasps.

As I walk the trail, a horsefly discovers my intrusion and attacks. There will be no peace until one of us is dead… if I had remembered the bug spray this wouldn't have to happen!

Whistling as I work, I hear the exact tune coming from the woods, and wonder if it's an echo, or my neighbor being funny. Eventually I realize it's a Mockingbird… I'd like to think its perfect mimicry was a compliment... but that would be taking it a bit too far.

The spare tire appeared to be just more to debris that I have to remove from the creek. Surprisingly, the old radial with the Chevy bowtie turned out to be a useful tool. With it, I could float four stones at a time across the creek, instead of precariously carrying one at a time. If it could float 100 pounds of

stone, it might also come in handy as life preserver. Even a slight current can be deadly if you're on the wrong side of a big log.

Went fishing today… the only thing biting were the mosquitoes!

Despite efforts to seal every hole, I'm constantly battling the mice. *Reluctantly* I use outside and traps inside the house. I'm getting pretty good, baiting the traps with peanut butter, cheese or frosting. The little buggers always have that same look in their eyes as I remove their broken bodies from the trap…but I don't care, this is war!

I've spent hours looking for mushrooms with minimal results, but at least I'm not a *mushroom virgin* like my wife. We suspect that deer and rabbits are getting there first, maybe squirrels and wild turkeys too. After 2 hours, I find three measly Morels... not even enough for an appetizer! At least the mushrooms stay put when you find them, most things you hunt for run for their lives!

Mushroom hunting is a solitary activity, though today I have a companion... it's a buzzing horsefly, but he hasn't bitten me yet. Eventually I decide to tackle the toughest terrain, where even Deer fear to tread. The problem is, I have a can of worms and two fishing poles in my hands... not the way to crawl through a briar patch! The thorns hold me like grim death as I yell to my wife to bring the *loppers.* Of course she's too far away to hear so I sacrifice my shirt, and leave mushroom-less, but with a hide full of thorns!

The next day, I found two huge mushrooms in my neighbors yard of all places and had to decide if I should share them, or secretly eat them all myself…umm, they were good!

The first thing I do when preparing to take a bath at the farmhouse, is drown the bugs. There aren't many, but even one is too much…I can't stand a bug in the tub!

The cable bridge has almost been destroyed several times when we have *gully washers*. I keep raising the bridge and Mother Nature keeps raising the creek... needless to say she's better at the game than me!

Group Think

"A type of thought exhibited by group members who try to minimize conflict and reach consensus without critically testing, analyzing, and evaluating ideas"… Wikipedia

Strong governments lead to "groupthink", which eventually threatens anyone unwilling to submit to preferences of the powerful or the majority.

Things may get worse before they get better… before *this* is over, we can expect to be imprisoned, or worse for speaking our minds. They'll do their best to control the rules of the debate, but in the end, their corrupt system will surely collapse!

It seems to me that knowingly or now, Ben was championing "new speak" and "Group Think." Instead of fighting for the rights of, and the opinions of who the government tells me to fight for, I'd rather fight (hopefully via the pen), for those who are not trying to take away the natural and God given rights of others.

Handyman Stuff

"I can't see anything in these goggles… what do I want vision or safety" - Mike Rowe

I'm finding that for *today's job*, there's no such thing as the "right tool" …it just keeps evolving into a bigger and bigger mess!

Ever notice that a good tool can be your best friend, while a lousy one can kill you!

Nothing works as advertised and nothing ever goes as planned… those are cardinal rules for the amateur *handyman!*

Folks… I'll gladly do *my* chores, just don't ask me to do yours too!

Things always break, it feels good to fix them, and sometimes it seems *that* is what we're here for. Eventually, we tire of it and long for heaven where things no longer fall apart… where warranties never expire.

Fix things! Don't automatically toss them, even if it's *more economical* to do so. Get a screwdriver, or glue out of the drawer and repair something!

Funny… the hardest screw to remove, is the easiest to put back.

There are many things I wish I could change about my life, some of them important other's trivial. Today while trying to repair the window frame I broke the glass instead. Unfortunately there's no way to go back and do it right... that's the story of my life!

I'm high on a ladder trying to *marry* a 2 x 8 to a damaged beam… It occurs that if this b.o.a.r.d. fell on my h.e.a.d., I'd be d.e.a.d. Think I'll wear a hard hat… its better than nothing! As usual, the *job* becomes more ridiculous as I go on… It would be an easy two man job, but doing it myself is nuts… I've lost count of how many times I've climbed this ladder.

Like terrorism, broken glass is nearly impossible to eradicate… no mater how much you sweep, one shard may *get lucky*. When working with glass, you can't be too careful… always assume the worst!

After the storm, I spent hours collecting branches, cutting limbs and burning them. Having no chainsaw, a *bow saw* was my tool of choice. It performed well, so I thanked it as I put it away. A good tool deserves thanks for a job well done!

Inevitably as you get better at something, in this case demolishing the chicken coop, you get a little cocky… that's when you get hurt!

"If you don't know how to tie a knot, you'll tie a lot!"… Rich Trethewey

The evolution of tools from; hand, to power to CNC has been as important as the evolution of the human brain... the two are inexorably intertwined!

Climbing high into the tree, I found only a very old rope to secure the ladder. It worked, so I guess an old rope can be better than no rope at all… but I hope I have sense enough not to trust my life to one again… that was scary!

Haste makes waste is an old adage, but a true one. It's better to climb a ladder three times, than fall off it once. Maybe that's why we are told not to walk under one, it may be less a superstition than just a warning to be careful and take our time.

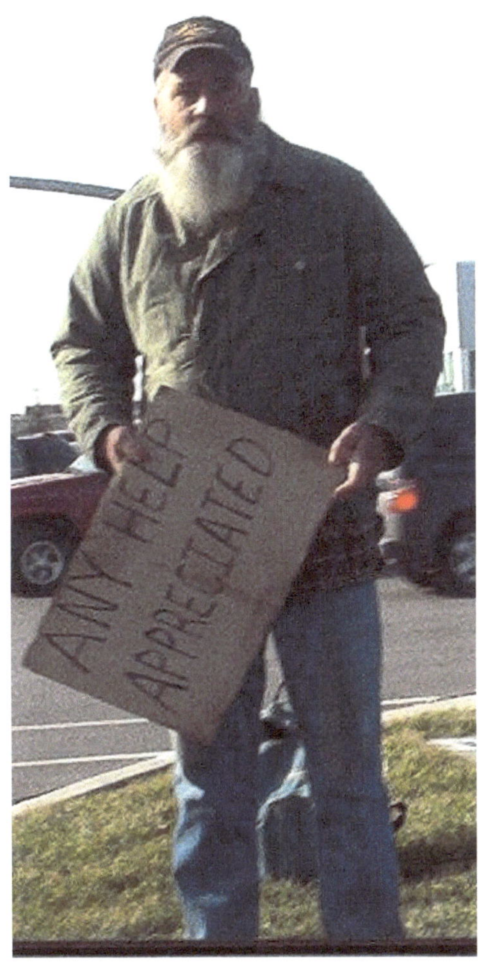

This is the last time I'm buying discounted paint... not until after using it do you find out its bad... at which point it's awfully hard to make the job right.

Have you ever seen or heard of Tom Silva and Rich Trethewey? I wish I could frame or plumb like they do!

How can I screw up these jobs so often? I keep saying it's cause I don't do it for a living... but that excuse is getting rather old!

I secured the rocking chair to the top of my Tucson and drove to Wal-Mart for supplies. Returning home, I cruised right into the garage and demolished the heirloom! Am I the only one who does things like this?

I just fixed an old wood screen door, partially returning it to its former glory. Long ago, someone added decorative details to it and strange as it seems, I feel a connection to whoever that was. Instead of being discarded, it will add more character to the farmhouse than a new screen door ever could. Working on the old house, I feel a bond with those who built it by hand long ago. It's not ancestor worship, just respect for the day-to-day accomplishments of those who came before us... who knows, maybe they are watching us.

I stared at the outlet for a long time... it wasn't complicated, but it worked, looked good and I had installed it myself. For a week, I couldn't walk by without stopping to admire my work… I wonder if other "handymen" do the same?

Regarding admiring my work, it's not just the barn door I built, or the electric outlet, the other day I found myself pausing to appreciate how nicely I had set out the trash for the garbage men. Now granted, it was after Christmas and there's quite a bit, but the cans were stable and would take quite a wind storm to knock them asunder… jeepers, I must me loosing my mind!

Haters, Sickos and Sociopaths

"Toward no crimes have men shown themselves so cold-bloodedly cruel as in punishing differences of belief"… James Russell Lowell

At the moment, its popular to call ones *adversaries* "haters" and it plays well in the press to blame the *haters* for society's ills. There certainly are haters out there, but like so many things, it's in the eye of the beholder and the finger pointers are often as bad as their targets.

I hear the word *hater*, in songs and interviews... usually by people who are considered *haters* by the people *they* hate.

Slandering someone who disagrees with your views by calling them a *hater*, is an effective way of discrediting them. Those who share your world view typically dislike, if not *hate* the so called hater. By calling someone a hater, his view is categorized as deviant... what better way to crush free speech and throttle debate!

Sociopathy, now that's a mouthful! Not to mention an excellent word to toss around if you're trying to shut someone up. I've heard it defined various ways, including meaning someone without a conscience, and I think there are a few people out there with no conscience. I wonder though… what is the definition of someone with a *perfect conscience?* Would it be the individual who does what ever society demands of him, or the person who questions the validity of those demands?

It seems to me, the more you conform to society's expectations, the less likely you are to be called a deviant or sociopath. Conversely, the more independent you are, the more likely you'll attract those words.

Our founding fathers would've been called sociopaths by the British, just as we called King George *insane*. Isn't; madness, hatred and sociopathy largely in the eye of the beholder, and is our vision not blurred by self-interest and other *considerations*?

Healing and Health

"Every human being is the author of his own health or disease"… Buddha quotes

Master your own; neurosis, addiction, foibles or obsession, don't rely on others to solve all your problems. Medicine, counseling and religion help tremendously, but in the end, *you* must change your own life.

My metabolism is slowing down, but my appetite isn't. Not an original observations, but relevant to my situation and my ever increasing battle of the bulge.

Regarding her constant coughing, I suggested trying to cough 1/3 less when she had a spasm, but this was dismissed as impossible and nonsense, "just wait till you're sick!" The cough is uncontrollable I was told, you can't use

mind over matter to slow it down. I hopelessly rebutted we won't know if it's impossible unless you try! Now prayer was another thing, they certainly believed it was worth praying for relief and I don't discount the effectiveness of that... I just think they may be related.

Okay, maybe it's *impossible* to reduce your coughing spasm by 1/3, but what about reducing it 1% ,for starters... again I was informed that such a suggestion is nonsense. To succeed, don't try *very hard* to cough less, instead just *barely try* to cough less.

I was told by the gals, all nurses, nursing students or experienced medical consumers that you can't slow down coughing by willing it, you must take medicine, or supplements... and that they certainly did, by the handful! I wondered why then, were the coughing spasms seemingly triggered by some one else coughing, or by words, looks, thoughts etc. There's also the phenomenon of yawns passing from one person to another. I'm not saying there's an absolute correlation, just that there's some validity to a mind body connection and we should control our impulse to over medicate.

When a child coughs uncontrollably might the *Pavlov Effect* be involved? What's strange about children subconsciously realizing their parents will come running when they cough? At night parents take turns waking up to comfort their coughing children. Without dismissing the fact that Asthma, allergies, sinus infections etc. are very real, we should not dismiss the advice of the elderly lady who has fifty years of experience... her advice, "train the child, or the child will train you!"

Just out of curiosity, did Superman ever need Band-Aids?

Funny how things have changed... we're an obese society requiring new products for our new *lifestyle.* We need air cleaners and breath rite strips to keep our fat laden breathing passages open so we don't snore, as well as CPAP machines and insulin at higher rates than past generations ... and we seem unable to control our appetites for happy meals and other indulgences.

The actress brushes her teeth in an effort to keep from mindless eating... most of us know this trick, but we've *outsmarted* it. She's gone a step further than most of us, she's outsmarted her sub-conscious!

The medical establishment is finally recognizing the connection between mind, spirit and body... at least some of them are. Unsurprisingly the

medical establishment will of course claim credit for discovering the connection!

Dang and thank goodness for the gag reflex… I almost choked to death on a vitamin the size of Milwaukee!

Maybe they call this thing hanging over my belt a "belly" because it looks like a big fat bell.

"Nothing is more fatal to Health, than an over Care of it" … Benjamin Franklin

Heaven

"See you in heaven if you make the list"… REM

Heaven should have no locks, keys, cords, cables, hoses or anything else that tangles. Things shouldn't fall apart, warranties never expire and repair men are honest. Everything's also completely wireless and the outdated stuff has been sent to the poor souls in Hades!

I wouldn't mind there being vacuum cleaners, tools and chores … just let everything be cordless. Heck what kind of place would Heaven be if there's absolutely no work, aren't idle hands the devil's play things? I'm advised that Heaven's *inhabitants* are too busy with heavenly stuff to do any work, and their spiritual bodies don't require food or shelter. Maybe it's a moot point, but I hope Heaven's interesting!

"Paradise, can it be all they say it is, I close my eyes and maybe I'm already there"… Kansas

I wonder if Heaven is segregated? They say church is the most segregated place in America, is Heaven any different?

Could someone kill a million people and go to heaven, and some else cure cancer and go to hell...just wondering? Would it depend on *who* he killed, or the sincerity of the killers repentance?

I hope dogs and cats go to people heaven and not animal heaven… on the other hand, what about really bad pets… where do they go?

An essential step in getting soldiers to join the army, is convincing they'll go straight to heaven, or paradise if killed. It's also *useful* to persuade them that the enemy *deserves* to be blown to kingdom come. I'm being cynical, but these are some of the reasons we have so many wars!

"Knocking on Heaven's Door" is on the radio, but the reception is poor. Moving my hand closer, I become the antenna, reception improves and the music enters my body like electricity.

I'm told God gives us free will, but due to our sinful nature we misuse it and foul things up constantly. This results in a high probability of burning in Hell, unless we repent and ask Jesus to be our savior. Mass murderers, reportedly have the same option… as long as they truly repent and accept Jesus, they go to heaven and their eternity will be wonderful. Meanwhile, their victims go to heaven, or hell depending on whether or not they've accepted Jesus... the whole thing seems wacky to me, but God does what he wants. Regardless, I can't help but wonder if all this is true, or some huge *misunderstanding*? Not surprisingly, other religions offer similar scenarios, albeit with different saviors and other minor variations.

"May you be in Heaven a half hour before the Devil knows you're dead"… Irish Blessing

Heroes

"The good Lord gives us but one death, we must not bungle it"… Trader Horn

I guess we need heroes, they encourage us to strive for excellence, but we shouldn't idolize them and should look for gentle heroes when possible. Interestingly today's heroes are often "everyday people" unlike the larger than life heroes of bygone days.

True heroes protect those in need out of the goodness of their hearts, others expect to be compensated. Heroes are also history's winners, if they were losers, they'd be remembered as villains instead!

Aggression is honored passivity is not and it's easy to be aggressive when you're powerful. Power and aggression is honored by all of society, even the weak… after all they aspire to be powerful too.

There's little honor in being brave when you're the strong one, and little shame in being afraid when you're the weak one. As a result, the labels hero and coward are often misplaced.

They're not my heroes, but I admire... Tom the carpenter, Steve the plumber and tow truck drivers who risk their lives everyday on the side of the road.

In the movie, the guy tells his buddy who's trying to make the team he'll fail and be a nobody, "like the rest of us." The hero goes on to prove him wrong, which is great, but it made me think that neither character was a "nobody"… nobody's a "nobody." Everyone's *somebody* even if we never get that 15 minutes of fame.

Heard another mention of heroes today… it was related to the rescue workers trying to save others in a mine collapse. Three of the rescuers died during their attempt… and I think they deserve being called heroes. On the other hand, the term "hero" is used so often these days that I have to wonder, are we are living in extraordinary times, or just *extra ordinary* times ?

Despite all the fancy talk, standing up for others usually involves a cost-benefit analysis... we don't talk about it, we just calculate it.

We honor some killers, as long as they are doing it for the "right reasons"… others we abhor, because their rampage is not directed at those we want eliminated. Ironically, some killers are loved and called heroes, while others are loathed and hunted down. An unfortunate "fact" of life, is that society has always sanctioned the killing of certain human beings in order to achieve certain "desired" goal.

"Heroism at command, senseless brutality, deplorable love-of-country stance, how violently I hate all this..." -- Albert Einstein

History

"History is stranger than fiction, because fiction has to make sense"... Mark Twain

Can history be used to predict the future? Heck, we can't agree on what *happened* in the past, much less what it meant!

There's always a dark age going on somewhere... if you don't have a real stake in a conflict, don't listen to those calling for blood, they're perfectly willing to spill yours - for their gain!

History's a great teacher, it can also be a big fat liar!

Don't look only at *your* books to learn your history, look at the *other side's* too and you will gain a valuable new perspective. These may not be flattering accounts...if that's all you want just read your own books.

Some people have a sense of history, others have a sense of fashion, don't let those in the second category making important decisions for you.

The phrase, "tide of history", explains a lot... some things ebb and flow, but in the end history moves like a tsunami.

The historian stated that Andrew Jackson's world was a brutal one, so he should be forgiven for such actions as the "Indian removal"... I think that's so much nonsense. Are we not living in brutal times today as well? When we excuse historic figures for atrocities -- will it not lead to more of the same?

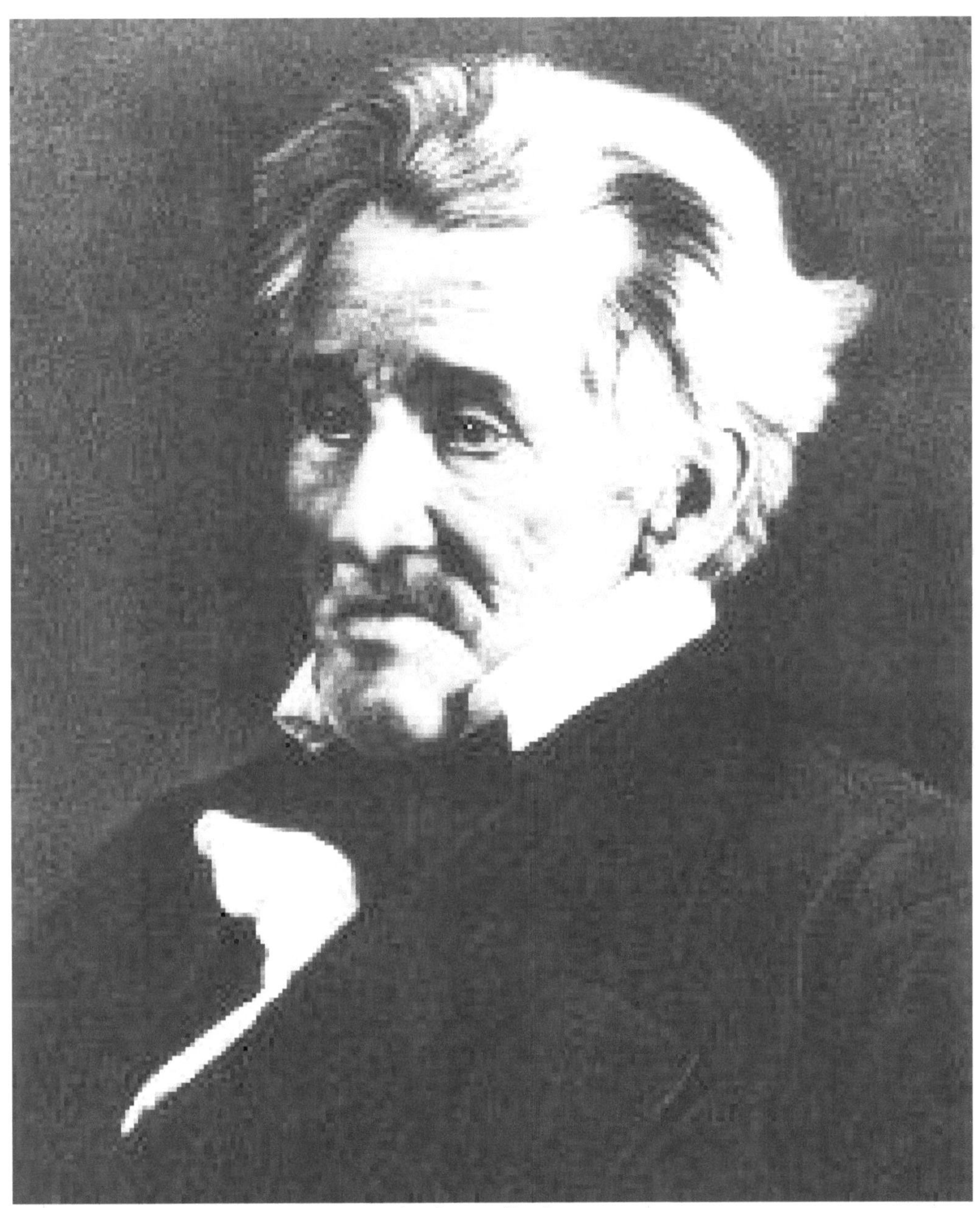

Andrew Jackson

Inevitably, someday in the future... people will talk about our civilization in the past tense, just as we talk about the Romans or the Greeks. Were the Greeks to ancient history what the British were to modern history, and does that make America to modernity, what Rome was to antiquity?

Most historians acknowledge the wrongs we did to Indians and Africans and for many Americans that's sufficient... but for the descendents of the oppressed, *acknowledgement* may not even scratch the surface.

Unfortunately I'm learning about history too much by studying, and too little by living it. The *dust heap of history*, may not be so bad after all...eventually those who put you there may replace you there.

The wonders of the ancient world, were built largely by conscripts and slaves as well as by paid craftsman. Unfortunately their names are lost to history... the only ones we remember, are the despots who ordered these monuments built to memorialize themselves!

"History is a vast early warning system"...Norman Cousins

Holidays

"Just as a puppy can be more of a challenge than a gift, so too can the holidays"... John Clayton

I am planning to do absolutely nothing this weekend... but even now, forces are conspiring against that plan!

What sometimes seems like sheer frivolity to me, is extremely important to my wife... think I'll grin and bear it!

Its days before Christmas and you have to be careful... harried shoppers become hurried drivers, as they try to full fill their "obligations." It's a stressful time of year, especially during the recession...incomes are down, but expectations are not.

***We* need non-Christians... otherwise who's going to work on Christmas and Easter?**

I've been accused of being a Scrooge, and as usual, I'm not terribly "into Christmas", but I have been shopping more than ever this year. For the most part, I'm buying little things, but getting in the spirit -- and oh yes, I'm supporting the economy!

Tis the season and we're worried someone will say we're cheap and lacking the Christmas spirit... which is exactly how the merchants want us to feel!

Christmas is approaching and I'm curious how my wife will approach the holidays this year. The *crash* is only a year behind us and our finances are tenuous, so will this be another year of keeping up with the Jones'? That's the problem with having friends who make twice as much as us!

Why don't they pronounce it "Christ mass" instead of Christmas... just wondering.

If they're still making holidays, I'd like to suggest "Pain In The Neck Day." I don't know if you'd give the *qualifying person* a card, or a kick in the behind!

Christmas? If nothing else, is when we're most likely to contact old friends, attempt to reconnect, or call that sick neighbor and see if there's "anything we can do"... and that's nice!

No one cares how many presents you've bought... they care how many you've bought *for them...*

Jeez, now they're selling $100 H*eirloom* Turkeys for Thanksgiving! The seller says this historic breed of Turkey can only be saved from extinction, if people eat more of them... sounds like circular logic!

"How many observe Christ's birthday! How few, his precepts! O! 'tis easier to keep holidays than commandments" ... Benjamin Franklin

Home Improvement

The remodeling project certainly tested my faith... not in God, but in man – I think God is what got me through the *ordeal*!

Contractors say they don't want the homeowner looking over their shoulders, because, we get in the way. I think its because the homeowner will see any shortcuts and shoddy work being done. Heck, I don't want my clients looking over my shoulder either and I'm a consultant!

The contractor scolded the worker for sitting while working on the new floor, "there's nothing you can do while sitting on your butt" he scolded. It sounded harsh, but later it made sense... like walking under a ladder, sitting on one's butt is likely to lead to accidents... can you imagine operating a circular saw in that position?

My clients? The less competent they are, the easier my job is... unfortunately, contractors rely on the same principal when working with me!

Dealing with builders and home improvement contractors, is a bit like dealing with my dogs... in both cases they spend most of their time trying to get what they want, not giving me what I've "hired" them for. I just want them to perform a service as per our contract... but they have other ideas, in the case of the contractor, its paying his bills... in both cases, I'm the gravy train!

The builder suggested several improvements for the rental house I was remodeling. "If it's nicer you'll get better tenants", he reminded me... but I'm not convinced. If past experience is any indication, there's no direct correlation between the quality of the property and the quality of the renter you'll get... there are renters and there are opportunists!

There are so many contractor related cock and bull stories! When the landscaper said, "I'll cut your grass higher so the weeds won't get any sun", he really meant he wants to cut it again next week, even though it won't need it!

Human Nature

"The problem with people is that they're only human"... Bill Watterson

Planet earth... when humans finally reached the top, you might say the inmates took over the asylum!

We are all "people in glass houses"...yet look at the stones fly!

Another difference between humans and beasts is, we plan ahead... at least some people do.

Life… you solve one problem and another one crops up, an imperfect system, but much better than the alternative!

I feel insecure in the air, or water, and though land is where I'm most likely to die, it's still where I'm most comfortable.

"I have often thought that God created the monkey because he was disappointed with man"…Mark Twain (of course.)

Just as some Indians thought the conquistadors were gods, I wonder if Neanderthals thought the same of Cro-Magnons?

"Lists" are another thing unique to humans, no animal makes a list, except possibly in its head, and that would be difficult to prove. Although animals exhibit superior memories in one area or another, their "to do lists" pale in comparison to our… not to mention our "honey do lists."

Everybody I know – me included, seems to operate under the premise that we're always right. We know we're not, but when it comes to dealing with others, human nature takes over and tells us we're in the right – this is hard wiring at its worst!

I may have A.D.D., but don't consider it problematic... it allows you to tune things out. Without it, you *have to* pay attention to the mindless chatter surrounding you. People with A.D.D., can focus on what they *want*, instead of what others want.

Some of us spend too much time preparing for eventualities that have an extraordinarily low chance of occurring. We check smoke detectors, install fire extinguishers, prepare for retirement and make sure we have a spare tire. Other's, spend no time preparing for these, or for things that *are* inevitable. Group one ends up playing a major supporting role for group two… it's the old Grasshopper and Ant story.

So… when is human nature going to change? Umm, would you believe never!

Humans are a complaint based species... we spend a huge amount of time complaining. I don't think animals are capable of that -- but I guess there's no telling what they're thinking.

"We don't make the rules, we just have to abide by them"… how many times have you heard this? Granted, there are lots of rules that make perfect sense, like not driving while drunk, but there are also lots of rules that should be amended or discarded. So don't be a sheeple, if a rule's ridiculous challenge it, and work to change it in a law abiding manner.

Humans have always come down hard on those lower in the hierarchy than themselves. In the Wolf pack or the lion pride, "underlings" are certainly put in their place, but rarely are they killed -- we could learn a lot from "beasts!"

Do I care about what other people think; how I live and earn a living? Of course! Probably more than I should, but not as much as others would like me to have. So rest assured, you have more influence than I like, just not as much as you'd like!

If you want to think ill of someone you'll easily find things to hold against them... conversely, if you like them you'll excuse any number of faults.

We have an infinite ability to blame others for our problems, but limited capacity to take responsibility for our actions... maybe it's a survival skill. Actually, it makes some sense, as it prevents us from "beating up" on ourselves… there're usually enough people doing that already!

Its funny, the things guys think about during those quiet moments… but the things we *dwell* on are even stranger.

The report stated that people speak an average of 16,000 words a day… my question is - how many *thoughts* does the average person have each day? Isn't what's going on in our heads at least as important as what comes out of our mouths?

"Beating a dead horse?" I've been known to wear out entire stables!

No wonder mankind invented weapons… unlike animals, we vary tremendously in physical prowess as a species. Some people are tiny, others are huge and powerful… Sam Colt is famous for making all men equal… but whoever strung the first bow and arrow beat him by ten thousand years!

It seems **some people do little more than convert oxygen into carbon dioxide… fortunately plants do the opposite.**

It's funny how much of our lives are on auto-pilot… conversations for example. We're adept at giving standard answers that keep everyone happy, leaving us clueless regarding what the conversation was about.

My neighbor was mad and wanted to kick the dog catchers ass –which made me wonder, how many people have actually kicked somebody's ass? It's not all its cracked up to be, but certainly feels better than the opposite!

It much better when we don't brag, since accolades sound much better from someone else's mouth. The problem is, even though, ***pride's a sin*****, we love being praised and love it even more when others hear that praise. The problem with waiting for other's to brag on us, is its rarity, so we end up** ***having*** **to do it ourselves.**

Walking through the Wal-Mart parking lot, I pass a very old woman, she glances towards me, then averts her eyes. She probably would like to hear a kind word… I smile and say hello, she beams and smiles back beautifully!

I think we're born with the equivalent of Tourette's syndrome, but it's ***educated*** **out of most of us… I'd like to get some back. A little Tourette's allows us to speak our minds... unfortunately civility suffers in the process. Let your Tourette's and A.D.D. shine from time to time, just don't let them take over!**

There are few things people enjoy saying as much as, "I told you so"… of course it's usually prefaced with, "I ***hate*** **to say it but …"**

Humility

"To be humble to superiors is duty, to equals courtesy, to inferiors nobleness" …
Benjamin Franklin

Is false humility worse than no humility, and where does politeness end and false humility begin?

When given too much, people appreciate too little. Most people would like to be rich and famous, but few attain that. Fewer still aspire to humble lives, which is at least as noble as being rich and famous.

Is being humble the same as being "down to earth", and is one preferable to the other? In both cases, these traits are rarely as genuine as we claim.

Whether or not I am humble, is debatable… what isn't, is the fact that I've been humbled… repeatedly!

False piety is exactly that…

Are you humble, arrogant or some where in between? Most of us are in between… and vacillating from one extreme to the other.

"If I had any humility I would be perfect"… Ted Turner

Hypocrisy

"Every man alone is sincere. At the entrance of a second person, hypocrisy begins" … Ralph Waldo Emerson

Hypocrisy is usually directly proportional to self righteousness… funny how it follow the chapter on humility and precedes the one on karma!

Is it hypocritical that so many founding fathers were slave holders and that they also produced such profound documents as the Declaration of Independence and the U.S. Constitution? Guess they wanted to have their cake and eat it too… and, like great men throughout history, there was indeed hypocrisy in their lives and in their worlds. Its as if they were able to produce these documents of liberty *because* they struggled with the hypocrisy in their lives.

"Politeness is the most acceptable hypocrisy"… Ambrose Bierce

Karma

"Like gravity, karma is so basic we often don't even notice it"... Sakyong Mipham

Two wrongs don't make a right... no justice, no peace... what goes around comes around... what ye sow, ye shall reap... do unto others as you would have others do unto you...cause and effect... shit flows downhill ...get the point?

If you poop on others, won't the chickens come home to roost...poop and all?

"Be kind, for everyone you meet is fighting a hard battle"... Philo

We are all part of the problem... hopefully we will all be part of the solution.

The problem with *divine* retribution and karma is that not enough people believe in them... if they did, the crime rate would be much lower.

"You cannot do a kindness too soon, for you never know how soon it will be too late" ... Ralph Waldo Emerson

Lanuage, Buzzwords and "New speak"

"War is peace, slavery is freedom, ignorance is strength"... George Orwell

The word "disarming", says it all, especially in contexts like, "he has a disarming smile." On a gut level, this should be a warning that somebody is trying to "disarm you" prior to taking advantage of you.

When you call for a strike, do you mean *labor* or *air*... there's a big difference. In both cases, someone's trying to get their way, but one method is infinitely more civilized than the other!

Words, by chance or design, are capable of influencing our thoughts. Consider the Pakistani cities *Islamabad* and *Lahore…* is it a stretch to think some Americans choose to interpret these as "Islam is Bad" and "La Whore." It reminds me of when a classmate stated that, "Saddam Hussein's wife is named Gamora." The class gasped when they realized the Iraqi "first couple" was named after Sodom and Gamora… the fellow laughed and said he was joking, but the connection, and his point had been made. How *evil* these Iraqis were... heck, they were even named after the evil cities that the Bible says were destroyed by God. We hear what we want to hear, and take from a message what we want to take. Does the expression "cobbled together" have anything to do with Kabul, Afghanistan… probably not, but I couldn't resist asking.

Regarding the *bad* sounding words above, I wonder if it works that way in other languages, do the names of our people and places sound evil to them?

An overused word is "absolutely"… it's applied to things that are hardly worthy of *absoluteness*, just as the word "awesome" is applied to things that barely exceed average.

Could "last ditch effort", come from trench warfare? When you finally got to your last ditch and there was no where else to go… ehhh, probably not.

I keep hearing "absurd" and "unconscionable"... used in partisan contexts, making these superlatives rather forgettable. It's to the point where they're only taken seriously by the choir being preached to.

Orwell may have coined the word, but *Newspeak* has been around forever. In the Civil War commanders were told to treat prisoners of war with "all economy possible", which basically meant "starve them." Newspeak is the art of leaders lying to subjects…the application of lipstick to pigs.

Funny how the words travel and travail sound alike... in the old days travel literally was travail!

According to some, clichés are lame, but I *beg to differ.* There always been a place for clichés, if something's been said nicely, why reinvent the wheel? If possible improve on them and by all means don't rely on them, but don't belittle clichés… they've survived for a reason.

"A lie told often enough becomes truth"… Vladimir Lenin.

Law and Order

"Laws are made for the guys making the laws!"... unknown

The Constitution was a great document from the start, unless you were a woman, Indian or slave – if so it lost much of its luster!

I heard a commercial on the radio for a law firm, stating that they "represent the seriously injured and wrongfully killed" –hmmm, who isn't *wrongfully* killed?

Life is like a court of law... anything you say, can and will be used against you. If it's not a lawyer twisting your words, it's your lover, or someone else who's equally "unassuming."

Whether or not we need religion in order to live moral lives and not take advantage of others is debatable, I think laws are good enough. After all, religion *takes sides* while in theory, the law does not. Without laws to deter us from following our base instincts, people would act even worse!

They had a *beer summit* at the White House, between a black professor and a white policeman. The president described it as a "teachable moment", but what was the lesson? To me it's that, police should give citizens the benefit of the doubt and not beat or arrest them unjustly. For our part, citizens should treat police with respect, these actions make for a more civil society... and help prevent civilians from getting injured. Let the wheels of justice turn in court, under the auspices of a judge, and not be administered at street level.

Leaders

"They dedicate their lives to running our affairs"... Metallica

If people have greater intellect than others, let them run railroads so the trains will be on time, or encourage them to become medical researchers... but don't let them run your lives! The majority of people are neither idiots or slackers and can run their own lives better than the *geniuses* can. If however someone wants to turn the *management* of his life over to others, then so be it.

Is it unnatural for people to actually think for themselves? Many prefer letting leaders do the thinking, as long as they "look out" for us. Is this an evolutionary adaptation that the human race has made *for its own good*? If so, it's not working at the moment.

When I see soldiers fighting for leaders they've never met, and ideas that make no sense, I'm reminded how humans can behave like ants. They act instinctively… what's our excuse?

Loyalty and Trust

"You don't earn loyalty in a day. You earn loyalty day-by-day"… Jeffrey Gitomer

I'm loyal to those who are loyal to me, and despite being taught to love my enemy… the people I love most, are the people who love me (at least I *think* they love me.)

Just about everything should have the caveat "within reason"... whether it's "obey thy parents", or "respect your elders", you should do so only when they deserve it. Don't fall into the trap of doing anyone's dirty work, or being their minion. Respect is one thing, subjugation is another, don't be lead astray by *honored* traditions like obedience to authority. At the same time, don't use being independent as an excuse for shirking responsibily.

My loyalty to others is roughly proportional to their loyalty to me... not a perfect arrangement, but better than being a doormat.

If we arrive at dire days -- I will help people when I can... especially those who have not mistreated me. I respect the teaching to *love your enemy*, but am unlikely to do so every case. After hundreds of years of people taking advantage of those who help them, that philosophy should be considered on a case-by-case basis. Gamers and abusers should not be rewarded at the expense of good, hard working people… do you want the lazy to inherit the world?

Loyalty is one thing, it should be earned and respected, but betrayal is another… it should not be done or taken lightly.

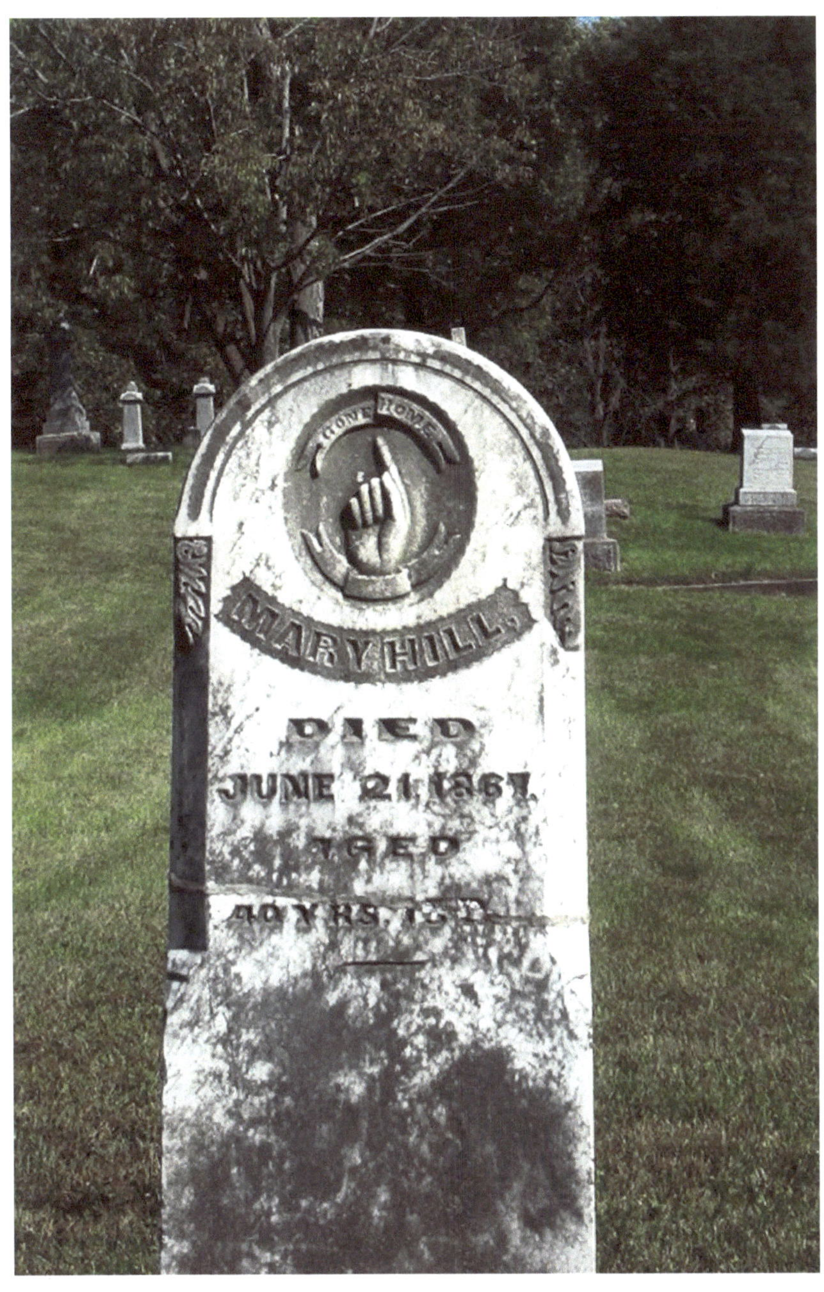

"The strength of a family, like the strength of an army, is in its loyalty to each other" … Mario Puzo

Machisimo

They take their cues from tough guys like the Marlboro Man... even though he's just an actor. Meanwhile, many good men are seen as weak and ineffectual, after all when was the last time they kicked someone's ass?

The way for young men to appear cool, is to do what the macho men do…if that means getting drunk, or cracking heads they're eager to comply. They play *follow the leader* and when the girls positively reinforce such behavior, it's impossible not to do the leaders bidding.

All you have to do is call them a "wuse" for not doing the macho thing and they'll fall in line… very few young men can stand being "called out." There's no up side to standing up for peace and reconciliation… doing so doesn't compare with the instant gratification available to those who *toe the line.*

So, is this tough guy thing *nature or nurture*? It's both… we're "blessed" with hormones that can be exploited and certainly our macho culture rewards *tough guys.*

"Coffee black, sunscreen hah!, beer, beer, beer, dressing on the side… hah, real men don't even eat salad… so it is with "real men." If such statements are not masking insecurity, I'll eat my hat and yours!

"Real men" won't put on gloves or a hat until the "head man" tells them its okay to… they'd rather get frost bite, than be the first one to *dress for the weather.*

We've been taught we can question anything, but the people we should question the most are the ones with the greatest power to retaliate if we dare to.

"The tragedy of machismo is that a man is never quite man enough"… Germaine Greer

<u>Marriage, Women and Wives</u>

"Before you get married, keep your eyes wide open, after you get married, keep them half shut"...Ben Franklin

My dear... you may not be perfect, but you're perfect for me!

I will never understand my wife and women, but I'm trying to at least develop a *working knowledge* of the female mind.

Full equality between sexes and populations is good... special privileges are bad.

Men are often called the dominant sex and this is said to be a man's world, but women have been battling for control since the garden of Eden and they've done quite well.

Don't we love to be complimented! Watching my Dad pluck the heart strings of his lady and still romancing the ladies at his age, is indeed interesting, if not an inspiration!

Animals roll in the scent of their prey, as it makes stalking easier. Humans also mask and enhance our odor when on the prowl for mates, but with more sophisticated, if not necessarily more successful means.

Men should listen carefully to the counsel of women, we just shouldn't be ruled by them. On a related note... how can you lead men, if you can't stand up to your woman?

Once in a while, one of us will ask the other what they're thinking... almost invariably we're in parallel universes of thought. She's thinking accessories, kids, holidays... I'm thinking lumber, politics and bills.

The dynamics of our relationship change when we enter our bedroom... and once again when we climb into bed.

The clock in our bedroom is purposely set nine minutes fast at the moment and that's no good. I don't want to wake up and have to calculate what time it really is... isn't that what the darn clocks for in the first place?

There always seems to be a fresh copy of Victoria's Secret catalog laying around, they arrive weekly, often accompanied with free panties. Those alluring *angels* remind me that the female form is designed to seduce us… it's perfectly designed to guarantee the survival of the species!

Don't argue with your spouse in front of others… they may egg you on, or take pleasure in it… but you will be the losers.

My wife has two functions to attend this week, so those evening I'll be living like a bachelor… it reminds me that without her civilizing influence, I might quickly revert to my baser instincts.

There's almost no such thing as a blonde… at least not in adulthood. Realizing society's preference, women want to look like fair maidens. Unlike Seal pups that start out blonde and turn dark, human females start out with various colors of hair, but usually end up blonde… at least during some part of their mating cycle.

I don't expect my wife to always understand me and vice versa, but if we tolerate and respect each other in spite of our differences, we just might do okay.

Women do not readily accept men's leadership… is it because we lead them astray, have different priorities, or because she has a mind of her own and a strong instinct to use it!

I've heard people say they cherish the wrinkles on their spouses face, because of the many loving years they've had together. I used to think such statements were insincere, but now as the lines accumulate on our faces, I'm beginning to understand what they're talking about. Rumor has it, I'm responsible for many of the lines on my wife's sweet visage!

Occasionally my wife seems to be losing her marbles and I wonder, *am I going to end up babysitting a crazy old lady someday*? Then reason prevails and I realize that if I'm even around by then, I'll probably be crazier than her. Hopefully we'll do our best to take care of each other with dignity and grace… as a friend recently reminded me "we'll all need someone to change our diapers some day."

Beautiful women may not be a dime a dozen, but there are millions of them. I'd say the price is about a million per dozen, that's why rich men do so well!

The male of the species has been disappointing females for a million years... so why expect anything to change now? It's a matter of different standards and priorities. Other than those few men who spoil things for the rest of us, we're nowhere near as picky as the average woman.

How can women be so sexual and at the same time so asexual? So alluring, yet so disinterested in sex at times? I suppose their desires are quite different than ours.

There must be a niche for macho bullies... after all a large percentage of the female population is attracted to them. There must be a good reason for that attraction... at least historically.

We find it difficult to live with each other and just as difficult living without each other. We communicate and operate differently on so many levels! Most women talk more than men, often sniping, snipping and badgering those around them. Men resort to violence more quickly than women and tragically often direct it at their women. We are not particularly well suited for living together, but when it is successfully accomplished, it is a very good thing… especially for the children.

The protector of the blood line is typically the male, his name is given to it and he wants it to continue into perpetuity. The female is less interested in his blood line than in the success of her offspring. She will select who she believes to be the best male, with little concern for his blood line or name, her main goal is to have a healthy brood. She is interested in survival and improvement, while he is interested in continuation of *his* line at any cost. She will look for the best male and he will look for the most attractive female... ironically both are often fooled!

Oxytocin, the scientist said is released after; nursing, orgasm and even after a pleasant conversation… I submit that it may also be released after a good cry.

We are basically just life support systems for our brains and gonads. All the other organs and systems are simply means of locomotion, or sustenance for the two organs that actually matter! Males and females have distinct anatomical differences, related to their brains and bodies, each designed to

maximize the DNA's chance to reproduce. The female of the species is designed to drive the male wild with excitement, and he is designed to make her think he'll hang around and be a big help!

I don't know why, but men whistle and women hum... hmmm?

"And all the bad boys are standing in the shadows and all the good girls are home with broken hearts"... Tom Petty and the Heartbreakers

I'm amazed at the large number of beautiful women in New York City... but it's actually not that high a number percentage wise. I'm guessing that several hundred people a minute are passing by, so the chances of encountering these beauties is considerable!

It's likely that there are many women out there who could be your soul mate. It's also likely that they all are looking for roughly the same thing in a man. If you come to the table with these attributes you can have a happy marriage to just about anyone... if you don't, then it's unlikely any marriage will be happy for you.

In many countries and many time periods, marriages were arranged, and their success and happiness rate probably didn't vary much from American marriages of today. True, the women in those marriages usually couldn't get a divorce, but our divorce rate of almost 50% is an indication that our *marriages for love* are not working out so well either.

Unlike the mountain man, I like having *a full time night woman*, but the *arrangement* certainly comes with a high level of consternation.

Our daughters have all grown up to be feminists or quasi feminists… after all, they have achieved hard won victories and whether they are liberal or conservative, will never voluntarily relinquish their *rights*… no one ever does, so why should they? That is why reform may be in vain and after the fall, they may face a backlash that will be most unpleasant.

Would it be wrong to make Stepford spouses? We *may* be able to get rid of the female *bitch* gene and the male *asshole* one... but would we still be human? It's one thing to *engineer* our babies to have our favorite eye colors, and another to alter their basic personalities. Meanwhile, aren't women disadvantaged if they lose the ability to bitch, and men disadvantaged if they're too passive? While there are scenarios where Stepford wives may be

desired by some, I will stick with the real McCoy and all the turmoil that goes with her.

Monogamy? Some of us are monogamous in theory but not in practice, some in practice but not in theory… in other words, they'd love to have an affair, but haven't found a partner. It's reported that neither sex is hard wired to be monogamous, but males are reputed to be the *worse offender*. Our eyes wander and our bodies stray for different reasons, men are wired to want to sow seed far and wide, women programmed to find the *best* possible seeds.

I'm guessing there's a correlation between men who don't fantasize and infidelity. There's probably also a correlation between; handsome, rich, powerful men and lack of a *rich* fantasy life. Such men don't need to fantasize, as they've always attracted *willing* women! The majority of men, *enjoy* a rich fantasy life and less need… or opportunity to philander.

We can be a team, we can be allied and we are by law and by nature sometimes joined at the hip, but we are also so different that we should not rule over each other… unless one of the parties agrees to it, which I suggest no man should ever do.

I'm home from the business trip and finally back in my own bed… I can tell I'm home because I'm being elbowed and kicked for snoring! Far away in my hotel room, I can snore as much as I want…

Another reason humans advanced beyond the apes, is that our women are far more demanding than theirs. Female apes are content with fruits, vegetables and beds made of leaves… our gals demand the means necessary to purchase every possible indulgence. Think about it guys, how much would we get done if the gals weren't constantly *urging* us on?

Men are called assholes and women are called bitches... this is logical. Women bitch and men behave like assholes. I mentioned this to my wife and she didn't disagree… in fact she *may* have smiled.

The funny thing about sex is, the things *nice* girls blush about and claim are weird or wrong, are often the things that turn them on the most! Women are probably kinkier than men when you get right down to it…we're content with a few variations, they require even more variety to remain interested. The gals may initially be appalled by *this* or *that*, but if they read in a

magazine, or hear from their girl friends that *it's okay*, they not only embrace it, they demand it!

I mentioned to my wife that I agree with experts who say men think about sex every thirty seconds. The more I think about it, that's when we're behind on the bills, when we're *caught up*, we think about it even more.

I love my wife, but resist being governed by; hormonal cycles, the moon, holiday traditions and super sales.

At approximately the age that a woman's sexual "power" over her man begins to wane, his potency decreases as well. Sometimes this occurs at an ideal rate allowing the older couple to find a new kind of intimacy based less on sex and more on friendship. Unfortunately these aren't always in sync and one partner may have unfulfilled urges leading to divorce or indiscretion.

Heck, my wife and I have joked that one reason we're still together, is that we've invested so much time and energy into "training" each other.

Although our marriage seems to get and stronger over the years and I love her more than ever, there're times when I think she gets a little wacky. After Christmas and early spring seem to be those times... but I would need to keep more careful records to be sure exactly when it occurs.

As I hit my early 50s and my wife her late 40s, I think we're having some of the best sex of our lives. We're more experienced, less self-conscious and we realize the clock is ticking. Whether we have five more years of good sex or 25, we understand that we need to get it while the getting's good!

I put up with peanut butter on knives and spoons and she puts up with me splattering the bathroom mirror… if that's the worst of it, then it's not too bad for either of us!

When I see these guys who have ruined their marriages by being unfaithful, I think to myself I would never do that. After all the *risk reward ratio* makes it clear it's not worth it... if you've got a real good thing, or even a pretty good thing, why screw it up? After all if you have an imagination you can just fantasize about the "other woman", not have to deal with the consequences including the sex which probably wouldn't be as good as expected anyway!

I wear whatever I find hanging in my closet, as my wife has good fashion sense and an inclination to shop. Occasionally there's something I'll refuse to wear, based on it being uncomfortable or me thinking I'll look silly in it. When it comes to looking ridiculous, I don't need any help!

While searching for a new vacuum cleaner belt in the laundry room cabinet, I come across many strange *female items.* In addition to the mini-marathon visors, there are ribbons, gift bags and several very small cushions -- the purpose of which I cannot imagine.

There are women SO good looking everywhere, that it blows me away… that's why it's *the package*, including brains and personality that are so important… not just great looks.

Friends says "this is what it's all about", the Super Bowl celebration and a big party. I'm looking forward to the party too... but get a lecture on the way there about not drinking too so much. Then I'm reprimanded for smoking a cigar, and lectured the next morning for saying the wrong thing vis-à-vis drinking and driving to the young folks… hmm! It's nice to have somebody *looking out for you* and usually she's right… but that doesn't make it any easier to take!

Strangely, I was *a victim* of "progesterone poisoning", when my wife's estrogene cream rubbed off on our sheets and I absorbed it. In addition to developing a sudden fondness for Abba music, I called the neighbors to apologize for missing their birthday part… what's next sending thank you notes after Christmas?

Why do they call of menopause... doesn't the menstrual cycle end at this point? Wouldn't "menostop " be a more accurate description?

My wife's looking for her watch at the bottom of her purse, and it reminds me of trying to find something at the bottom of my tool bucket. After removing combs, brushes and other female necessities, she finally arrives at the multitude of smaller items that have settled to the bottom. Many a time, I have removed screwdrivers, drill bits etc. in an effort to reach the bottom and locate a certain tool… all I get is a bloody knuckle!

When our assets increased in value, I'm torn between bragging about it to my wife, and keeping my big mouth shut... ***asset appreciation*** **is a "buy signal", as in let's go to the mall and buy something!**

I went to the store and bought nine healthy items and a delicious Pumpkin Roll, so guess what… instead of getting an "A" for scoring 90%, I'm scolded and given an "F" for fatty food!

"Single men have consciences married men have wives"... Samuel Johnson

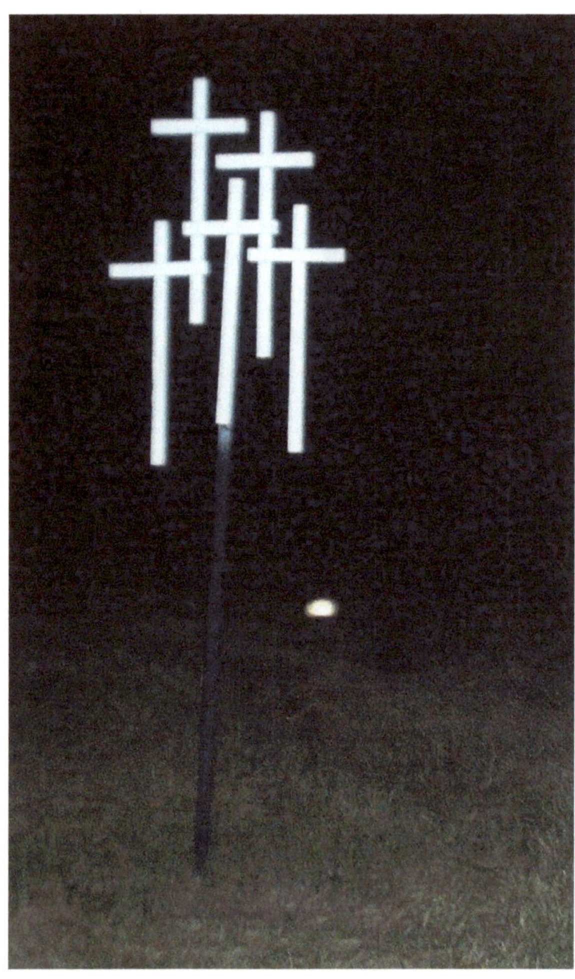

Meek Shall Inherit the Earth…

***"The meek shall inherit the Earth, but not its mineral rights"*… J. Paul Getty**

What better way for the meek to inherit the earth than by the vote… what better way to cling to power than by force.

If the meek inherit the earth, will it be instantly like the rapture, or will it be slowly and by degrees? Will the meek hold sway forever, or just till they become as wicked at those they've replaced?

When the meek take over, will they show the same aggressive tendencies as the formerly powerful…I think so, human always seems to prevail!

How are the meek ever going to inherit the earth if they can't rig the rules like the powerful have done? The overlords are Goliaths, the meek are like David scouring the ground for stones… but somehow David prevailed!

The Nanny State may be the ultimate expression of the meek inheriting the earth. It's also the culmination of society turning into an ant colony. Do not forget the vicious efficiency in which ants eliminate any who don't submit to the Queen.

Maybe *the meek shall inherit the earth,* means there will finally be justice for all.

When "many who are first will be last, and many who are last will be first", it may not be a more peaceful world for anyone, it may just be that the shoe that kicks the down trodden will be on a different foot.

Military Industrial complex

"… we must guard against the acquisition of unwarranted influence, whether sought or unsought, by the military-industrial complex"… President Eisenhower

Although we have the largest military industrial complex (MIC) in history, we don't *appear* to be highly militarized. Only the tip of the iceberg is visible, as most of our military assets are deployed overseas in countries we are

"protecting" or liberating. Our economy however is highly dependent on the MIC, we're the largest arms dealer in the world, and our "defense" budget is reportedly larger than the rest of the worlds combined!

What we need is a larger *medical research complex* and a smaller military industrial complex. Each year, more Americans die from disease than the number that have died in all of our wars throughout our history. We would also be helping more foreigners, by curing disease than by nation building… of course our; war mongers, ideologues and investors, have a vested interest in bombing instead of healing.

I realize there are regimes that should be toppled, and genocide should be interrupted whenever and wherever it occurs. As often as not however, we support those willing to do the bidding of our corporations and other special interest groups.

It doesn't matter what anyone thinks, the MIC, is a fact of life and has been since the first bow and arrow assembly line commenced thousands of years ago.

We face legitimate threats to our security from time to time, but they may be rarer than our leaders would have us believe. Threats are often exaggerated to rouse the masses, and garner support for adventures that do nothing but enrich the arms dealers and financiers.

The U.S. reportedly has sixteen intelligence agencies, but a man almost blew up an airliner with an *underwear bomb*. Do these meddlesome and often violent organizations do much good, and do we need so many of them? In their evil *prime*, did the Soviets or Nazis have this many clandestine *service* organizations?

I agree with those who say we need a robust military industrial complex, because if we dismantle ours, and other countries don't, we'll be sorry. The important thing is to use it responsibly and not let those profiting from it control our foreign policy.

How ironic is it that our former and possible futures enemies are the ones financing our incredible war machine?

Not surprisingly the interstate highway system was designed around our defense requirements and is part of the MIC. Straight stretches of interstate

at regular intervals are incorporated into our highways, in case military aircraft needed emergency landing strips.

The advent of the interstate highway system also meant the end of light rail commuter lines and made us into the most oil dependent society in the world. Eventually, we declared our willingness to use the military to defend our right to procure oil, and any potential interruption of our foreign supply of oil was deemed an "act of war" against the U.S.A.

In one fell swoop, the MIC had justified its existence for perpetuity. Along with their cronies, the oil and auto companies, the MIC's owners grew rich, while the rest of us grew fat, lazy and dependent on cheap gasoline.

I'm watching the business news and the *ticker* mentions today's sponsors… is it a surprise they are virtually all defense contractors?

Moderation, Willpower and Delayed Gratification

"Freedom is not procured by a full enjoyment of what is desired, but by controlling the desire" … Epictetus

The aforementioned are un-cool, old fashioned and corny, but quietly practiced by the healthy, wealthy and wise.

We do most of the damage to our bodies on weekends and holidays, when we *show off* our eating and drinking skills. It's Especially important moderation and self-control at these times!

Depriving oneself of reasonable indulgences leads to the worst binges of all, but once you've ID'd your worst poison, don't' get near the stuff! *If* you have *normal* self control enjoy life! It's when we totally forgo *treats* that we fall off the wagon and binge drink, or eat a quart of ice cream.

"If you can't be with the one you love, love the one you're with!"…has been a popular attitude since time immemorial. How "square" is it to suggest that if you can't be with the one you love, you should exercise self-control?

Willpower, self-control, moderation and restraint... so easy to say, so hard to do!

Moderation, willpower and delayed gratification are potent antidotes to, sloth and gluttony, two of the "Seven Deadly Sins!"

You may have nerves of steel, iron will and rock hard abs, but that doesn't make you *better* than the rest… just more capable, so don't squander your abilities!

Even guilt can be a good thing if it keeps you from doing that which you shouldn't.

There are people of strong will and people of strong character… the latter is better. The strong willed are often just bullies, or people with the power to put your *stugats* in a vice.

People have written books on "will" … it's not so much part of the brain, as part of ones character. Some are blessed with enormous willpower, others come up short, but in all cases, it ebbs and flows.

When your willpower flows strong, take full advantage and make progress in your life. On those days you find it ebbing, fight hard to regain it and hold onto your gains.

Moderation like his friend *delayed gratification* is a lonely fellow! How can these gents compete with the parties being thrown at *misery's* house?

I've eaten a thousand burgers, and partaken of other vices a hundred times, there's no gain in having more…there never was! Ignore those who egg you on towards getting fatter, drunker, or stupider… it doesn't add up! If your friends are determined to go down the wrong path, find new ones… unlike relatives, you're not *stuck* with you friends. It takes gumption, but if most of your friends are in *low places,* upgrade to people who aspire to more than being drunk and disorderly! If your misguided friends are willing to come along for the ride, that's great… if not just wave good bye.

Money and Wealth…

"A penny saved is a penny earned"… Ben Franklin

There is *another* age old battle going on… it is between the rich and the poor.

Money… why is it that the more you make, the more you need!

There are asses and there are assets. Having a nice ass is an asset... being an ass is not.

Yes, I've been harping on it, but if you want to spend more, earn more! On the flip side, if you don't won't to work more, then spend less.

It's easier to make money by exercising your brain, than your back. You can also do it the Al Capone way but eventually you'll do hard time.

It's been years since those who are frugal could openly *ply their trade...* during the roaring 90s and early 2000's, the thrifty were considered *losers*! Waste not want not, had been thrown out the window and *shop till you drop* was the mantra. We fell for anything with a fancy label, or a nice paint job.

Funny, we often resent those who are doing a little better than us, yet admire and defend the actions of those doing a hundred times better.

The rich say they can always pay half the poor to kill the other half of the poor, and so on and so on. Perhaps the restraining factor is that if they kill them all they'd have to take the trash out themselves.

The economy can tank while the stock market reaches new highs, as companies move manufacturing offshore where labor is incredibly cheap. Meanwhile, the working class has little clout, it's more difficult to move their labor than for the rich to move their money.

At the rate the government's printing them, dollars could soon be a dime a dozen!

How you take care of your "things", determines if your ownership will just be *taxing* or literally break you.

We sometimes gauge a persons "value" by the size of their bank account. When someone says, "I'm worth more than him", they may be referring to bank accounts, but they're making a broader general statement too.

The elite, will do anything to hold on to the institutions allowing them to amass wealth on an unprecedented scale. Fiat and digital storage not only allow them to plunder wealth from others, but unlike pharaohs or kings, they can easily move their fortunes to friendlier environs when necessary.

I heard that there's more gold on the ocean floor than on land… there's probably also more boats on the bottom of the sea than on it's surface… but that's another story.

A few years ago an infamous international financier reportedly made 41,000 times as much as the average American family... is it just me or is that crazy?

Money for humans is like blood to a vampire, to survive we must constantly replenish our supply.

Via the widespread acceptance of; derivatives, credit default swaps, subprime loans, futures, puts, shorts and the like, humans have been *reprogrammed* to accept fiat money and debt slavery as the natural state of affairs. How else could we *creatively* finance our conspicuous consumption and how would the government be able to spend so much? The "bee hive" needs to be restructured, but not along the lines of rewarding the greediest brainiacs among us.

Having a large bank account and full larder, does not mean you're wealthy... especially if you're never satisfied with what you have. Money like any other addictive substance will slip through your fingers, or go up in smoke.

There are investors, there are gamblers and they overlap... you shouldn't invest at the Roulette Wheel, nor should you *gamble* in the stock market but that's what many people do. Reagan wanted wealth to trickle down from the top, Obama wants it to start of the bottom... what about starting in the middle? That's where the greatest concentration of people who work hard and pay taxes are.

One good thing for the US dollar, is that it's still the currency of choice, for everyone from narco-traffickers to Somali pirates. Meanwhile "respectable"

businessmen around the world are increasingly asking for payment in euros or yen... that's not good for the greenback.

The fact that such a small percentage of the US population control so much of America's wealth is an indication that financial disaster has already occurred.

If it's true that behind every great fortune there is a great crime, what does that say about those of in the *upper middle class,* are they *petty* white collar criminals?

There's nothing wrong with wealth re-distribution schemes, as long as it's done with the proponents wealth and not everyone else's. It's also no surprise that the wealthy want to redistribute the average family's money while holding onto theirs.

Queen Elizabeth is visiting the U.S. and she's brought lots of fancy hats! I'm not excited by the visit of monarchs... why don't their *subjects* give them brooms and put them to work!

As long as the investor class keeps the lower working class "poor enough", there will always be a steady supply of soldiers to fight for *the investor class.*

If you learn to use the financial system intelligently it will work for you, if you don't its likely to ruin you.

Everyone's trying to *get by*, and *get more*...it makes for a very 'interesting' world.

Pennies are not sacred, I sweep and throw them away... but quarters, I still pick up. Pennies hardly contain copper anymore and are almost worthless. Since my aching back has only *so many bends* left, I'm determined to make at least $ 0.25 when I use it.

You don't make a man strong by lifting weights for him and you don't make a man wise by thinking for him. You don't make winners by rewarding losers and you shouldn't throw good money after bad.

"We are all pieces of each other's puzzles"... Native Americans saying

Are you living in overdrive too? Sometimes I feel like a bartender, hustling to make each movement as efficient as possible, in order to make more money for other people to spend! I need to drive a harder bargain with all the people competing for my money… whoever they are!

Don't get hung up on being productive all the time… take time to smell the roses and watch the clouds go by. These people telling you to be more productive, will never be satisfied until they have spent you like so many dollar bills!

I'm on a cruise watching gamblers use their *systems* at slots, and card games. In the end, most lose their money – I don't think they understand basic math and elementary statistics!

I wasn't a good student and didn't learn much in business college… what I did learn was; hire an accountant, the law of diminishing returns and pay yourself first.

Regarding the criticism I receive for how I earn money, it's interesting that the critics have no problem demanding their share of that *tainted* money!

We're "invited" to join the investor class and grow rich too, but it mostly benefits the puppet masters that the pool of investors keeps growing. They need to maintain the proper ratio of puppet masters to *working stiffs*… since the latter segment is always increasing. Since working folk around the world reproduce at a higher rate, the puppet master's must constantly increase their ranks… otherwise the ratio of rich to poor will become so low that even money and manipulation will fail to maintain "order."

During the fund drive, the announcer describes what separates his radio station's listeners from "ordinary" people. He said his listeners have a "deep concern for the community." I interpret that as meaning his listeners have more money than "ordinary" listeners. Almost everyone is concerned about their community, but some people have more money to oil the machinery!

Hate to say it, but you don't score points by working hard, you score by making money…that's what friends and family want to see.

As you wake up, stagger to your old car and hope it starts, remember the brain produces greater results than the back. I'm just the messenger, and

this is how it's been for thousands of years. There is nothing wrong with manual labor, it's as noble as any other type of work... its just not rewarded accordingly.

There are two different types of bank robbers, those that rob banks, and those who *own* the bank. Conventional robbers steal a few thousand at a time from the vault, while bank owners steal a dollars at a time, but from thousands of people, via fees and charges… guess which robber makes more money?

So far there has been no decoupling of the worlds economies… the rest of the world has hitched their wagon to our star. When we collide with the sun, there will be serious consequences for everyone…or at least for those who work for a living.

Being a devoted protégée of Ayn Rand is scary enough, but when the chairman of the Federal Reserve starts takes advice from the host of Mad Money, look out!

"The golden rule ... those who have the gold make the rules" - unknown

Mother Nature

"Nature must not win the game, but she can not loose"… Carl Jung

You tell me not to eat meat and to treat the various species of animals as tribes of equals. If you remake the lion to lay down with the lamb, is it still a lion…will you tame gators and sharks as well?

It's funny how westerners, who are responsible for driving many species towards extinction, spend so much time studying animals. Historically, indigenous peoples hunted animals, but didn't kill them purely for trophies, or to destroy their habitat on a massive scale. Instead, they utilized them sustainably and often revered them, now however, the roles are increasingly reversing…what gives?

The wind is gusting 40 miles an hour, I'm trying to stake a pine tree so it won't blow away and my fingers are bloody. I'm fighting Mother Nature so I

have a good idea how this is going to turn out... but being involved in so many losing battles, one more doesn't matter. Don Quixote where are you!

I'm watching a TV show about decimation of the whales, and it makes me wonder… what's more valuable to the planet Earth – another billion human beings, or the survival of a few thousand Blue Whales? I value humans over whales, but think we must protect these wonders of nature too.

Do animals wake up after a weekend binge, hung over and thinking, "Geez, its freaking Monday and I've gotta get a Zebra!"

I'd never want to be a bat, snake or chicken… horses on the other hand would be near the top of my list. So, who's responsible for a horses beauty and grace, God or man? I would give God most of the glory, but selective breeding by mankind deserves credit as well. Mother nature's Zebra may be better able to survive in the wild, but they're not nearly as elegant and beautiful as the horse.

What is it with some fish, the Salmon for example… the male doesn't even penetrate the female, he just masturbates next to her as she releases her eggs… spawning they call it… I call it boring!

In the news today, a family released a 300 pound Seal back into the wild, after rescuing and nursing it back to health. On its flipper, they put a "medical history" tag, in case it's rescued and needs care again. I hope it doesn't meet up with a Great White or Polar Bear…they can't read!

Mother nature's job is to birth you, and eventually to kill you. She's charged with keeping things; orderly, moving and making sure the earth doesn't get to crowded.

They say a horse designed by a committee is a camel... but what would you rather have if you were crossing the desert?

Why do they call zoo animals "residents", wouldn't prisoners be more accurate?

Entropy, rust and decay, are "Mom's" way of making sure nothing lasts forever. Whether a human body or skyscraper, it takes more energy to build and keep them up, than bring them down. Just consider Humpty Dumpty –

“all the king’s horses and all the kings men couldn’t put Humpty together again.”

There’s an entire infrastructure devoted to making sure that things fall apart. Whether it's Mother Nature, Father Time or the wrecking ball -- creativity and imagination constantly face these foils. Whether you call them; good and evil, Ying and Yang, sun, water and wind, or God and the devil, the same forces that create beauty and life, eventually erode and destroy them. Within our body, the miracle of orderly cellular division, which makes a child grow, eventually gives way to disorderly division, and kills us with cancer or old age.

Obviously rabbits are not be very bright, otherwise my dog would not be regularly catching them in the back yard. God made them dumb for a reason - so they would feed others... he also gave them a prodigious rate of reproduction so they may thrive anyway.

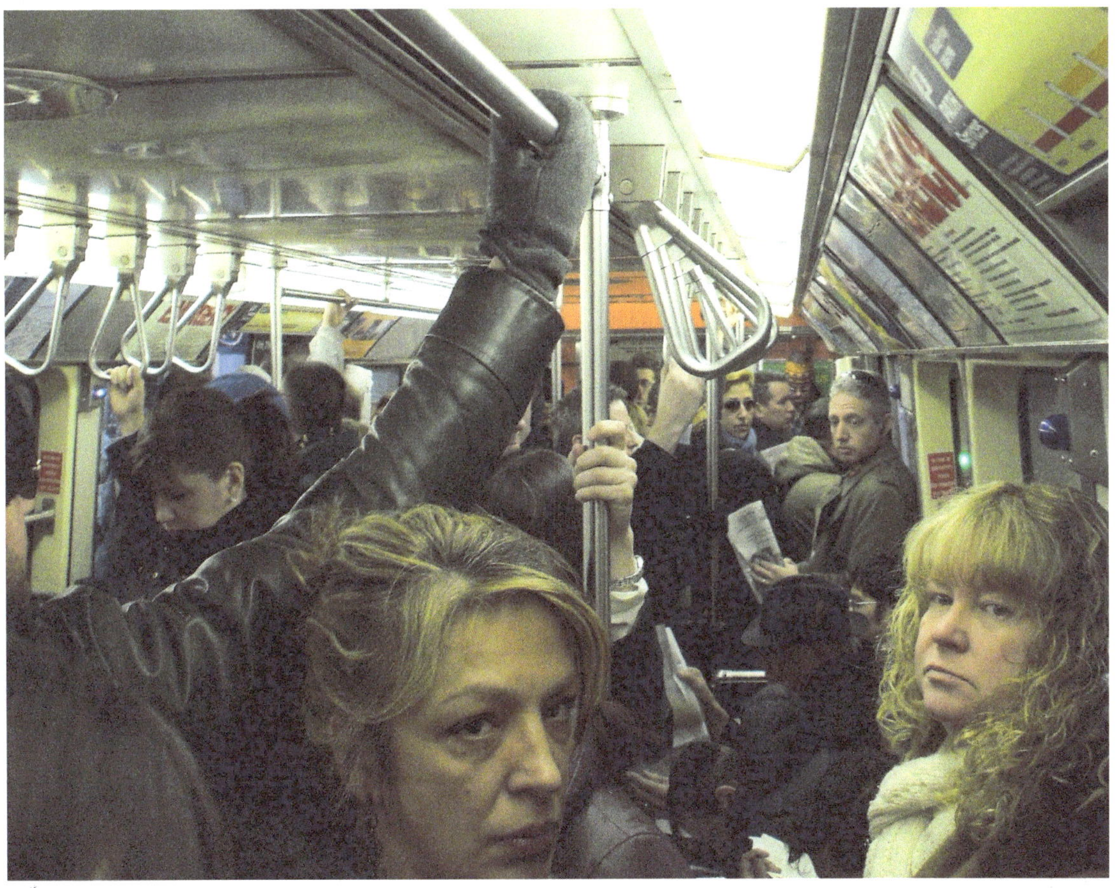

On TV, the "Driver ants" attack the Termite colony in an attempt to overpower and consume their larva. From the lowest to the "highest" we prey on other species... just another one of "Mom's" methods to prevent overpopulation? On the same show, ants of a different species "shepherd" Aphids like humans shepherd sheep. The Aphids provide a sweet nectar that sustains the ants, who in turn protect the Aphids from predators… is this symbiotic or slavery?

We certainly don't want to model our society after that of Ants or Bees, but we can learn a few things from their behavior. They are orderly, but mindless... we have minds but are disorderly!

Mother nature is one "rad" bitch, she has to be… after all, she's Momma Bear to the entire world!

Nobody makes parts like "Mom"... so take care of your body. Medical technology's come a long way, but it's still far from able to replace an eye or a hand that works like the original.

"Nature, Mr. Allnut, is what we are put into this world to rise above"… Katherine Hepburn

Is it possible for animals to contemplate suicide? Is a chained dog or a cage chimpanzee simply miserable, or does it want to end it all?

As I start grinding and mashing the apples for a batch of hard cider the Bees and Flies descend. I hate these bugs, but they're just doing their job… filling their niche, same as the rest of creation.

Why is it that wild Orcas don't attack humans? Somewhere along the line did they learn it's better to leave people alone? Maybe it was during the whaling era, when so many of their relatives were hunted to near extinction.

Does the lioness revel in the carnage she commits in the course of feeding her family? Does she feel guilty, or is her brain programmed not to realize that emotion in the least?

Regarding the "lunkers" we caught, I like photographic souvenirs better than the one's you mount on the wall. Photos take advantage of camera

angles and are a better basis for fish stories, the trophy on the wall is finite and easily measured!

Animal intelligence? Horses and deer probably aren't as dumb as we think they are, but with their speed and senses, they don't have to be brilliant, they simply have to recognize a threat and giddy up!

Thanks to my sore hip, I have not walked in a month... but today I've walked a mile and I pass a spot where the possum and her spawn met their maker, and where the skunk met its demise. The last time I passed, there were traces of all three of them. Now the rains have washed the street clean and to the naked eye there's not the slightest trace they ever existed.

I squashed the tiny spider as it traversed the kitchen floor… unless you eat ants, we don't need any more critters in here… I didn't do it with glee… but I did it.

Earth... isn't it basically made of rock covered by poop and *dead stuff?* Each year it gets bigger... *stuff* has to go somewhere…and magically it supports life!

"Nature is resilient, it has survived worse things than us"… unknown.

Music

I hate it when a song gets stuck in my head and I sing, whistle or hum it all day long... well actually I don't mind, it's those around me who hate it!

Music is like a chemical reaction, we like it or we don't, but we react to it. There's music we like, music we can't relate to, "crap" we don't consider music at all… its different for each of us.

Is it a paradox that the descendents of slaves created such free form music as jazz and R&B? Probably not… why wouldn't people longing for freedom create free form music while those holding them in bondage create more *orderly* music?

When John Mellencamp sings, "if you're not part of the future that get out of the way", I hope he doesn't mean, if you're not part of the future as your "supposed to" see it, get out of the way!

How many songs have been written since *the beginning*? I have no idea... but billions have been composed in people's heads.

"Packed like lemmings into shiny metal boxes, like chestnuts in a suicidal race"... The Police

At the Festival, we listened to a young rock band and I noticed their lyrics were utterly party line about the war. Appearance wise, they look like rebels from the 60s, but their music sounded like sitcom theme songs. Meanwhile, old farts were making out on the dance floor… With few exceptions, rock 'n roll has been PC for years… chalk it up to the usual suspects.

"I worry that the person who thought up *Muzak* may be thinking up something else"…Lily Tomlin

Nukes

"Nuclear weapons can wipe out life on Earth, if used properly"… Gareth Owen

America's "nuclear deterrent" is different now than it was in the cold war days. Instead of being intended to keep the Russian bear at bay via mutual assured destruction, it is now being contemplated as an instrument of persuasion. It has become the *logical* last step in our foreign policy, when conventional means of "diplomacy" do not achieve the desired results. Nuclear weapons are the ultimate stick for when carrots don't work! Will we destroy half the world for ideology and economic domination?

When I was young I never felt particularly threatened by Russian missiles, even though it was the height of the Cold War. Now in the midst of the war on terrorism, I don't lose sleep over Al Qaeda's schemes… I was always more concerned with more immediate problems. When I was younger, it was things like meeting girls and learning to *drive a stick* … now it mostly revolves around paying the bills.

"I know not with what weapons World War III will be fought, but World War IV will be fought with sticks and stones" ... Albert Einstein

I hear people suggest that we bomb various countries back to the stone age... but these countries are virtually in the stone age already! We on the other hand are "highly advanced" and may not adjust very well to going back in time. We should think long and hard before using nukes and possibly ending up back in the stone age ourselves... aren't there better ways of influencing others than force?

One of the reasons we think twice before nuking our enemies, is the fear it might create a nuclear winter that could severely damage own civilization. Other than that, I some of our leaders and populace would have no problem blowing "insubordinate" nations to kingdom come. Now if our leaders think they can use nukes on a limited basis without repercussions, then Katie bar the door!

I suppose a nuclear apocalypse is almost inevitable, since eventually many countries will have these weapons and the will to use them. Because of ideology, self-preservation or religion, countries will think they have the right to nuke their neighbors... it's certainly been done before. Superpowers might think they have the right to impose their will on others, but if they cross the line too many times, smaller nuclear armed nations might pull the trigger first... after all, it's the only *ace up their sleeve.*

From the sling shot to the machine gun... inventors of more advanced weapons have eventually had them used against themselves... we are dreaming if we thing it will be otherwise with nukes. Don't they warn us that those who live by the sword, will die by the sword?

"Free nations are peaceful nations. Free nations don't attack each other. Free nations don't develop weapons of mass destruction"...George W. Bush.

Like Smith and Wesson making all men equal a century ago, Einstein's discovery could make all countries equal too. Not that it's anything to look forward to, but the genie is out of the bag.

"I am proud of the fact that I never invented weapons to kill"... Thomas Edison

The USA may be backing itself into a corner, yes we have enough nukes to kill everybody in the world several times... but an increasing number of countries will soon have enough nukes to kill some of us once -- and that's all it takes. If we keep imposing our views on others -- how can this not come back and bite us on the "you know what."

Instead of curing disease and helping billions of people, we squander our national treasure developing new bunker busting nuclear bombs that are more "usable" and "environmentally friendlier." If and when they are used, will they save humanity, or simply maintain the status quo?

I'm curious - how long would it take a highly industrialized country, with an existing *peaceful* nuclear program to develop nuclear weapons? I wonder how many of them have plans on the drawing board - just in case?

"It would be our policy to use nuclear weapons wherever we felt it necessary to protect our forces and achieve our objectives" ... Robert McNamara

Obligations

"The thing is, Bob, it's not that I'm lazy, it's that I just don't care"... Office Space

I think we're primarily *in it* for ourselves and our loved ones, and being in it for our loved ones, is much like being in it for ourselves, since their success trickles down to us. When we do nice things for those outside of our little circle, are we doing it for the right reasons... who cares, do it anyway!

If someone has a reputation for being a doormat, they will find it a hard *rep* to unload. People like having doormats around and will resist your attempt at liberation ... that's when you'll need to be at the top of your game!

When we spend too much time accommodating others, we have little time to do what we believe we're put in this world to do... some call that selfish... I don't.

Most people would like to simplify their lives and focus on the things of greatest importance to them selves. Unfortunately, the PTB are determined

to complicate our lives and make it impossible for us to focus on anything other than being a spoke in their wheel.

Funny, it seems everyone I know is dissatisfied with my "performance" in one way or another. Having been raised to be *responsible,* I give a darn and that keeps me spinning like a top, in an effort to please everyone. I think people who *don't give a damn* have it a lot easier… I'm trying to become one.

Everyone's so busy! In fact we're *conditioned* to think we should be busy all the time. The implication is, the busier you are, the better person you are.

With all due respect, I have too many people asking me to jump through too many hoops… it can't be done! My new motto is, "I'll get around to doing it, when I get around to doing it." Of course it falls on deaf ears… after all, we have obligations! The problem with jumping through all these hoops, is we end up; injured, worn out and old before our time. Worst of all, we end up never having taken the time to do what we believe we were put here to do.

Obligations, expectations, anticipations – these "a*tions*" can be overwhelming!

We all create obligations, were all subject to obligations, we all keep track of obligations... and even when we don't, the other fellow does.

We didn't create this system, certainly cavemen created obligations too... this system has been around for a very long time!

Our obligation system, *may* actually be a positive thing for the human race. Since we do better when we cooperate, obligations might have *evolved* to help us strengthen ties to those around us. The caveat is, it's not always equitable, but when it is, it's not any worse than any other system,

It's less problematic to borrow a cup of sugar from the neighbor, then to accept advice. You can simply return the cup of sugar, but when you accept advice, he thinks he's done you a great favor!

We borrowed 2 cups of oil from the neighbor two days ago and returned a bottle containing 4 cups yesterday. I asked my wife why she got such a large bottle? She told me that they were all the same price... now instead of

"evening things", we've unintentionally created an obligation on their part… it's a viscous cycle!

When you do something nice for someone you create an obligation, most people will try to repay it even though they may resent you for it. Some will forget that you've done them a favor but they won't forget that they resent you for "something."

It's better not to do favors if you're doing it to create an obligation... favors should be like gifts, don't give them if you expect to be repaid. I bought lunch for my friend, hoping to *mend fences*, but instead created an obligation he neither wants or needs.

When I say *I'm going to do things my way for now on…* I mean I want to tweak things… I'm not going to *intentionally* be a butt hole.

Oil

"This conservation crap has gone too far... why did we take this country from the Indians if we aren't going to use it" -- Al Bundy.

Now that Iraq *appears* liberated, pacified, and a compliant Iraqi government has indicated that American oil companies will get lucrative contracts, everything appears hunky-dory. Time will tell if we have done the Iraqi people a great favor and if their oil reserves will help us during this period of transition from a world of cheap oil to one of expensive oil and new energy technologies. I am hoping for the best, but not necessarily expecting it.

It may have been Reagan who popularized the trickle-down economy, where the wealthy receive tax breaks which encourages them to create jobs for the "working class." The Saudi Arabian system of huge oil revenues belonging to the princes, results in similar trickling down to the working class - I'm not a big supporter of either "scheme."

It's possible the only way the US will survive is for it to inflict on its own citizens, or on other nations. When people riot because they can't pay for gasoline or heat, and their taxes are through the roof, will there not be an executive order for them to be rounded up and *sent to camp*? Will we not also increase the use of our military in order to obtain the oil that others have and we "need?"

Many Americans have decided the Iraqis *owe us* their oil... after all, didn't we liberate them? Come to think of it, aren't there other oil-rich countries that *need* to be liberated… sounds like a growth industry to me! You could survey the Iraqis about their feeling and depending on who you ask, you'll get whatever result you want... but there's no way to ask the hundreds of thousands of Iraqis killed since the invasion.

I've heard it said that our country is based on cheap energy, I would go a little further and say we are based on cheap everything and we are quite willing to procure it anyway that is "necessary." Historically slavery and cheap immigrant labor have been as much the basis of our economy, as cheap oil, free timber and free land thanks to the Indians.

Many American's who say we can't afford to convert to clean energy, are willing to approve trillions for oil wars. I guess they consider it a better way to investment in *energy independence*… after all he who controls the oil, can consume all he wants!

The explanation some give for our actions in the middle east is that we're doing God's work… I hope they're right, if not we may be doing the devils.

Order or Chaos?

"We are always just nine meals away from anarchy"… Lord Cameron

Its interesting how the two things we need the most - water and oxygen, are among the most destructive substances on earth. In the form of rust and oxidation, they reduce everything they come in contact with to debris.

The concept of "orderliness" is largely a myth, chaos always lurks just around the corner and things invariably fall apart!

When the "shit hits the fan", do you think computers will keep working? Do you think 911 operators will answer your calls? Forget about buying food and fancy clothes... sadly, like the phrase WTSHTF implies, it will be utter chaos.

"My grandfather rode a camel, my father rode a camel, I drive a Mercedes, my son drives a Land Rover, his son will drive a Land Rover, but his son will ride a camel" ... Sheikh Rashid bin Saeed Al Maktoum

Likewise…Grandpa used the telegraph, Dad a phone, we use cell phones... the kid's send text messages… will theirs use tin cans and a string?

In an emergency, experts say that 10% of people keep their wits about them, while 80% become paralyzed with confusion and wait for an *authority figure* to lead them… I'm guessing the other 10% go completely nuts.

They say people with A.D.D. are like hunters in a farmer's world, and that under certain extreme circumstances, A.D.D. would once again be advantageous. … I wonder if chaos is that circumstance?

"What did they use before they had candles and oil lamps in Zimbabwe? Electricity!"…unknown

There's always a dark age somewhere and civilization in general may collapse, but no one knows if it will in two years or two hundred. Hopefully it never happens, but if so, the later the better… only then will humans have a realistic chance of successfully heading for the stars.

Since there is order in the universe, (as well as entropy, chaos and disorder), perhaps mathematical equations can explain that order, as well as the disorder. I won't take; Galileo, Newton and Einstein over Jesus, but I'll take them over those who have anointed themselves to speak on his behalf, starting with the apostle Paul, right on up to the latest crop of kooks.

"Anarchy means rowdier sheep, but sheep none the less"… unknown

Reform is fantastic and should be occurring constantly. Total collapse on the other hand is horrendous and should be avoided at *almost* any cost. God help humanity if there's another dark age… hopefully our and actions won't make it inevitable.

"When the peasants show up at the castle with their torches and pitchforks, you don't want to be in the castle"… unknown.

When society's in chaos, it's "every man (or woman) for himself." That's bad… its even worse that some people behave like that even when society's functioning *properly*.

It's almost always preferable to reform than to rebel, and it is never preferable to usher in chaos and anarchy. Doing so may overturn corrupt leaders, but they are likely to be replace with equally corrupt leaders and war lords. Under anarchy, the technologies we take for granted might disappear eliminating not only the comforts of civilization, but also the essentials that keep us alive.

"Those who make peaceful revolution impossible make violent revolution inevitable." – John F. Kennedy

Patriotism

If I'm seen as critical of our great country, it's because we're not going to make it better by patting each other on the back... that's a recipe for destruction.

When your neighbor's hauled away, it's Homeland Defense. When you are, its oppression.

Is it unpatriotic to love one's country but not its government?

Peace

"Blessed are the peacemakers, for they shall be called the children of God"… Matthew 5:9

Peace and justice go hand in hand…it's like the soup commercial, "you can't have one, you can't have none, you can't have one without the other!"

Son, there will be enough fights without picking any… try to be peaceful!

There's plenty of hope for mankind's survival, but less hope for peace on earth. That might actually require supernatural intervention… not just human meddling masquerading as the supernatural.

Peace appears to be but a brief transitional phase, occurring only when we have what we want and ending, when we determine that we *must* have more.

When we safely harness the power of the sun, wind, tides, atoms, can feed everyone and move out into space, could there finally be peace?

Have people ever been able to just live in peace and also posses the ability to express themselves freely? I don't think so… we've always had to belong to a clique, clan, or something whose strength affords us "protection." That protection comes at the price of sacrificing a degree of freedom and individuality… like it or not, we usually accept the *necessary* sacrifices.

As long as there is life, there will be death. As long as there is pleasure, there will be pain, as long as there are people, there will be conflict.

To some extent, we're like sharks, doing whatever's necessary to survive. I've heard that some sharks eat their siblings en utero – at least we don't do that!

Sadly people are more likely to have the "opportunity" to destroy life than preserve it. We can join the military and "legally" kill the "enemy", but unless you're a doctor, nurse or medic how often do you get the chance to save someone? If you ever get that chance take it! Don't worry if the person is friend or enemy…saving a life must be thrilling and a badge of honor no matter who it is! Hardly anyone's life ever needs to be taken, yet humans go around culling each other like they're cutting the grass!

If a person is so talented as to be capable of tremendous good, they're also capable of tremendous harm. The same applies to nations, both should be encouraged to do good, and prevented whenever humanly possible from running amok.

As much as possible, your agenda should be yours and mine should be mine... let's stop shoving ours down each other's throats! The only thing we should be able to force on anyone, is peace.

Peer Pressure

"Repeat after me... I promise to be different, I promise to be unique... I promise not to repeat what other people say." - Steve Martin's Non-Conformist's Oath

We're taught to stand up for what we believe in... eventually it becomes apparent we're to do so only if we believe in the "right things." We're given some leeway, but there're certain core beliefs we're expected to uphold. If we don't extol those, we're advised to keep out mouths shut, failing that, we risk a variety of repercussions.

You can conform and be *allowed* a measure of acceptance, or you can resist and *earn* a measure of respect. The latter is more difficult, but you'll feel better about yourself in the long run.

Where does *hard wiring* end and peer pressure begin? Why do we feel we have to be *knuckle heads* when we're with *the guy?* The *leader of the pack*, is usually the biggest jerk of all... unfortunately his buddies are defenseless against his powers of persuasion.

Don't settle for being *the person you're known as* - I'm known as someone who loves cake...but I don't want that to be my legacy!

Peer pressure is one of the most *educational* forces in our lives. People with an agenda find it invaluable for "getting people off the fence" and addicts are experts at employing it to entice others to accompany them in their misery. Those who master its use usually win the day... especially when the contestants are im*pressionable* young people.

There are many reasons that peer pressure is so effective, especially with the young...they want to fit in, prove they're tough and they have yet to see how damaging blind faith can be.

Admit it or not, adults are interested in influencing, if not indoctrinating young people. Some use the direct approach, some speak in parables and other's methods are even more "discreet."

Where do our young people learn negative behaviors? For starters, they're human and humans are not *really* taught to think, we're taught to *agree.*

Whether it's work, school, parties, most people don't like to make waves... we try to do what we think the "alphas" want us to do.

I received curious looks as I cut the lawn with my "Leave It to Beaver" lawn mower. Friends thought it ridiculous and asked, "why don't you buy a real mower?" I explained it's a very small yard, no one wants to steal it and it *starts every time!* That didn't fly and I was considered a woose for not using at least *3 1/2 horses* to cut my eighth of an acre… maybe they were right, I finally gave up on it, since the darn thing couldn't cut dandelions!

Those who claim they aren't concerned about being judged on appearances, either haven't been, or have been judged favorably… the rest of humanity has been and admit it or not, we're concerned.

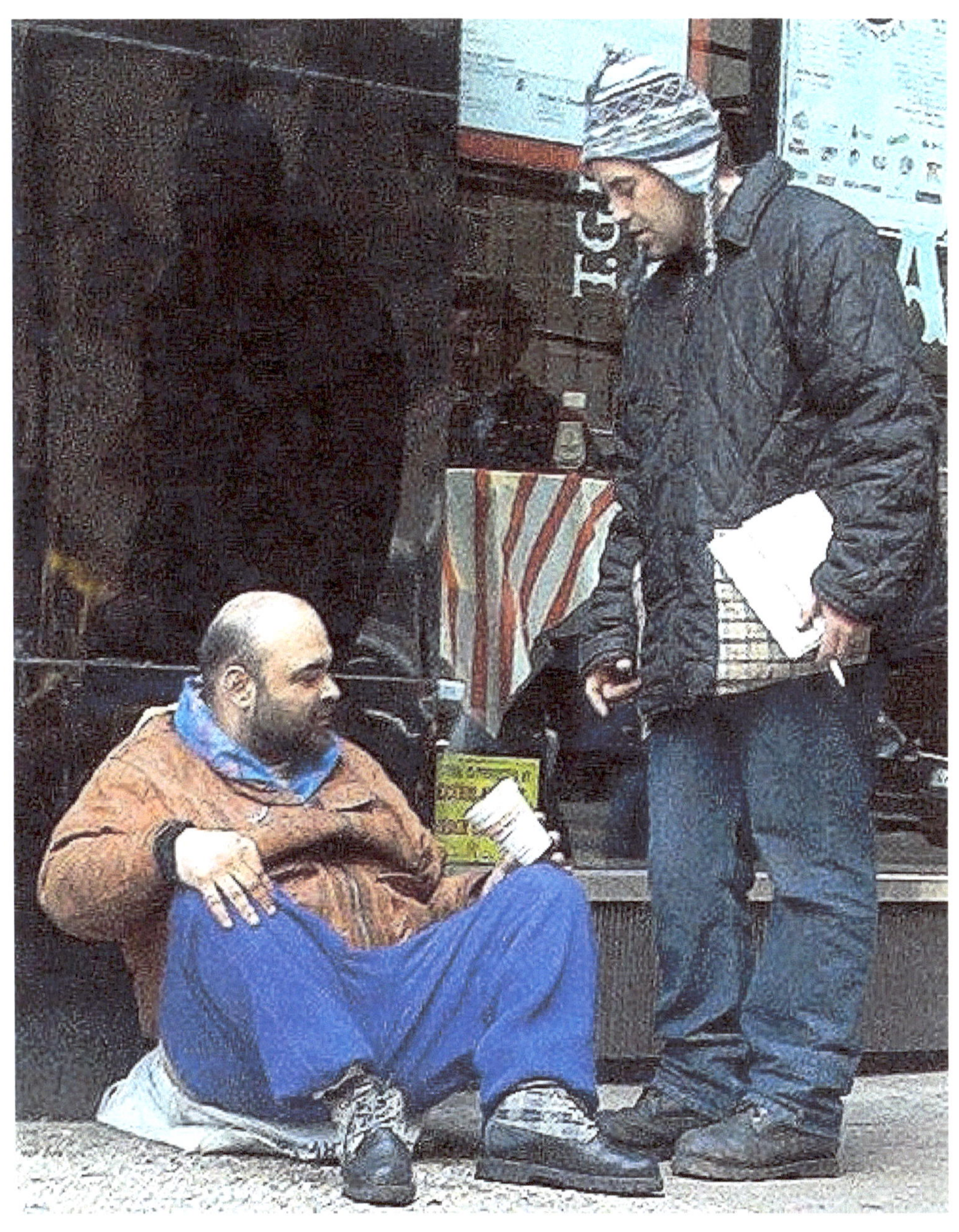

At the "guys retreat" I learned the following; real men don't; wipe their feet, turn on the exhaust fan after number two, pick up trash, say they're sorry… or admit they're wrong!

There are so many reasons for people not to excessively; eat, drink and self medicate, but peer pressure almost invariably overrides them and we end up; fat, addicted or dead.

I have repeatedly given my kids, bad advice and set bad examples... but they're resilient so there's an excellent chance they'll survive or even flourish …at least I hope so!

I've yet to meet anyone who's not *somewhat* "brainwashed" by their; upbringing, education, religion or the popular media.

At what point do "high aspirations" become "delusions of grandeur?" I think the line in the sand, is where your ideas clashes with those around you. As long as your aspirations jive with mainstream views, you're applauded. When you are at odds with the majority, you're no longer commended, instead you can be apprehended!

Vote with your remote! Don't support anything you find offensive, monitor what your children watch, but don't go completely overboard. Watching what they and their peers watch will inform you about what's going on. You can exercise control over their viewing and hopefully counter what the media is drumming into their heads. Reacting angrily, will only play into the garbage purveyor's plans, since you're fighting against peer pressure and psychological warriors. A frontal assault may have the opposite effect to which you desire.

Our boys are influenced if not ruled by; peer pressure, testosterone, machismo and alcohol. They're also influenced by the media, movies and music, and the *bill of goods* they're being sold is not a pretty picture. Many are "conflicted"… since they're taught to "turn the other cheek", but also "take no prisoners"… they end up unsure if they should walk the walk, or just talk the talk.

"Where the crowd runs, run in the opposite direction and you'll probably be right" … Nietzsche

Police

"We live in an age when pizza gets to your home before the police" … Jeff Marder

Of course I live in a police state… I'm married.

Police are a *necessary evil* and by no means evil all the time… just often enough to tarnish their reputation.

As long as you're intent on turning America into a police state, why not make it one that helps hard working people, instead of those living off the "generosity" of the taxpayers.

Humans are the only creatures that don't trust their instincts... can you imagine what would happen if Deer didn't rely on their instincts? Rely on yours too… just in case the police aren't around when you need them… you know what they say, when you need a cop in seconds, one will there in minutes.

I see hundreds of police carrying lethal weapons, in some places they carry automatic weapons and apparently it makes us feel more secure. Modern society prefers a few *authorized* individuals carrying massive firepower to everyone strapping a six shooter on his hip.

Politics

"Limit politicians to two terms. One in office and one in jail"… unknown.

The fact that we have third-party candidates is a joke... when's the last time one of them were elected dog catcher, much less senator or president?

I've never felt represented by any politicians... maybe that's why I complain so much!

"The difference between death and taxes is that death doesn't get worse every time congress meets"… Will Rogers

Death and taxes is as certain for man, as feeding the Lions is for Zebra.

I'm not particularly interested in which party's in power, because I can't predict which will treat me better… I just hope for the best and plan for the worst.

Even if we're all are rounded up and *sent to camp*, it will have little effect on our politics. The average person will continue blaming the "other" party for their problems. In the long run however, whoever provides more "bread and circus" is likely to gain our support.

I was waiting to see what the new president's policies were before applauding or criticizing too much. I wondered if the new administration would; help us feed our ox, gore it, or give it to someone who deserves it more than we do… guess what's happening!

"Enlightened statesmen will not always be at the helm"… James Madison

We're quick to criticize the *other* party, but few are willing to criticize our country…that's considered crossing the line.

Liberals, Conservatives, Independents… everyone uses the same tactics and venomous attacks. It's what separates us from the beasts... we're able to organize, agitate and cause mischief on a massive scale! Not surprisingly, each group believes *it's* the one with the noble cause.

Being *unaffiliated*, I have different views and unlike my friends, I have the option to change my views… they're committed to their party's platform to the bitter end.

Caroline Kennedy wanted to be *appointed* to the Senate, where she would replace Hillary Clinton who got their largely because of being married to an ex-president. The other main rival, was the son of the former Governor of New York… am I detecting a pattern here? Why not bestow titles like Duke and Duchess since we already have nobility here… nepotism is alive and well!

Watching the president in his State of the Union Address, I wondered... how did this guy ever get elected? Then I remembered – he stole the thing!

Is it just me, or are we turning into a country full of; lying politicians, predatory lenders and speed traps? I guess the rich have to maintain the status quo some how.

Politicians aren't really into fixing things, they are into "fixing" things. They're not into finding *solutions*, they're into finding *fixes*. Thusly our system is continuously "fixed" instead of being repaired.

There's a reference in Orwell's Nineteen Eighty-Four to the "Two Minute Hate." Similar *rallies* have been a part of humanity since time immemorial and we're seeing more of them than ever!

Just because one party's probably wrong, doesn't mean the other one's probably right.

Poverty

"For even when we were with you, this we commanded you, that if any would not work, neither should he eat"... 2 Thessalonians 3:10

The *social safety net* has become ridiculous… it's become a cornucopia of freebies for the Grasshoppers courtesy of the Ants.

I saw a construction worker's body on the side of the road... his death never made the front page. When the rich and famous die, its front page news... for the rest, it's a few lines way back on the obituary page.

Hardworking taxpayers are constantly fighting the welfare state to hold on to the fruits of their labor. The welfare state constantly increases its *membership* along with the number of bureaucrats and others profiting from its existence.

The widow's mite... is there a point where compassion for the unfortunate should be tempered with dissatisfaction for those who're gaming the system? Is there a point where we recognize that for some people *needs* end, and *freeloading* begin?

The Bible says, "render unto Caesar what is Caesars's", but emperors are insatiably greedy and citizens have the right to say enough is enough… but will he still throw us to the Lions?

What is the welfare state, but *serfdom* with a color TV? The sad thing is, more and more people are opting for it.

"The financial policy of the welfare state requires that there be no way for the owners of wealth to protect themselves" … Alan Greenspan

I suppose it's worth asking why *shouldn't* people simply enjoy material things? We're only here for about 70 years and if we don't have "lofty" goals, there may be little else to do but indulge one's "worldly" desires.

It's difficult to "forecast" anything but increased socialism, poverty and dependence on the government. One good thing for the powerful, is that impoverished citizens make great soldiers... they're plenty smart enough to operate war machines and thanks to the violence in our culture, desensitized enough to perform like robots.

This is the dilemma, do you let the bums on the inside destroy your country or those on the outside… obviously you try not to let either destroy it. One reason society allows so many bums to eat off the taxpayers plate, is that the rich need cannon fodder for their wars… occasionally poor folks come in "handy."

Bill and Melinda have earmarked $ 10 billion to vaccinate for poor people the world over… I hope they've earmark the same amount to feed them.

If the destitute don't acknowledge and address their own problems, they'll never pull themselves out of poverty, and the well intentioned people on the outside who try to help them, will eventually be replaced by those they are trying to save.

The common man is sometimes *put to work* killing people, the rich *benefit* from this dirty work, but keep their hands - if not his conscious clean. The establishments' job is to convince the *little man* that killing "certain people" is moral and needs to be done... it's a lousy system. The little man is to be used as canon fodder…that's what keeps the rich in fancy homes and secure jobs.

I don't mind income re-distribution as long as you only do it with yours! Taking it from hard working middle class payers and giving to people who disdain hard work and education is not just a crime, its also ineffective and unsustainable. If you want to take it from the *super rich*, go right ahead and try… but be forewarned, they hold onto to money like grim death!

Seventy percent of Americans reportedly live paycheck to paycheck, and the pundits say you shouldn't take financial advice from the destitute. Meanwhile, my broke friends proclaim the rich are all crooks and only the poor are honest. Anyone who looks at it objectively will realize there are rich crooks and poor crooks and the same applies to honesty.

Bar tenders, sushi chefs, hairdressers, roofers, cashiers and others, work like well oiled machines, and are a marvel to watch, yet they make a pittance compared to Wall Streeters and the like. You make more using your head than your hands, and donations from the rich to politicians has lead to a playing field that isn't even remotely level… heck it's vertical!

If knowledge is power, and power corrupts, does that mean the most knowledgeable people are the most corrupt? Would this also apply to societies?

"You can always hire half the poor to kill the other half"... Streets of New York.

The homeless, indigent and panhandlers frequently suffer from substance abuse, which in America is often a crime. The government incarcerates, or leaves addicts on the street, which doesn't rehabilitate them. Meanwhile, the public is subjected to panhandling and crime at the hands of some of the indigent population. If we do nothing to help them overcome substance abuse there's little chance for progress… it's a classic vicious circle

Kindness is great, but vigilance and preparedness matter greatly too… especially if you want to being *around* to be kind to others.

Should the *advantaged* be disadvantaged, to advantage the d*isadvantaged*? Should we raise taxes on the middle class to give more to the poor?

"When you subsidize poverty and failure, you get more of both."- J.D. Davidson, National Taxpayers Union

Power

"Whom the gods would destroy, they first make mad with power" … Charles Beard

What's worse? Somebody ruling because they're stronger than you, or because they think they're smarter than you... both are abhorrent.

Are the CEOs, financiers and politicians who run our lives today, anymore benevolent than the princes and kings of the past?

It's a fine thing to protect our nation, it's wrong to think you're justified in doing anything you want in the process.

It's been said, "God created man, but Sam Colt made us all equal." Certainly Sam Colt made us more equal, but the first caveman to bash a bully's with a club also deserves credit. Ingenuity evens the odds… just look at David and Goliath!

We don't like bullies, unless they're on our side… then we call them champions. Sometimes the only difference between a bully and a champion, is whose interest they're acting on behalf of.

Many *strong men* develop their bodies because they don't want to be bullied, so why do many *inadvertently* become bullies?

Intimidation is a common strategy seen in animals as well as in humans. Unlike humans however, *beasts* are far less likely to *cross the line* than are people.

"Those in power write history and those who suffer write the songs" -- Irish saying.

Mob rule would be worse than domination by the rich -- which is what we have now. Moderates should run the show, but such people are portrayed as "lukewarm" and usually loose to leaders who are *passionate.* It's much easier for the charismatic to attract a following than for the rational to do so.

Our foreign policy of "beating them into submission", isn't much different than some peoples philosophy regarding personal relationships.

I'm for an individual's right to be as *sovereign* as possible, but it's a loosing battle when faced by governments that demand we be spokes in a wheel, or bees in a hive.

Like in the Land of Oz, wizards are *currently* behind the curtain frantically pulling levers, but they are loosing the battle. They know what their goals are, but greed keeps getting in their way... meanwhile, humanity suffers at their hands.

Comedian Tom Lehrer said, "Might makes right, no matter what the fight" and dictator Mao Tse Tung said "Political power comes from the barrel of a gun" ... the difference is Lehrer was a comedian and Mao a commandant.

For hundreds of years, a few hundred men in the west, have largely ruled the world… now they face competition from men and women all over the world. You can be sure, what remains of the *old boy club* doesn't like it!

Human history has been one long battle between the elites of different societies. Most of the dying has been done by their minions who aspire to someday become part of the elite, but end up cannon fodder instead.

Dictator – *dictatress…* wow it didn't trigger the "spell checker", I guess it's actually a word!

So, who are the ultimate pawns - poor men, poor women, or some other *class* of people? While the poor are undoubtedly exploited, they are by no means powerless… they're mostly just outgunned and disorganized.

"Power tends to corrupt, and absolute power corrupts absolutely. Great men are almost always bad men" … Lord Acton

Presidents of the United States

George Washington reportedly suggested the president be addressed as, "His High and Mightiness", but accepted "Mr. President" instead…. hmmm.

George Washington's birthday is no longer a separate holiday, instead he shares "Presidents' Day", with the rest of the rogues gallery. That's too bad,

because despite his shortcomings, he was greater than most of our presidents. That brings to mind the question of whether our founders were great, or just greedy? I think they were somewhere in between... We're told that it was principles not profit that motivated them... but I'm not so sure. Many were slaveholders, making their fortunes from the forced labor of unfortunate Africans. On the other hand they did risk everything their lives and their fortunes for what they believed in... a good part of which is very inspiring stuff!

One year, George Washington produced 11,000 gallons of Whiskey at Mt. Vernon, making him the single largest distiller in America. Some years, he and Thomas Jefferson reportedly also paid their taxes with hemp... I don't think that would fly anymore!

The more I learn about Thomas Jefferson, the less I like him... he may have been the most hypocritical of the founding fathers... but do your own research.

"Did you know that all 43 U.S. presidents have carried European royal bloodlines into office? ... Nineteen of them directly descended from King Edward III of England. In fact, the presidential candidate with the most royal genes has won every single American election"... this according to Burke's Peerage. So, have we simply traded old tyrants for new ones, or is this just the mathematics of exponential growth and the fact that so many American's are of European descent?

What is the Secret Service, if not our own version of the Praetorian Guard?

In *days of old*, those who did the King's dirty work became *noblemen* and were rewarded with titles and land. Today such men are called General or Ambassador and rewarded with appointments, money and land... the more things change, the more they stay the same!

It's a bit scary that every Tom, Dick and Harry I know has decided to buy a 9mm semi-automatic. Though not entirely attributable to the last election, it was the final straw for many of them. If the *#%@*!* hits the fan, will they sell their weapons for cheap, or use them to requisition what they *need*?

The President faces economic, geopolitical and environmental problems, and I hope it works out, but I'm more concerned with my own quandaries. Like

the President, we attempt to solve our problems with the limited resources at hand… unlike him, we can't make money out of thin air.

Why have we allowed our presidents to become Imperial rulers? During their four or eight year reigns, they wield more power than mad King George ever dreamed of having!

Quips

All I can say about today… which is a Monday, is it's certainly living up to its name!

Ever notice the tar lines on asphalt roads and can you imagine being the guy who *dribbles* that tar into millions of cracks to maintain our roads. These unsung heroes are rarely seen, their work appearing overnight like crop circles. It's cool though and our older roads with their tar lines, look like living, breathing organisms. I want to be one of the guys making those lines… but only for an hour.

Just wondering… would a taser work on someone wearing rubber underwear?

I got another butcher shop haircut... that's what I get for wanting to be in and out and in 10 minutes… I still tipped her two dollars on a $12.95 haircut -- my goal was to get in and out quickly and she accomplished that!

You imply I'm a good egg, but a bad seed... thanks a lot!

There he sat in the outer space prison, so happy to see a Fly buzzing around his face. He'd hated Flies all his life, it felt good to see another Earthling… a Mouse would totally make his day!

" I like hammering nails and speaking in tongues, Cause it doesn't remind me of anything… "... Audioslave.

It's easier to forgive than to forget…that requires a lobotomy.

Why is it that lately, everything I do is either a fiasco or a disaster… I'm having one of those days when you just can't get that last bit of shrimp out of the tail.

Is it strange that I can never find what I'm looking for, until I stop looking for it... actually that's a universal experience.

"Are you working, or lurking", I asked…"no, just out doing nefarious and sundry things", he replied.

I suffer from chronic conditions; pain, anguish and joy – the funny thing is, they're inexorably intertwined.

Socks are ridiculous! What sketchy products…whoever came up with them should be spanked. You buy a pair and a week later there's a hole in the toe or heel… it's scandalous! We should boycott socks and go around bare footed until they start offering us something that wears like iron.

You know you're bored, when you're looking forward to reviewing the contents of your spam folder.

It occurs to me that garbage trucks must compact the heck out of trash—how else can they get the entire neighborhood's refuse into one truck?

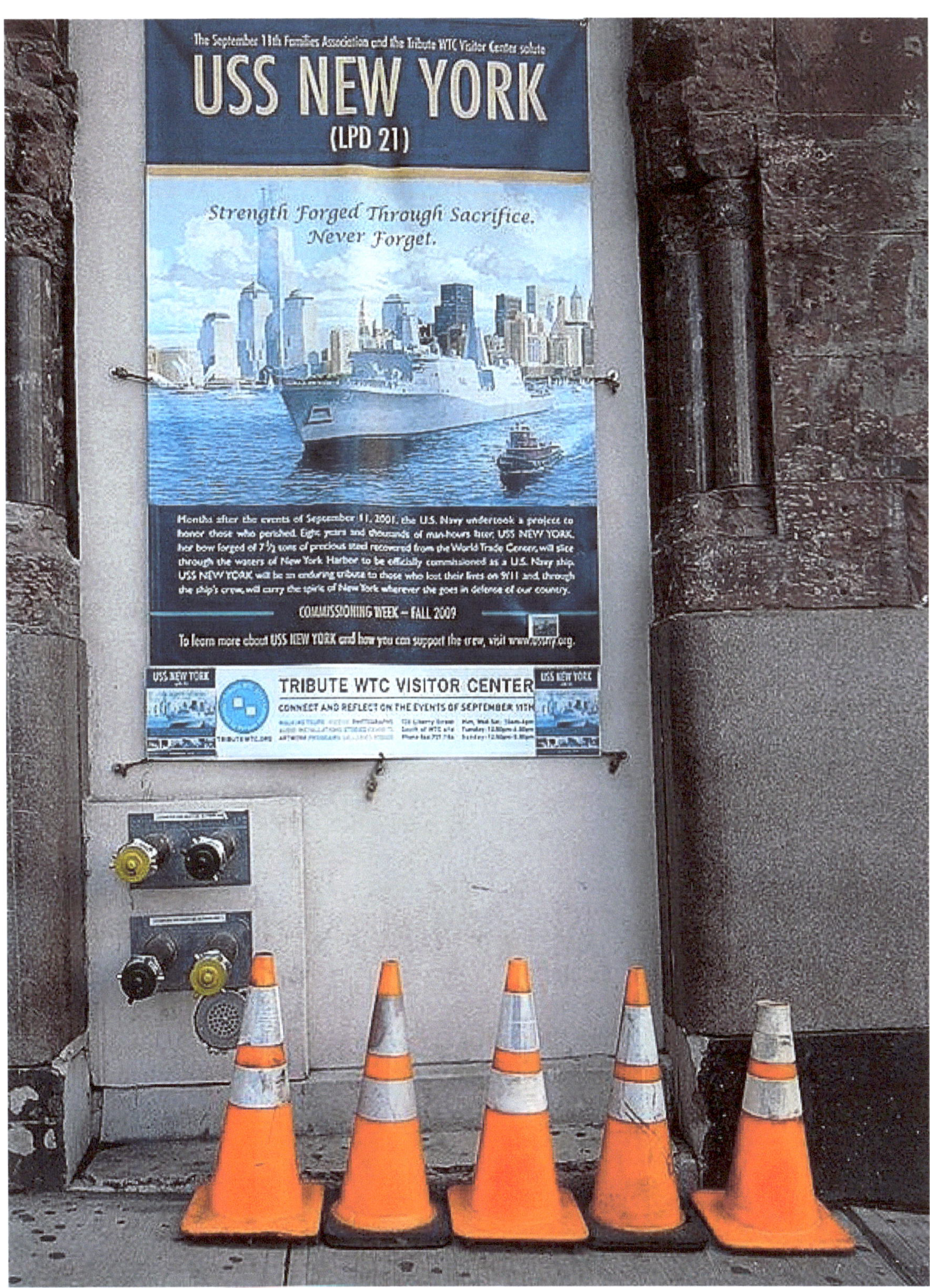
The September 11th Families Association and the Tribute WTC Visitor Center salute
USS NEW YORK
(LPD 21)
Strength Forged Through Sacrifice.
Never Forget.
Months after the events of September 11, 2001, the U.S. Navy undertook a project to honor those who perished. Eight years and thousands of man-hours later, USS NEW YORK, her bow forged of 7 ½ tons of precious steel recovered from the World Trade Center, will slice through the waters of New York Harbor to be officially commissioned as a U.S. Navy ship. USS NEW YORK will be an enduring tribute to those who lost their lives on 9/11 and, through the ship's crew, will carry the spirit of New York wherever she goes in defense of our country.
COMMISSIONING WEEK – FALL 2009
To learn more about USS NEW YORK and how you can support the crew, visit
USS NEW YORK
TRIBUTE WTC VISITOR CENTER
CONNECT AND REFLECT ON THE EVENTS OF SEPTEMBER 11TH
TRIBUTEWTC.ORG
USS NEW YORK

Having a tattoo used to mean you were a sailor, or Marine and had seen the world... now it just means you've been to the mall.

Is there anybody else out there still using the word "fuzz" for the police? Just curious, because it was common in the 70s but now it would be considered silly.

Does anybody remember the smell of pencil shavings in their elementary school classroom? It's no longer a common aroma, but one that many of us were once familiar with.

Why does folding shirts and putting them in a suitcase, bring to mind putting a body in a coffin?

It's nice to know there were over 40 attempts on Hitler's life… but how could so many assassins have failed?

Does anybody else remember when Band-Aid packages had red threads in them to make them easier to open? That was state-of-the-art for many years, now it's gone completely by the wayside.

They built a new fire station here and named it station 133… funny, there're only five stations in the whole town… why are they exaggerating?

The saying, "clean as a whistle" makes perfect sense… who wants to put a dirty whistle in their mouth?

Frequently I'm left speechless… other times, I wish I'd been!

Regrets

"A man is not old until regrets take the place of dreams"… John Barrymore

"Sometimes I lie awake at night, and ask, 'Where have I gone wrong?' Then a voice says to me, 'This is going to take more than one night.'" … Charles M. Schulz

If I had a dime for every regret, I'd be able to buy dinner…but not at a fancy restaurant… not yet, anyway!

I'll admit to having *at least* a few regrets… I'm just trying not to dwell on them.

In the time I have left a lot of things are going to change, but I say a lot and follow up on very little... so time will tell.

There are times in our lives when things could "go either way." We teeter but avoid the fall…we're not so different from those who hit that slick spot and take that nasty plunge.

Have you ever *looked around* and said "is this really my freaking life?" I have… and the only *upside,* is it's better than the alternative!

Should I admit to my screw ups, or try and hide them? Actually, I do both…but mostly the latter.

I've stuck my foot in my mouth so many times, I should carry a shoe horn. Foot in mouth disease results from talking to much and thinking too little. What comes out are remarks that; annoy, offend or irritate others… I think Mark Twain put it nicely – look it up!

Agreed, I've done lots of stupid things... we just don't agree on exactly what they were. Of course, your list of stupid things *I've done* is longer than mine.

Why is it I spend half my time "straightening out" what I've done the other half?

It's been said, many of us miss the point of our own lives and the *story we tell* is not what we're really about.

"I'm not what I want to be, not what I ought to be, not what I'm going to be - but
I'm thankful that I'm not what I used to be"... John wooden

Many of us crucify ourselves between two thieves - regret for the past and fear of the future. ~ Fulton Oursler

Renting

So what came first… the slum lord or the slum renter?

Landlords get tired of the excuses, "you've been so good to me... I'm going to pay you everything I owe, if it's the last thing I do." The excuses would be funny if they weren't costing me so much. I hate to think of all the grandmas that have "died" on rent day… and don't get me started on houses trashed after all the kind words. Landlords are despised and I've deserved to be on occasion... the question is what came first the chicken or the egg.

Fixing a rental house for sale is like selling clothes... the secret is *cheap materials and poor lighting*! After the renters "left" I found the usual stuff... as well as dog poop, especially in the garage, but they didn't forget to leave some in the house either.

A certain percentage of renters realize that with the housing crisis there are lots of investors buying foreclosed houses and converting them to rentals. This segment of the market, has already gamed landlords half their lives anyway and see this as a golden opportunity to continue jumping from house to house without paying rent... I feel sorry for the rookie landlords, at least the good ones.

Painting the rental house I feel a little bit like Michelangelo... not that I'm a master by any stretch of the imagination, but I am trying to get the most out of my little brush and roller. *Cutting in*, I work with precision and rolling the walls, I try to get the most bang for my buck. Like a dummy, I've bought the economy paint... because of the poor coverage, I end up having to paint some of the rooms twice!

It's amazing how many mops and brooms I find… my renters always buy cleaning supplies, they just never use them!

I'm trying to get out of the landlord business… it's a pain in the neck, and I'm usually either too nice, or a jerk. When I'm too nice it's usually to a jerk, when I am a jerk, it's usually to a renter who's nice… I wish that wasn't the case.

As a landlord, I've had two kinds of renters, those who can afford to stay but don't want to and those who can't afford to stay, but intend to anyway.

I'm trying to rent this apartment, but everyone whose come to look, seems to be a drunk, an addict or someone looking for a place to offload a troublesome relative. I don't know if this phenomenon is a sign of the times or if I just haven't fixed up the place enough to attract a "better class" of renter.

When housing is subsidized over seas, many call it socialism and object, but when these same people don't pay their rent here, they call it social justice or "getting even with the man"… hmmm?

By the time I was done cleaning the fridge and oven, I had used a variety of cleaning products; oven and bathroom cleaner, laundry spot remover, dishwashing detergent, even a fork, the tongs of which were effective for cleaning the over grill… anyway, they both looked pretty darn good by then!

Respect

"Never take a person's dignity: it is worth everything to them, and nothing to you"…Frank Barron

Treat people with kindness and respect and insist on receiving the same. If you are not treated with these, don't get upset or *even*, instead look for other's to hang out with, who will give you the respect you deserve.

Disrespect is a lack of thoughtfulness and consideration for another person's feelings, nobody likes to be treated that way and it can't be made up for with cakes, cocktails, or presents.

Everyone wants and deserves respect, meanwhile some spend time bemoaning how they've lost respect for *so and so, or so and so…* what a waste of breath!

<u>Rome</u>

Truly Rome wasn't built in a day, but it was burnt in one… and Nero fiddled all the while!

America is a great country, but I wouldn't say it's the greatest in the world any more than Rome was the greatest country in the ancient world. Both are/were the most powerful of their times, but the greatness depends on one's definition of the word.

Julius Caesar's conquests of Gaul and other areas were vile and despicable, he killed millions of people. Still he's honored, while those who opposed and were murdered by him are forgotten… of course Caesar's cronies wrote the history books.

Like Rome, will our success be our downfall? Will world trade allow disease to cross our borders, and will uncontrolled immigration overwhelm *us*? Romans, like American's, considered their country to be the "mother of the world", but like Mother Rome, are we also terminally ill?

We like violent sports, but being even *more civilized* than the Romans, we don't want to see our athletes killed. We don't mind watching them staggered, or knocked out, but few fans want to go back to the days of thumbs down.

America has people from almost every country in the world living here, which reminds me of Rome. In ancient times, Rome had citizens, residents and slaves from all over the known world. We're a lot like them… and that worries me!

On the evening news the commentator says, "now let's go to our correspondent across the pond." As Rome considered the Mediterranean it's "lake", America considers the Atlantic and the Pacific it's *ponds*.

I think we're closer to a one world government than we've ever been, and that government is "US." Not even Rome at its peak was anywhere near as powerful as US has been the last couple of decades. While we are not an evil empire, our *elitist* leader's motives are just as suspect as Rome's.

What happened to Greece? They were a superpower of the ancient world, but unlike Rome, which *as* Italy is still a fairly significant economic power, Greece has fallen from the great heights it reached in antiquity, to a relatively insignificant country economically. Despite its early embrace of democracy, Greece has not followed the course of Rome, Britain and the colonial powers… it seems instead to have followed in the footsteps of other ancient empires like; Egypt, Persia, Assyria and Babylon which for centuries declined. Actually this model is by far the more common one.

My friends believe we are greater than any civilization ever, that God's on our side and we should reshape the world in our image. I wonder if history will show us to be anything more than the latest incarnation of Rome?

Secrets

"Three may keep a secret, if two of them are dead"… Benjamin Franklin

It's funny… there're things we tell no one, and other things impossible to keep to ourselves!

Despite intending to be *closed lipped*, I usually tell "one person too many", and my attempt at privacy turns into a huge advertisement.

If you record a thought, or tell it to someone, your brain can process it better, because it's been solidified… it's no longer just a passing thought. Just be careful, anything you tell *anyone* may eventually be known by everyone. Someone will ferret it out, perhaps after a few drinks...or, your confidant will sing like a Canary for the heck of it. A little pressure, or the hope of some reward tempts people to unlock the safe.

Stop telling me secrets… I don't want to be burdened with keeping them! I'd rather wait for the gossip via the grapevine or other "approved" channels… its just as juicy and unlikely to get me in trouble. When I hear secrets, I end up in hot water for not sharing them … or more often, *for* sharing them.

I don't mind telling you what I think, even if there's no upside, but when there's a definite down side, I *try* to stifle myself.

Does the fact that it's so hard to keep a secret mean that "squealing" is a useul evolutionary adaptation?

"If you reveal your secrets to the wind you should not blame the wind for revealing them to the trees"... Kahlil Gibran

Sitting on the Fence

"Sitting on the fence is a dangerous course - you can even catch a bullet from the peacekeeping force"... Dire Straits.

There're lots of reasons to get off the fence... and many reasons not to casually enter the fray. There are always prophets, demagogues and war mongers calling for soldiers...be wary, their motive is power and you are just fodder.

By all means, get off the fence... but not until *you* decide what "side" to be on. They are not selling you a used car, you may be ordered to take lives, or sacrifice your own... don't give in easily.

If you're on the fence and unconvinced by either of the sides courting you, gird your loins, move to the hills and pray for deliverance from the smooth talking war mongers. You may be the only ones left to rebuild society.

Politicians and demagogues court the *swing vote,* doing their best to sway people with their often bogus arguments. V*illains* don't advance their agendas gently or logically... they rely on emotional appeals that target our most basic instincts.

I'm not on the fence, I'm just unaffiliated... resoundingly so, that's different than being on the fence.

"The hottest places in hell are reserved for those who in times of great moral crises maintain their neutrality"...Dante Alighieri. He has a point...just

don't let Dante or anyone else be the definer of *great moral crisis*... do your own due diligence!

When there are two misguided *teams on the field*, the fence may be a good place to be. From there you can watch their antics and judge whether or not you should enter the fray.

"And if you choose not to decide you still have made a choice"... Rush.

I'm accused of being indecisive, but I don't see the willingness to change ones mind a weakness. Issues aren't always *black and white*, so give them considerable thought...it is only considered weakness by those convinced they have *all the answers*. Surrendering the right to make your own decision is the real weakness!

Calling someone a "fence sitter" is as effective as calling them a coward, it touches a raw nerve, insults one's masculinity and pushes the peer pressure button. Sit on the fence for a while and watch the crazies on those killing fields they adore. Just keep your powder dry, because sooner or later they'll need a new game and a new opponent.

"Forward he cried from the rear and the front rank died"... Pink Floyd.

Smoking

"It's easy to quit smoking, I've done it hundreds of times!"... Mark Twain

I keep lighters and matches up high... out of reach of children and my wife... she might dispose of them for my own good.

My wife doesn't like to kiss me when I've been smoking cigars, but we only kiss once a week anyway – a guy's got to do something with my mouth in between!

Smoked a cigar in my wife's car, ate two of my daughters *reserved* cookies and finished off the last marshmallow "Peep"... I'm a guy, that's par for the course!

A woman and her daughter were in the next car next as I enjoyed a Churchill... what were they thinking about this guy with a huge cigar in his

mouth! I keep thinking of reasons not to smoke cigars, but that little devil on my other shoulder keeps telling me to "do it, do it!"

One cool thing about keeping a stogie alive - you're doing what men have done for eons... practicing the art of keeping a valuable ember alive.

I have to stop using *roach clips*... no matter how much these stogies cost. There's a reason you throw them away when they get too small to hold..., it's not worth burning holes in your lungs any sooner than *you have to*!

She asks how many cigars I smoke per week and I say I don't know. I'm a guy, aren't I supposed to have bad habits?" How do you know how much of the cigar to smoke...you smoke till the ashes fall on your lap.

I'm discovering that one of the requirements for effectively lighting a cigar, is having a decent lighter. The four I got at the dollar store, weren't worth a single greenback. They may be okay for cigarettes, but they only light my cigar, under *ideal* conditions.

The "Italia", tastes like chocolate... didn't like it at first, but now it's a favorite. You pay three times as much for a hand rolled cigar, but they last twice as long... you pretty much get what you pay for, although there is a point of diminishing returns.

Heat rises, but cigars burn from the bottom of the cherry... I keep that in mind while trying to get it to burn evenly. You can enjoy an $ 8 cigar a lot longer than an $ 8 cocktail, but the combo's even better... or worse depending on how you look at it.

The water logged Cohiba's been drying out for a few days... and looks like it's "getting there"... I'm listening to Agnetha singing "P &B" and looking forward to her pronunciation of *coax* and *cajole*.

I'm *learning new tricks* and today discovered how to relight big stogies... you light the wrapper, not the carbonized center, just the -- that's all it takes!

I don't inhale the cigar smoke, I just puff them... so maybe it's killing me more slowly.

I have plenty of reasons to get up in the morning... cake, sushi, beer, a good cigar, and most of all friends!

I enjoy the forbidden Cuban, aware that if it were legal I'd probably be hooked. There's nothing like savoring a contraband stogie while soaking in the tub with a good cup of java. Later, the resin in my nostrils is somehow *reactivated* and I'm reminded of the pleasure the cigar provided. I'm also reminded of the addiction potential of the herb's nicotine and I desire more… if it were legal on this side of the border, I'd have yet another monkey on my back.

"Sooner or later, everyone stops smoking"… unknown.

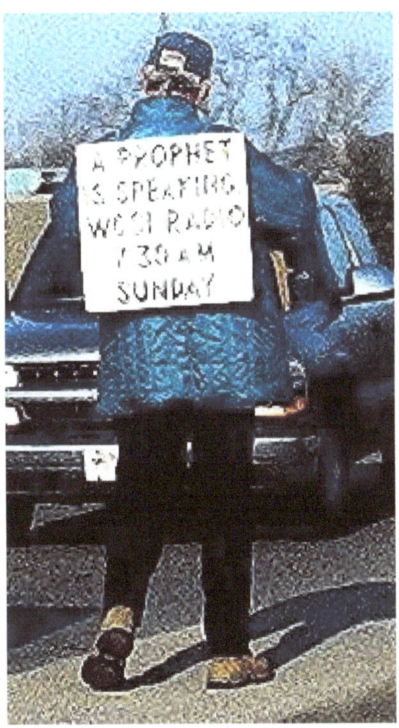

Society

"The danger of the past was that men became slaves. The danger of the future is that man may become robots"…Erich Fromm

Society needs all kinds of members, and as long as we fill some acceptable niche we're *valued.* Society needs; workers, soldiers, nurses, salesmen and rulers… sounds like a bee hive! If you make a *contribution* to society, you'll

be kept on the payroll. If not, you'll be frowned on, but as long as you don't rock the boat, you can still count on a free lunch.

Whether it's the African plains, selling widgets, or being a single parent, survival of the fittest is at play. The difference is that on the Serengeti, there're no bailouts or welfare... in human society there're both... the question is, how long can they be sustained without bankrupting the country?

What's better, being "in the vanguard" or being "ahead of the curve?"

The human race, nations and society are all like the stock market... they ebb and flow, rise and fall. When it appears they've "bottomed out", there might be further to go, and when they ascend, it's amazing to see how high they can soar!

It feels like the government's telling me, "don't tug on Superman's cape, don't spit in the wind, don't pull the mask off that old Lone Ranger and you don't mess around with Jim." Another words, *toe the line...* well folks, isn't it about time to pull the mask off that old Lone Ranger?

"Suburbia is where the developer bulldozes out the trees, then names the streets after them"...Bill Vaughn

Soldiers

"Soldiers generally win battles; generals get credit for them"... Napoleon Bonaparte

Sometimes ones sword can't be beaten into a plow shear until its terrible work is done... but that is the exception, not the rule we have made it. We have been convinced that permanent war is the norm and not such a bad thing...exactly the opposite should be the case!

One type of soldier I respect as much as those who have beaten their swords into plow shears, are those who clear minefields and defuse bombs... God they're brave!

Maybe I'm over analyzing things, but it is Veterans Day and I'm wondering - should there be any limit to our gratitude towards veterans? I am grateful

for some of the things they have done, I also think that to a considerable extent – they've been corporate mercenaries… of course I'd be crazy to publicly state that!

That being said, I believe soldiers are almost universally brave men and women… especially those who volunteer to serve, and even more so those who join the marines or special forces.

Unlike dead soldiers, an army can be resurrected… so as long as there are new recruits, there will be new wars.

Hundreds of thousands of young Americans are doing their "duty" the Secretary of Defense said... in other words they're following orders from their *superiors*.. I wonder, in the greater scheme of things, is it more important to follow orders, or follow your conscience? If you can do both that's fine, but if simply following orders from *above*, is not the same as following orders from *on high*.

It disturbs me to watch young people play violent video war games, but I'm told they are honing their skills for the future, when they will use futuristic weapons to *guarantee our freedom.* In the past, boys who were masters with a Squirrel gun, adopted nicely to the M1-Garrand's that helped us win WWII… today's marksmen are as likely to control Predator Drones with a mouse or joy stick and never fire a rifle.

Young men willing to kill at the drop of a hat have been useful to *the powers that be* since the dawn of time, that's why so that gene is so prevalent. That's not to say they haven't helped preserve freedom on many occasions, but just as often, that willingness to kill has wreaked havoc on the innocent. Young men with little fear or conscience make some of the best soldiers… and assassins. In war, killers earn shiny medals, in peacetime they're *awarded* life sentences.

When it comes to military technology we've made great *progress*... one modern soldier with a Phalanx Gun could wipe out entire Roman legions -- those who were once mighty could be laid low by a simple conscript. When it comes to saving lives however we have not accomplished nearly as much.

Regarding post traumatic stress disorder for returning soldiers, the Veterans Administration is doing everything it can to help "cure" the afflicted. Their methods include; convincing soldiers that they've done the right thing,

rationalizing what they've done to civilians and teaching them *techniques* to help them forget what they've seen and done. It would be more effective to encourage the soldiers to consider whether or not they have been misused by their government and empower them to speak out as they see fit.

The best way to cure PTSD is for soldiers to beat their swords into plowshares and work for peaceful solutions. A TV show on the *art of war* raves about the sword's beauty and notes that far more skill is required to produce one, than to make a knife or ax. Plowshares are not as *exciting* as swords, but they're far more useful to the human race. Of course we need to defend ourselves and our land, but if more time was spent planting *quality* seeds, less time would be spent reaping fields of sorrow.

February is "Sniper Month" on the military channel… isn't that just dandy!

"If my soldiers were to begin to think, not one would remain in the ranks"… Frederick The Great

Space Case

"The journey of a thousand miles begins with one step"... Lao Tzu

Space is the place! It will not be utopian, but it offers an infinite region to attempt to replicate the good things society offers while avoiding as many pitfalls as possible.

The Chinese space program now includes the capability to shoot down satellites… if this doesn't lead to an arms race in space, then I don't know what will… but isn't that just the normal course of affairs?

If there are advanced aliens out there who are less violent than us, they must be watching us with troubled anticipation. I wonder if *in their councils*, they've already decided what to do with us?

I like the name *New Chicago* for a future space city, it's not original, having been used years ago in a movie. What are some other good names? Some will be names of old cities with the word "New" in front of them, like *New Washington,* while others will be entirely new and exciting words.

What will the star ships be called that carry pioneers beyond the far reaches of our galaxy… perhaps the Mayflower, or the Nina, Pinta and Santa Maria!

Scientists estimate it might take 60 million years for humans to colonize the Milky Way galaxy... they would travel on huge spinning space colony ships. That may sound like a long time but in relation to the age of the universe it's miniscule.

When the Earth finally freezes or burns to a crisp, will anybody really care? Will there be anybody left anyway, or will we have moved far into the cosmos by then? I imagine there'll be a few stragglers left, but conditions may become unbearable centuries, or eons prior our lovely home's demise anyway.

A simple Tomato plant on a spaceship might be cherished as much as a mighty Oak tree on earth... it's all relative.

To be viable, starships will have to be large and sophisticated, and it will likely be a hundred years before pilgrims attempting to reach for the stars. We're no where near ready to attempt such journeys, but you have to start somewhere… "a journey of a thousand miles starts with one step."

Even in space, there will be conflict as humans, and perhaps aliens fight over *prime* real estate and resources! We've always congregated around fertile land, and that's been the cause of so much earthly conflict. Space pioneers will have to contend with; disease, famine, war, piracy and every other affliction wrought by man and nature. So why even bother colonizing space? Because as earth gets more crowded, things may get a lot worse for its inhabitants.

Is life miraculous and exclusive to earth, or might any heavenly body with the right conditions also spawn life…especially if the necessary seeds blow in its direction.

Whenever humans travel to new lands, they look for the resources and riches they need or desire. Historically it's been fertile soil, lumber, freshwater and mineral wealth. As we travel the cosmos we will look for the same things in one form or another, as well as atmospheres and climates we can tolerate or modify.

It's unlikely there'll ever be a human utopia, no matter who you recruit, they will be at each other's throats eventually. If these are democracies, which is most desirable, surely the same problems we have, will once again rear their ugly heads in *New Merica.*

It is unlikely there will ever be peace on earth as long as there are people who think they, their religions or their ideologies are chosen above all others. Separating from such people is an important reason for going into space, but it is also an issue that should be *addressed* on earth.

Jupiter's moon Europa and Saturn's moon Enceladus are reportedly icy orbs, comprised largely of water, which can be converted into; hydrogen fuel, oxygen to breath and water to drink. Some day these moons will surely be outposts or interplanetary *truck stops..*

Mars and the moon reportedly have reserves of water that will support human life as well. Both also have deep caves which might shelter future *cave men* and women.

So you go off to space to *escape* problems on earth, but find the same problems continue to *crop up* where ever humankind occurs. That doesn't mean it won't be worth it, in fact it will be necessary in the long run and may give us the few thousand years we need to *mature* into responsible human beings!

"The Earth is just too small and fragile a basket for the human race to keep all its eggs in"... Robert Heinlein

Sports and Extra-cise

"It's not the mountains ahead that wear us out, its the grain of sand struck in our shoe"... Anonymous

Nobody's perfect, not even close, and no "body" is perfect, but some come darn close... especially after a little air brushing!

The World Cup of Football is on again and I'm enjoying it... but have you ever "headed" a soccer ball? Dang, It hurts!

Walking past the golf course, I see a rare sight... a few people are walking instead of riding golf carts. I hear clubs clattering in their bags as they amble along... far different than the usual sound of motorized golf carts!

Exercise… does that mean that in the old days the goal was to achieve "extra-size?" Being large was an advantage back then… a little extra weight was useful in a fight, or in case of *lean times.*

The brain is vitally important body when it comes to loosing weight, for example taking a swig of mouthwash at a moment of weakness can help you resist eating. Unfortunately, our brains are too large to be outsmarted by such a simple tricks… so do the smart thing and be outsmarted!

The toothpaste, mouthwash trick doesn't work all the time, but it works some of time and that's positive. If it *never* works, then you're using no willpower whatsoever, and nothing will help if that's the case.

When someone makes a meal and insists you overindulge, you've been given an opportunity and a challenge. You have the chance to demonstrate that you can enjoy a reasonable serving and graciously decline their invitation to be a glutton. If they're okay with that great, otherwise, it's not your problem… its theirs.

Does anybody else remember gym class as being a bit like prison? Weren't the bullies like prison gangs and gym teachers like guards? They seemed to enjoy watching the fights instead of breaking them up!

A lot of men want to be "big" and I'm wondering why. Are they afraid they'll be *messed with* if they aren't *large and in charge*? Unfortunately, they don't adequately consider the implications of being large, which includes an increased risk of numerous medical conditions.

The human back bones are like a bridge, and should be treated like one when carrying a load. Make contact with something so that you are effectively a tripod instead of a hanging arch. When bending, rest your elbow or forearm on your thigh, or lean your shoulder against something to redistribute the weight…don't make your back do all the work. By doing so, you make what could be an injurious event into a beneficial exercise. With a little practice you can do it *without* your friends noticing... then you won't have to make excuses for being sensible!

Have you ever had a back itch, but nothing to scratch it with or against?

Maybe they call them *dumb*bells because they don't ring... in any case, I like the word dumbbell, it's funny!

Doing a *little better each day* may be impossible, since invariably we have our ups and downs. The trend however is the important thing and the trend *must be your friend* if you hope to improve yourself. Try to do more than just "one thing right" every day... although better than nothing, that's too slow an approach.

If nothing else, a little housework provides a little exercise and helps your wife, who's usually doing more than her share house anyway. You may also be pleasantly surprised when your wife shows her appreciation... if you know what I mean!

"Probably the Battle of Waterloo was won on the playing fields of Eaton"... George Orwell.

Success (Failure)

"God gave us two ends. One to sit on and one to think with. Success depends on which one you use"...Unknown.

Forget about the stocks and real estate - our major asset is our brain and the willingness to use it.

There's nothing wrong with tooting your own horn, especially when everyone else thinks it's a spittoon!

If you want "the job", go there looking and talking like the person who can do it, and if given the opportunity, you'd better be able to.

I've hear the expression, "good little worker bees" for people who get the job done and I wonder, why do people work like bees? On Wall Street, they do it because they're well compensated...but other classes of workers put in long hard hours for very little pay. "Worker bees" perform, because of compensation, fear or loyalty... misplaced though it often is.

My wife does not like being called a "good little worker bee", nor does she like to be honored simply for her looks... understandably, she wants to be recognized for her talent and accomplishments.

Success in life is largely about rising to challenges *and* resisting temptation.

***You* were led to water and drank, the other *horses* didn't… now tired and thirsty they demand that you carry their load… what a surprise!**

I know people who have nothing and it reminds me of the line, "freedom's just another word for nothing left to lose." They may be free, but is that what they want? Other's who appear to be materially *blessed*, but far from being free, they're owned by their "stuff." Somewhere in the middle there's a happy medium – I'm still trying to find it!

If you have the attitude that the deck's stacked against you, and you surely can't win, then surely you won't.

You can be all about winning and not be a winner, so I suggest valuing things other than winning, then you might be a winner regardless of how the chips fall.

Use your head to make a living, or you'll have to sweat…you can do some thinking, or you can do some stinking…both types of work are equally noble, but the pay is not.

Hang around with smart people... if you surround yourself with idiots, stupidity is bound to rub off!

For most of us, life is a series of victories and defeats, some minor and some major. We can improve our chances with; education, preparation and hard work... but as anyone who's been around the block can tell you, there're no guarantees!

There's guilt by association and *value* by association… sometimes success or failure depends on who you know, or who you're related to. We can't do much about who we're related to, but we have considerable control over who we know and even more over who we hang out with.

If you spend money like there's no tomorrow, you'll quickly find out you were right!

It's a waste of time to reinvent the wheel, but not every good thing has already been invented. If you have ingenuity use it, and regardless of whether or not you're a genius, be ingenious!

If you listen to those who complain *the deck is stacked*, so there's no use trying to get ahead, then you'll never get ahead. He is telling you a half truth and some very old news. Don't let *anyone's* advice restrain your ambition! If you listen to people whose words of wisdom are *you can't*, then *you won't…* but if you educate and apply yourself, you'll find out that *you can*!

Another *quality* essential for success is wherewithal… *without it* you're lost, *with it* you can do anything!

Listen selectively, embrace wisdom and ignore nonsense. Usually the advice of the successful leads to success, while that of the ruined and leads to ruin.

If you want to be successfull, every once in a while, you must go out on a limb!

Whether its business, marriage or war… a *win, win* outcome is better than demanding unconditional surrender.

With everything in life, the new day is another chance to do a bit better, or a bit worse… you'll obviously choose the former!

Inertia is the opposite of momentum, and something to be avoided. Not everything we do needs to be productive, but we should avoid being counterproductive. If you want to survive tough times, may I suggest *strong will* and a *marketable skill.*

You can be anal and prepare too much for a sales call, but that's unlikely. You can improvise if you have to, but preparation trumps improvisation 90% of the time.

Is life, a race to win, to finish… or should it be a race at all?

I'm not a great business man, but no worse than acquaintances who are so keen on dispensing advice. Most of them are broke, but that doesn't stop them from dispensing advice as if they were oracles! Meanwhile the

successful people I know dispense far less advice, but a morsel from them is better than the constant stream of unsolicited nuggets the vagabond offers.

Most of us don't work terribly hard, nor are we brilliant, but we're consistent, so we get a fair amount done. Compare that to those who're lazy or inefficient and ask yourself – should the competent subsidize them?

I heard that Lions are only successful in 5% of their hunts and thought that was pretty bad. After some rough calculations, I realized I'd love to be that successful when it comes to selling!

When you're trying to make sales, there's nothing wrong with just going through the motions especially if you put a little emotion into those motions. The key is you have to show up and give the presentation – the more emotional you are, the better!

You need the will, intent and desire to succeed at your goals... that's what separates you from those who *only* have the *ability* to succeed.

To effectively prioritize, you must first understand what your goals are… do you?

"Failure is simply the opportunity to begin again, this time more intelligently"…
Henry Ford

Work a little, play a little, work a little more, play a little more. If you live this way, things will usually work out. If you do neither of these, you're likely to have problems. Even in nature we see this, the Lioness sleeps then she hunts, the Wolf hunts then plays... the deer pays attention or dies!

"The road to failure, begins with self-pity"... anonymous.

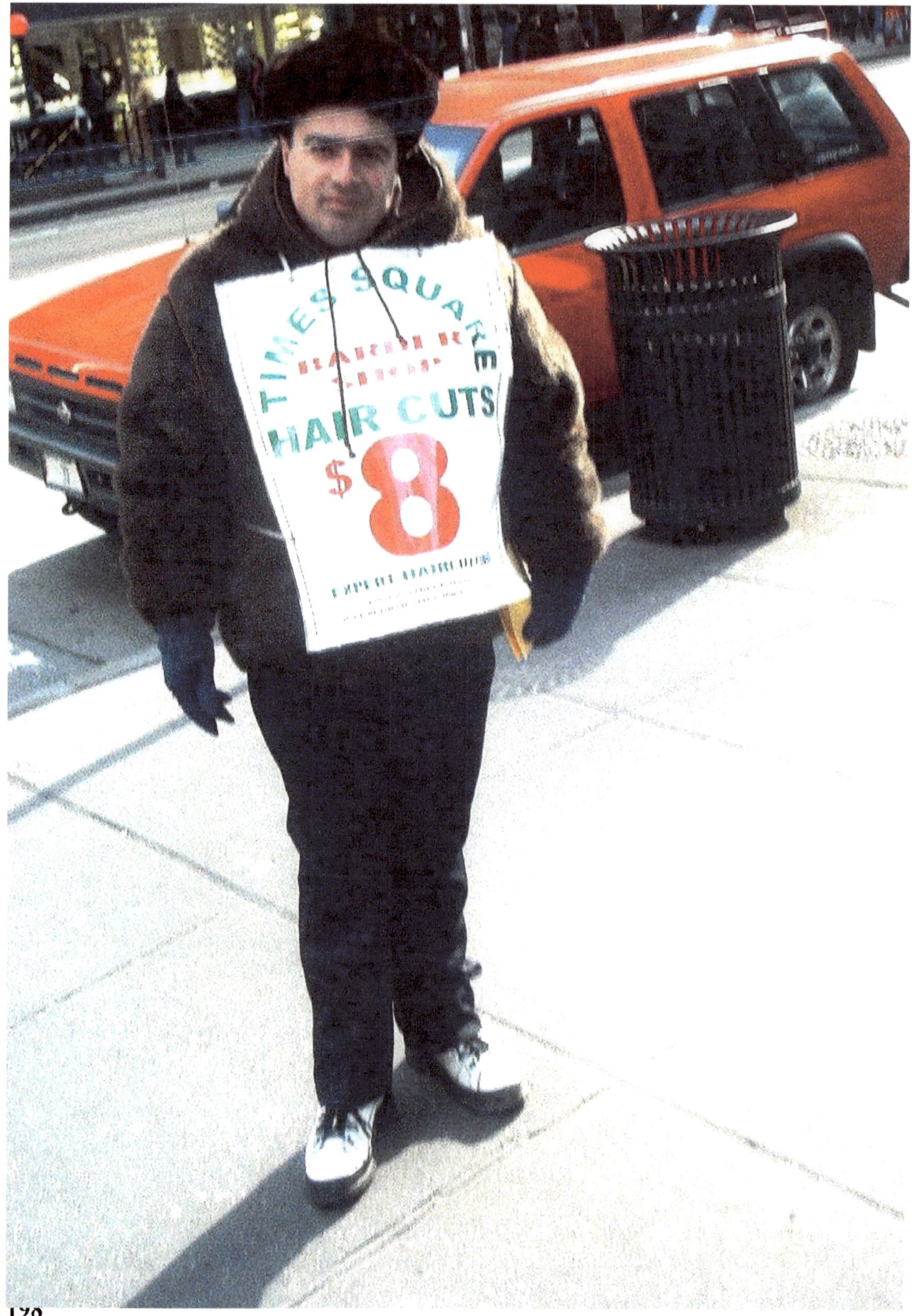
TIMES SQUARE
HAIR CUTS
$8

Surveillance Nation

Surveillance isn't always negative, as it can stop crime and terrorism. Unfortunately it can create digital trails of everything we do and every transaction we make... its just a matter of time before the IRS uses these to make sure we're all paying our *fair share* of taxes.

Forget the mark of the beast, drivers license photos will increasingly be used for facial recognition. Cameras catch us speeding and we're sent tickets in the mail. Emails, phone calls, mail and faxes are subject to surveillance. When we pay an outrageous tax bill, the IRS can deem our ability to pay suspicious and demand to know, *where the money came from!*

We're living in a police state... and its something rulers have always strived for... how else can they keep large numbers of people in line? When you think about it, what's the alternative... anarchy, or warlords -- not very appealing if you ask me! For the time being, just tweak the system and make it better, if that doesn't work, stronger action might be required!

We are *blessed* with a police state that protects *some of the people, some of the time...* in return we're constantly surveilled, with every move and transaction traceable. With 300 million people to manage, the best they can do is use ant colonies as their model. Between the popular media and our education system, we've become a fairly compliant herd. Meanwhile, the wizards behind the curtain still fear the masses who at any given time could rise up against their *masters*!

I'm noticing more and more women employed at security guards and it occurs to me that they're excellent at surveillance. Women are famous for *keeping an eye on things* and people... after all, how else would they know what shananigans their men are up to... or their kids for that matter!

We may be the most surveilled people in the world – between; phones and e-mail being monitored, surveillance cameras and nosey neighbors -- the government seems capable of finding out everything we do. On the positive side, they rarely seem to bother the average Joe... so if we know what's good for us, we'll remain average!

Think Tanks

Think tank names are such nonsense.... nothing but subterfuge and deception, designed to advance their members agendas, while sounding civilized, humanitarian and smarter than the rest of us. Here's a good one, "The Institute for Peace"... perhaps they should add the words, "on Our Terms."

The "expert" stated if you spend one dollar to fight hunger in sub-Saharan Africa, you have done $40 worth of social good... while one dollar spent on the Kyoto protocol does only 30 cents worth of social good.. I wonder how he *calculated* these numbers? Not only are the numbers ridiculous, one man's *social good* may also be another's *meddling* in someone else's business.

The "Center for public integrity"...an impressive sounding name for another special interest lobbying group.

If you are right about something, but violently force it on others, then even if you are right, you're wrong.

"Nonprofit" doesn't mean nonpartisan, although these organizations intentionally create confusion regarding their objectives. Nonprofit organizations often have extreme ideological agendas cloaked in a veil of faux-compassion.

"Committed to building a more just, verdant and peaceful world", is the foundation slogan, but I wonder for whom are they building it?

Here's another amusing think tank title... "Senior Fellow". These *fellows* may indeed be senior and even *scholarly*, but that doesn't mean they're anything but biased lobbyists. Simply members of elitist groups intent on reengineering society as per their *prescription*. Society could certainly use improvement, the question is whose vision of improvement will be promoted... the answer is, money talks!

There is no such thing as nonpartisan... When I hear a think tank described that way, I wonder who started it in the first place? Certainly the founders had a worldview didn't they? When they state their sole purpose is to help society I have to laugh. Certainly helping society is subjective and a think tank's agenda is inevitably biased in favor of its members and their agenda.

Time

“Time is a great teacher, but unfortunately it kills all its pupils”…Louis Berlioz

Time is something we have lots of when we’re young, and run out of when we’re old. In between, we waste this precious resource like there’s no tomorrow.

Ever notice very little happens in the short term, but everything, happens in the long run…everything is just a matter of time!

Haste makes waste whether you’re getting out of the shower or off of the freeway.

The problem with being efficient, is that it leads to haste, which leads to waste… or smashed fingers at the very least. So slow down, the boss isn’t worth injuring yourself over and you’ve all heard that thing about *what do you want your epitaph to be…* haven’t you?

These darn bills and all our work will still be here tomorrow… if your spouse is the “cause” of your rushing about, then lovingly stop doing it! My wife and I rush to make the bed single handedly thinking it will lead to bragging rights…more often it leads to a stubbed toe!

Boring as it sounds, the best antidote to *haste making waste*, is planning and preparation.

“Men talk of killing time, while time quietly kills them”…Dion Boucicault

Torture

"Charges of torture don't spill much beer down at the Legion Hall"... anonymous.

There are things we’ll allow to be done to others, that we’d never *allow* to be done to ourselves.

Newspeak... torture equals "enhanced interrogation" and *occupation* equals liberation.

I can't think of any one who doesn't think, "the ends justifies the means", when their loved ones, or their "way of life" is at stake.

Our system isn't that different from that of the middle ages when inquisitors tortured *heretics*. Now they prefer water boards to racks and thumbscrews. The dirty work is *contracted out* today, but it's still approved by the ruling class who's hands still don't get *dirty* in the process.

Aren't "Intelligence officers" the same guys referred to as inquisitors in the Middle Ages? They no longer burn people at the stake, but they're still very *persuasive!*

Our interrogators use; water boarding, beatings, stress positions, death threats, sleep deprivation, loud noises etc... but rarely do anything that "leaves a mark!"

After World War II, America prosecuted Japanese war criminals for water boarding American prisoners... so how's our Karma doing?

Despite being against torture, I wouldn't oppose it if a city was threatened with annihilation and we had the people who knew where the bomb was. On the other hand, to use torture as a *fairly routine* method of extracting information is sick and relatively ineffective. What *might* be effective, would be addressing the root causes of any of the wars you've declared, be it on; terror, drugs or poverty!

Now there's a "water board" thrill ride at the amusement park... isn't that nice.

Tradition

"Tradition is the dead governing the living"... Auguste Comte

Those with a vested interest in the status quo, have a vested interest in preserving the traditions they uphold and that sometimes hold others down!

Should we resist the *traditional* obligations foisted on us during the holidays and other times? To some extent we probably should, but we should realize that it's good to celebrate, to give thanks and share our bounty. What we should resist is the notion that others can and will determine any of the above for us… in other words, make up your own mind!

"Every generation laughs at the old fashions, but religiously follows the new"… Henry David Thoreau

Tribes and Natives

"We will drive them along with the wild beasts to the Rocky Mountains"… Thomas Jefferson

"All the tribes tell the same story. They are surrounded on all sides, the game is destroyed or driven away; they are left to starve, and there remains but one thing for them to do - fight while they can" … General George Crook

There are national tribes, nations of tribes, tribes of nations and nations of nations. That's what diversity is all about, if we become a world with only one tribe, diversity will be lost. Historically, some tribes excelled at business, others at sport or war and a few have largely sat on their butts. As the social engineers mold us into one tribe, which attributes will they nurture?

I'm not opposed to us being a nation, instead of a hodgepodge of tribes. What I'm opposed to, is bullying those countries that are tribal, instead of being a shining example to them. Human nature and national behavior being what it is…powerful nations don't enlighten tribes, they abuse them.

Tribal societies would be better off if they joined together to protect themselves against aggressor nations, but they rarely do. Nations with strong central governments, understand this weakness and take full advantage of it. Strong nations have the power to compel their bickering factions to come together for the "national good." Funny how the national good usually has something to do with the need to invade someone else.

The north was built on the bones of exterminated natives and exploited immigrants. In the south, the same occurred, but much of the work was

done by enslaved Africans. What goes up, must come down… no justice no peace… this just might be a law of nature.

It's arguable that some native tribes were barbaric and deserved "what they got", such as those that practiced human sacrifice. So instead of giving the conquistadors and pilgrims an F, maybe they deserve slightly better.

What is a nation other than a conglomeration of; clans and tribes joined together to be stronger than neighboring clans and tribes. A *united nation* can defend itself against its disorganized neighbors, or even make war and steal their resources. Ironically, tribes often outlive powerful nations, which eventually fall apart from within.

Personally I'd take tribes over nations, but understand the weakness of tribes when they're confronted by nations. Nations have greater numbers and organization, and go far beyond simple strategies like, "the enemy of my enemy is my friend." Nations believe in dividing and conquering tribes and history has shown it to be an effective way for great powers to get their way.

America has a lot of problems, but that doesn't mean we're finished. America has a long tradition of making lemonade out of lemons.... Americans are not to be trifled with, there are numerous *tribes* and nations that can attest to that.

You never know… maybe some day the Indian nations *will* return. They lost their land by force, doesn't that mean they have the "right of return?" On the other hand those who won land by conquest or paid for it with money believe they have title to it… so things could get messy some day. The Indians fought each other for land as well although I'm told their definition of ownership was different than ours. In the final analysis, land goes to the strong, every tribe, nation and race has killed and died for it and it is only possessed for as long as a people is strong enough to defend it.

With their natural resource wealth, the Indian tribes of the Americas might have been wealthy and could have prospered in whatever manner that they saw fit. Instead, lagging in the science of war and divided among themselves, they lost virtually their entire world.

Western nations developed war machines to defend themselves against all manner of *old world* aggressors. When they unleashed canon and ball on the native American's the eventual outcome was predictable…

Hearing "Waltzing Matilda" on the radio, I wonder why don't we hear more about the Aussies extermination of that country's natives? I don't know if they were any kinder than us... did the land support fewer natives in the first place? What's a billabong and a swagman anyway, and who was Matilda... hopefully not a Wallaby or Roo.

Truth, Lies and Videotape

"All great truths begin as blasphemies"...George Bernard Shaw

"Seeing is Just Seeing"... unknown

If two wrongs don't make a right, how can - three, four or five?

You know *this*, you know *that*, you're *all knowing*! I don't know much, but realize he who claims to know everything, doesn't know squat!

There is justice and there is *justice*...it is sometimes poorly defined, but those who are on the short end of it have a pretty good idea what they're missing!

The phrases "sitting on the fence" and "the truth lies somewhere in the middle" have a lot in common. Both phrases are used by the ideologues to recruit followers to fight for *their* agendas.

The powerful don't have to lie but they do... the weak feel they have to lie to survive, but that's debatable.

For the last time...what am I supposed to believe, your mouth or my eyes?

Lying with a straight face is an unfortunate quality that has helped humans get ahead for a million years. Whether its done to friend or foe, most humans are guilty of lying from time to time, and have reaped it's *rewards.*

On a related subject, what are actors other than convincing liars? Does that make Oscar winners, the biggest liars of all, or does that dubious distinction go to certain lawyers?

Is it wrong to always "do good", even when doing so might harm the innocent? On the flip side, we're told that sometimes you have to do harm in order to do good. In either case the law of unintended consequences often rears its ugly head.

If it's true that when a lie is repeated often enough people eventually except it is the truth, is the opposite also true?

Are we forced to lie, because telling the truth is sometimes more expensive? If so, is it wrong to lie in such cases? I'm thinking about returning things to the store, and lying to make the exchange easier...I haven't always done the right thing.

There is something wrong with our legal system if you can't enter into evidence the fact that a plaintiff or defendant has abused the legal system before, via frivolous lawsuits. If that information isn't relevant to a case than what is!

"Innocent until proven guilty"... to me, that sounds like it's a foregone conclusion that you'll be found guilty... shouldn't it be "innocent unless proven guilty?" It's a catch 22, just like *pleading the fifth* is often construed as an admission of guilt.

Meanwhile back at the ranch, our revolving door justice system is absurd... who would you rather see released back to society? A pot smoker who has never committed a violent crime, or a pedophile who has, or may commit murder? The chances of the pedophile being released may not be much lower than the pot smoker.

If you truly are a man of your word, you shouldn't have to advertise that fact... chances are, the word will get around.

What is integrity? It's easily defined if you look in the dictionary, but it's also in the eye of the beholder. A man believed to have integrity by some, can be considered a shyster by others. It depends on how he conducts himself on that occasion and even more so, what is the outcome for the parties involved. We're back to that old bell curve... no one's a paragon of virtue all the time!

One person's "worthy cause" is to someone else, an intrusion or invasion of privacy. The "beneficiary" of our well intended efforts may not even agree there is a *problem.* They're likely to consider outsiders *solving* their problems

to be the problem – not the solution. If you're going to interfere in the affairs of others, you'd better be darn sure you're right… and that's not easy to ascertain.

Beware…statements beginning with phrases like, "frankly speaking" and "honestly though" are often the preface to a lie.

I am happy to live in a nation of laws… by all means I prefer society of laws, as long as they are just and equitable – and therein lies the rub!

Peace and justice…it's like the old Campbell's *soup and sandwich* commercial…you can't have one, you can't have none, you can't have one without the other."…

You claim to never lie, so maybe you're telling half truths. What do two of them equal… a whole lie, or the truth?

"A foolish faith in authority is the worst enemy of truth"... Albert Einstein.

We believe so much of the nonsense we hear, because we desire *certain things* to be true. I'm thinking of things that are said so "authoritatively" on TV, radio and newspapers, as well as by friends and acquaintances. When something unsubstantiated, is presented in an authoritative tone to a willing audience, it's taken as the gospel truth. Everyone is feeding us lines, but what they say is merely *their* truth not *the* truth.

Another evolutionary adaptation that helps us maintain our sanity, is the refusal to accept the "truth" about certain things. You could also call it "eternal hope", but whatever it is, it helps us get through some pretty tough things.

Now they can determine via MRI and brain wave analysis if you're telling the truth. They claim it's more accurate than a polygraph, so why not use it in law enforcement? I have no beef with that… but like water boarding, will they eventually decide to use it on a routine and wholesale basis?

While it is possible that some people are almost always wrong, it's impossible that anyone alive is almost always right.

"Truth is not determined by a majority vote" - Cardinal Ratzinger

TV, Media and Movies

"The morning disinformation break"... anonymous

You know you've been away from home a long time, when you forget the numbers for the stations you regularly watch. It's confusing to try and remember two sets of numbers, one for your home town and one for a town you've spent a couple of weeks in.

If TV shows didn't have *laugh tracks* would we still think they're funny? I wish they'd let us decide for ourselves what we want to laugh at! So why do they have laugh tracks? An obvious reason is the producer's use of peer pressure to achieve their goals. We're encouraged to laugh along with our "peers", even though the *track* is nothing but canned laughter. If we enjoy the show, we'll tune in again and be influenced by the sponsors advertising. But there are also nefarious and sundry reasons for the laugh track...for example, the writers and producers use of TV shows to promote their world view. We're indoctrinated with their values and laughing along with the *track*, reinforces what's; hip, acceptable and proper. The more we laugh along with the *track*, the more likely we are to accept their world view and gradually discard the *antiquated* values we were raised with.

I've had my fill of Meerkats on the nature channels, they may be cute and interesting to some people, but I'll take Lions and Tigers and Bears any day! A couple more shows I'm getting tired of are Ice Road Truckers and Deadliest Catch... I don't want to see any more Crab legs -- unless they're on my plate.

When I hear the talk show hosts spewing their divisiveness, I'm turned off... but there "loyal followers" are even worse when they call in. Hopefully they're just trying to cozy up with the host and not as mean as they sound. The ironic thing is that pundits on both side will eventually be proven partially wrong, but it won't matter... they'll be forgotten and new generation of soothsayers will have replaced them. The cycle of rabblerousing that's been going on forever shows not sign of ever letting up!

Headlines are what we see on TV, newspaper and internet... these frame the debate, and whoever controls the headlines, controls the debate.

We have five different TV remotes in our house… half my brain is devoted to trying to remember where the "recall" and mute buttons are. Why won't they standardize these things!

Instead of being PO'd when commercials come on and having to surf, I should be grateful. Like the comedian said, it's not just *what's on* that we're interested in, it's *what else* is on!

Increasingly I watch the news to see the anchorwoman as much as to find out what's going on in the world.... funny thing is, the prettiest gals are on the business channels!

I wonder how many other guys are switching back and forth between Conan the Barbarian,and 20th Century Battlefield tonight?

We've gone from citizens eager to be informed and learn, to *subjects* content on being entertained… the result is we're indoctrinated with the cores beliefs of our masters.

I'm not watching quite as much news are before… after all, it's an endless account of who's bombing who and how many have been blown up. All I care about is when will it hit the fan and should I head north, south, east or west.

There I was rushing to finish by 6:30 so I could watch the evening news. Then it occurred to me…why risk falling off the roof, just so I can watch the daily propaganda session?

Some of the talking heads read the news to us like we're five-year-olds. It's part of the dumbing down process… their tone of voice sounds like elementary school teachers reading to their class!

Bloomberg has a brunette business babe during the time slot that Fox business features a beautiful blonde… is each targeting a specific market segment?

It's a slow news day, and that's good… fewer people have been laid off, or blown up!

Now days, there's a lot of "breaking" news... just not much "fixing" news.

The special offered by the cable company expires soon and I'll probably revert to the basic package. There'll be fewer channels to watch, so I'll have to settle for "inferior" programming... as if I'm not doing that already!

Two great inventions for obtaining accurate information are the scan button on a radio and the TV remote control. Without using them, you're just indoctrinated by one side or the other... if you park your eyes and ears on only one station, it will brainwash you.

I don't know which is worse... NPR or FOX…to many independents, they seem hugely biased, but to their core audiences, both are *fair and balanced*...hmmm?

You know they've been successful, when even pot smokers are for the war… apparently government and corporate media propaganda are more powerful than Cannabis!

It's difficult to divide and conquer, when people have good information. So they have to prevent access, control content, or divert people's attention with something more *entertaining*.

Not only do all three major networks cover the same news stories each evening, they also broadcast the same commercials... "ask your doctor about...and side effects may include a certain sexual blah, blah, blah!"

We're watching "A Night At The Museum" and despite the *latest* special effects, it's the same slapstick they fed us in the 1920s -- the sheeple are easily entertained.

Funny, I'm watching the infomercials at five in the morning and addition to penis enlargement, how to make a million and how to lose weight... there're commercials for growing hair on men and removing it on women!

Why is it that in the movies, they just wrap the horse's reins once around the hitching post? Wouldn't you lose a lot of horses that way?

Violence

"The man who strikes first admits that his ideas have given out"...Chinese Proverb

It's said that in societies where young people perform rites of passage to become adults, violence is reduced. We have few such rites, compelling our boys to prove their manhood by joining gangs, the military or just beating the crap out of each other.

Too time and energy is spent trying to *do something about* people, who we think are infringing on some aspect of our lives. No matter where you live, who you are or what time in history, people have always been at odds with each other. Too often *being at odds* escalates into violently *doing something about them.*

The average American is not a thug but our crime rate is higher than most developed countries. Our history is more violent than most countries and to often our society rewards aggression.

Voting

***"It's Not the People Who Vote that Count; It's the People Who Count the Votes"...* Josef Stalin**

Vote with your remote and speak with your keyboard!

Free people need iron clad constitutional guarantees as much as they need elections. Our rights were won by a revolution, not by votes and elections have robbed some Americans of more rights than foreign enemies... I hope it doesn't require another revolution to win them back.

I won't fight for your right to vote, I'm not sure I'd fight for my right to vote... but I will fight for our God given rights. Tragically, there are people determined to "vote" away the rights you have remaining.

They say you have to vote for someone, otherwise you shouldn't complain about the government. Does anyone else think that's but a cunning tactic to shame us into supporting an increasingly corrupt system? It reminds me of

the gang leader telling the gang member, "here you shoot him too… now you're one of us."

When I look at the major candidates, I wonder should we vote for the lesser of two evils, or not vote at all? For me, the answer is no vote, just tea in the harbor!

I'm criticized for not voting when I explain that nobody represents my views. Your advice is to vote for *the best of the worst* or keep my mouth shut. Adding insult to injury, you want to be sure I "throw away my vote" to the *right candidate*… namely yours!

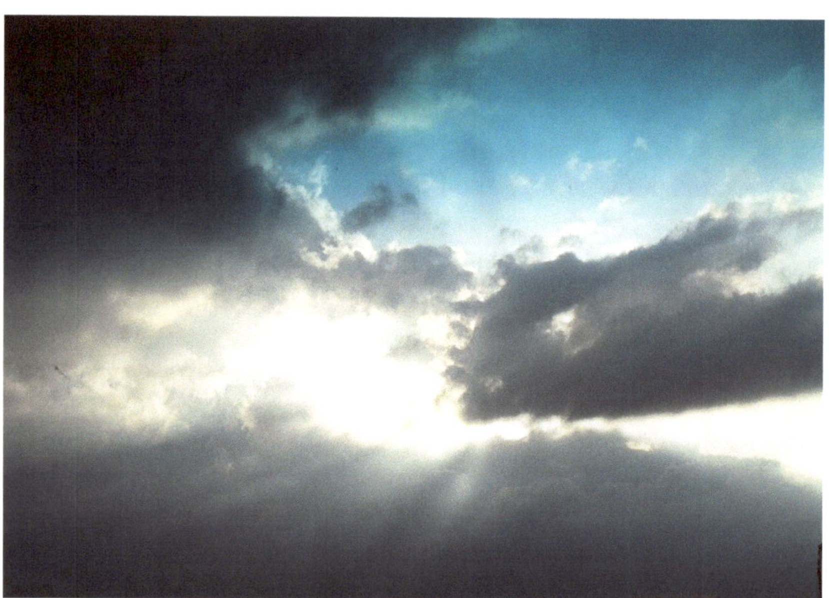

WWW

"The Internet is so big, so powerful and pointless that for some people it is a complete substitute for life"… Andrew Brown

With the net, you can discuss religion and politics anonymously, which is better than discussing them with friends… that's like shitting where you eat.

According to reports, Google has kept every search its users have ever done, and *may* be able to connect each one to whoever did the search via their IP

address. Through the Patriot act, the government can subpoena these, lawyers in general can do this as well… isn't that nice!

At the UN meeting on the future of the Internet they focused on how to get more poor people around the world "connected." Proponents say they are concerned with everyone having access to information, but I think they're more interested in selling *junk*. I hope these people don't mind losing their privacy and having every possible bit of information about them entered into the merchants databases.

"During my service in the United States Congress, I took the initiative in creating the Internet"… Al Gore quotes

Weeds and Gardens…

"Gardening requires lots of water -- most of it in the form of perspiration"… Lou Erickson

After it rains is the most productive time to pull weeds, they give up without a fight and you can devastate their ranks! Even so, after 15 minutes, it becomes apparent they're too many and in the end they will prevail. The weeds, with their allies the mosquitoes overwhelm me and I must retreat.

I put on heavy gloves and trim the garden-variety rosebushes in our yard. I chuckled while carrying the prickly canes to the fire pit and thought, "you guys are a joke!" Compared to the wild "Roses" at the farm that puncture tractor tires on a regular basis, these "domestic" rosebushes are Pansies.

I would like to grow a garden with plump tomatoes and pretty flowers… but first I must kill the weeds!

What's prettier, the flowers blooming in the spring, or the trees turning colors in the fall? As far as I'm concerned it's a beautiful tie!

The Cottonwood seeds land by the thousands creating a mess on my deck and in the hot tub, but I sweep them up. Thousands also land on the grass, where the *weed and feed* kills them. Unfortunately, hundreds of them successfully sprout in various nooks and crannies, guaranteeing a new generation of this annoying species!

Scots **must be desperate, their new commercial features a young man killing the dandelions because he "doesn't want to be a bad neighbor." I've noticed that in this down economy, dandelions are going crazy all over the city... people must be buying less weed and feed. Scots' knows this, thus their desperate appeal using guilt and peer pressure. Guess it works, I went out and bought weed and feed, but it was the store brand, Scots was too expensive!**

If **there's anything** ***nice*** **thing about weeds, it's that the more successful they are, the harder it is for them to hide. There's no reason to rush out and spray everything that's sprouting. Wait a week or two until you can tell the flowers from the weeds and then deal with them!**

Weeds are smart, you have to crawl through the brambles to pull them by their roots... brilliant! Later, while cutting the grass the weeds have positioned themselves too far under the bushes to mow them down. To attack, I'd have to dismount and pull them by hand… that's too much effort!

Even Mother Nature assists the weeds, as I pull wild vines off the Wegia, dropping the red weed seeds in a bucket, the wind comes up and blows them under the bush. Next year a whole new pesky crop will sprout! Even if I could accomplish the nearly impossible task of removing all the vines and berries, the birds would ***pitch in*** **and poop them all over the place! Nature is one vast conspiracy against mankind, no wonder we have struggled against "Mom" since time immemorial.**
I've struggled against the wind to keep the little Pine tree upright for three years. It's currently supported by seven wires and looks like something out of Guliver's Travels.

Trimming the Lilac I feel like ***Edward Scissor Hands*****, occasionally stepping back to appraise my work, then moving in to continue the** ***haircut…*****later my dear wife, who requested the trim job not only forgot about it, she couldn't even tell it had been trimmed!**

This should be an ideal time to knock down that Hornets nest... if I get stung a few times I'll have an excuse for not going to ballroom dancing class! On the other hand it's important to my wife that we attend, so I must be careful. Ever since they stung me after accidentally jostling a box next to it, we've been a war! I relentlessly persecute them , so far spraying three cans of pesticide into the nest - they're greatly weakened, but not dead yet!

Sitting in the hot tub looking at the yard, its Arborvitae, fruit trees and the rest, I'm reminded that I'll enjoy it for just a few years, while *this spot* - in one form or another will be around "forever."

Mulch has become ubiquitous, thirty years ago it was rare... now it's available in endless types and colors... we can't seem to live without it!

I don't mind cutting both the front and back yards... it's no secret I end up doing less work that way. Every time my wife cuts the yard, she finds things that need to be trimmed, planted, sprayed or God forbid mulched!

I'm not trying to get an A+ on my lawn ... they don't give prizes for perfection!

I ran over the Apple with the mower and to my surprise, instead of being squashed as usual... it emerged nicely peeled!

This year, I'm not pulling many weeds, I'm just spraying them, I figure my back has *just so many* bends left...its time to start rationing them.

Once again I am outside spraying the weeds in our yard, it's a losing battle, but one I engage in each spring. No matter what the cost in plant life and treasure, we must strive to make the yard look like the neighbors yard... only better. As usual, many flowers are falling to friendly fire... they're young, innocent, and as in any war a certain amount of collateral damage is "acceptable."

Spring has arrived and I hear the sound of lawn mowers *singing* through the neighborhood. I guess its time to fire my engine, be a *good neighbor and* cut the grass!

Winter Take all!

"In the winter it was luge lessons, in the summer we'd make meat helmets"... Dr. Evil

It's just mid-November, and I've already seen two pickup trucks with snowplows attached to their front ends. Either these guys are eternal optimists, or they know something the weatherman doesn't.

"When worms come out of the ground in winter, an earthquake is imminent", says a Japanese legend. In a thousand years, we may also know precisely when a quake is coming and that will be wonderful. Perhaps quakes will become minor annoyances, or even opportunities to go out and *play in the quake* like it's a thrill ride.

I wouldn't mind spending winters in; Florida, California or Arizona, but one thing they don't have, is the incredibly crisp cold winter air... I like it!

As I get dressed for some winter chores, I see ant spray on the shelf and think … I'd rather deal with summer problems than winter ones any day!

One of the nice things about shoveling a long driveway covered with a foot of snow, is you might lose a couple pounds in the process... that's if you don't die of a heart attack!

I'm becoming like the retirees in the neighborhood, they shovel or snow blow their driveways to perfection. I'm just trying to get a little fresh air and exercise, since cabin fever's a problem on these frigid days and indoor air is not the answer.

Finally I'm done shoveling and like a kid who's made a snowman, I stand back to admire my work. There should be some way to *sign* this Picasso, although like a snow castle, it will be gone in no time. I look around for some way to finish it with a flair, and decide to widen the mouth of driveway, as that's where we usually get stuck. Makes me wonder if surgeons sign their *work…* or would they even want to? Heck, my surgeons always say *everything went perfectly*, when in fact they each time they've screwed up. They'd have to be nuts to put their *John Hancock* on me… I can only imagine what they've left inside me!

I want my driveway to look perfect, but don't the neighbors to think I'm obsessed, so I leave a few streaks of snow and ice… imperfection mean I'm normal!

Despite my *occasional* sarcasm, I'm pleasantly surprised to see good Samaritans out and about using their trucks to pull complete strangers out of ditches were they've slid... free of charge at that!

Technique wise, it's a lot easier if you have an ergonomically designed snow shovel and push the snow downhill. I found such a shovel about five years ago in the middle of the street and it's the best one I've ever had. Don't worry about getting your driveway perfect if you're shoveling, that's for guys with snow blowers. I'm just trying to make it possible for the letter carrier to get through with that box of cigars I ordered!

Shoveling, like other physical pursuits can be quite enjoyable… just don't overdo it or you'll get the proverbial hernia or heart attack. If you do it in moderation, it's good exercise and you're accomplishing something productive at the same time. Finally, consider it an *open ended* activity – don't expect to ever finish because it's just going to snow again.

Inevitably, the County plow comes by and seals every driveway on the block in with a three foot snow drift snow. Maybe they're doing us a favor, keeping us off the street since we really shouldn't be driving under these conditions unless like the TV anchorman says, it's "absolutely necessary."

I hope no one saw me using my Tucson as a snow plow… it wasn't a complete debacle, nor was it a success.

The second big snowstorm of the year has arrived, and my shoveling standards have diminished considerably. It's debatable whether or not I'll want to stand back and admire my work this time… this time it will be *quick and dirty.*

Then the third major storm hits and shoveling is a drag… this time the snow's wet, heavy and killing me! After two hours I can finally see the light at the end of the tunnel, but there's still another ton of snow to remove.

As my herniated body cries out in pain, I'm reminded that it's only $ 50 to hire a plow, versus a $ 3,000 deductible and three months to recover if I require another surgery! Regardless, I shovel on, after all, I need the exercise after gaining ten pounds over the holidays… yikes, is that what they call penny wise and pound foolish?

After shoveling the driveway for seventeen years, I still hit the same expansion cracks and the shovel gouges me in the stomach… some things never change! You'd think by now I'd see them coming and change the angle of the shovel in time.

It's 22 below with the wind chill, but it feels great in the hot tub, where the house protects me from the wind. We've had over a foot of snow in the last two weeks and I've been re-filling the hot tub with shovelfuls of snow! Today I've thrown in some great big chunks of ice, 10 pounders at least – they look like icebergs floating in the ocean… all I need is a rubber ducky, or a toy boat to have some real fun.

It's a cold morning indeed, the kind when wet flesh freezes instantly to metal. Each of the last three days, while climbing out of the hot tub, my leg touched the fire pit and I've lost a layer of skin… ouch!

Those of us in the snow belt get pretty good with a shovel or snow blower, and we're proud of our work. It's the same in the summer with the mower, we like to look at the lines…the straighter the better! We refine our technique and compare our work to the neighbors... however when we move south, very few of us miss the shoveling!

An era has ended … after fifteen years, the hot tub has bit the dust and I can't replace it. Now, I soak in the garden tub and enjoy the winter wonderland though the bathroom window… not a bad deal!

The rest of the family doesn't like Indiana in the wintertime, they say it's gray and gloomy. I don't find it that way at all... of course that's in comparison to Baghdad and Kabul!

Wisdom

"The next best thing to being wise oneself is to live in a circle of those who are" …
C.S. Lewis

A philosopher might be more profound, but a comedian is more popular. We'd rather hear funny stories than *wisdom*… after all, don't we have that subject covered? Not to mention, philosophy often *is* a joke and comedy can be first class philosophy!

Obviously it's more difficult to do something great than something average, or nothing at all … but that shouldn't stop us from trying.

Wisdom is usually common and un-common sense combined. It's also equally *distributed* between both brilliant and ordinary folks.

Wisdom and intellect overlap, but aren't the same... the lucky ones come with a measure of both.

Thinking about things too much is like anything else... after awhile you reach the point of diminishing returns.

The wise man gives but scant advice, the fool heeds even less!

"It is the province of knowledge to speak, and it is the privilege of wisdom to listen."
Oliver Wendell Holmes

Work

"My father taught me to work; he did not teach me to love it"... Abraham Lincoln

Funny.,. the more I work, the more I need to work!

Some things never change... you still get paid more for exercising your brain than for breaking your back!

Behind most of the comforts we enjoy, are men and women with dirty nails and bloody knuckles... they deserve our respect!

Most of the *working stiffs* I've known suffer from the double whammy of substance abuse and minimal education. They spend thousands on drugs, alcohol and cigarettes while working at low-paying jobs. Forget about getting ahead...how can they keep up? They make vital contributions to society, but their lifestyle also can make them more of a drain on *the system* than other people.

Whether they know it or not, low paid workers have the ability to improve the lives... unfortunately many of them never do. In fact some blame society and few admit that getting the monkey off their back is their responsibility.

There's a bell curve related to *Working stiffs*... at one end are *temporarily* down and out skilled craftsmen, while at the other are people with no marketable skills, nor drive to attain them.

If you like your job and it pays well, you're ahead of the pack...most of us have jobs we hate, that don't even pay the bills!

"Nothing is more reliable than a man whose loyalties can be bought with hard cash" ...Boris Balkan

Work for a living, is like hunting... to feed the family, don't aim for Rabbits... shoot for Moose!

Like most folks, I live for the weekend, anxiously waiting for it to arrive... during the week, I just try to survive the rat race.

If you tell someone they've *done a great job*, they'll let up and things will go down hill fast. Whether it's a waiter, contractor or your kid...don't praise them exceeding, it just leads to trouble.

It's a lie to tell clients I have five employees and I'm not proud of it ... can we leave it at that, or are you going to keep beating me up? I could construct a reasonably good defensive, but I'd rather not. Some businessmen lie, others exaggerate...admittedly or not, many make misrepresentations when we "have to."

Actually, I think we're just looking for the easiest way of making a sale. Any lie resides somewhere on the bell curve...some may be worse, but they are all misrepresentations. We justify lying, by saying or thinking that we cannot feed our families grass, nor can we live on the sidewalk. That not withstanding, any salesmen feel's better when he's made an "honest" sale.

Never underestimate the destructive force of a Monday... there're will be fires to extinguish and grief to face!

Driving home after eight appointment, I am exhausted and wonder, *why am I doing this!?* Is it to pay the bills, or to afford things we don't even need? If I eke out a subsistence level lifestyle, will I be any less exhausted... chances are I won't, the problems will just be magnified!

How many of us, by fate, events or circumstance end up not living the life we expected to?

It's 8:00 am, I'm walking the hood and have been up since 4:00, but have I done anything productive? It depends on how you define it... I know I've been trying to!

Sometimes we're efficient, sometimes we're not, but most people strive to become better. Others are inefficient, make no attempt to become so, and expect the rest of society to pay their tab and make up their slack.

I've made dozens of cold calls for appointments - now like a hunter who has set a snare in the woods, I sit back to see what I'll catch... if anything!

You must force *certain* words out of your mouth to make things happen. If the words don't come, the desired outcome won't either. If you never *specifically* ask for the sale, you'll almost never get it...even if you're the foremost expert on the product.

You begrudge us a week vacation in Florida, but idolize the Wall Street gangsters making $ 600 million a year... meanwhile you languish in squalor. You've swallowed their crapola – hook, line and sinker.

When somebody pushes you hard to work at a frenetic pace, compromising your safety in order to enrich them, turn the tables and slow down instead. You'll kill two birds with one stone... not only are you telling them you won't be their slave, you're also reminding *yourself* that you're free and will not be exploited. Rushing about at someone else's bequest is when you're most likely to whack your elbow, stub your toe... or worse.

I'm like the guy in the movie "Office Space"... unmotivated that is. Why should I work harder, when it just means I'll pay more taxes and people will find more ways to spend it.

"You can't make someone understand something if their salary depends on them not understanding it"... Upton Sinclair

Writing

"There is nothing to writing. All you do is sit down at a typewriter and bleed"… Ernest Hemingway

Despite having a cynical streak, I believe in taking chances, and trying to leave the world a better place than it was when we arrived.

If you can't be cryptic, at least be vague and enigmatic... what?

If I was a writer in Iraq or Iran, I'd have to fear the knock on the door in the middle of the night. Here, for the most part, all I have to fear is being ostracized by friends and family… our system is much better, but not perfect enough to should rest on our laurels.

It's therapeutic to journal and good to edit our work in hopes of getting published. Editing encourages us to rethink our opinions, but we shouldn't water them down too much in an effort to appeal to a broader audience.

If you're writing for 1% of the population, you have to accept that 99% will not take kindly to you.

Just as people who talk all the time waste a lot of time, people who write *constantly* are wasting their time. You have to listen, read or *view* to absorb useful information.

I keep hearing that the Internet is allowing huge numbers of people to become authors... well maybe they are becoming "authors", but that doesn't mean anybody is reading their work.

One of the reasons I stopped smoking, was that I thought it was holding me back them accomplishing my goal of becoming a writer. Now almost 15 years later, I still have not accomplished that goal... does that mean I should start smoking again… I don't think so.

What's worse for a writer, being discredited or being unknown? I think the latter is worse, as being discredited can "come and go." If there's anything good about being unknown, its that you aren't discredited… yet.

Writers are always trying to make sense of the world they live in and there're plenty of resources available to help. There're holy books, science, observation and experience, but even with these, we never *really* figure out what the heck's going on.

Should authors write things that; burst bubbles, raise questions and destroy fantasies? I'd say for the most part *yes*, but some believe - if you don't have anything nice to say, don't write anything at all.

Don't state the obvious… if something's obvious, let readers recognize it themselves, only if they miss the point should it be explained.

Every once in a while, you'll change some one's mind…more often, we have to be *content* with chronicling the world around us.

Writing is often a reaction and backlash against that which we do not like… it's also as necessary as breathing!

The written word can reach a large audience *if* you get published, which is no easy task. The spoken word reaches a smaller audience, but is less subject to editorial manipulation and rejection. In this country, you can still stand on a street corner and rant… at least a few people might hear you!

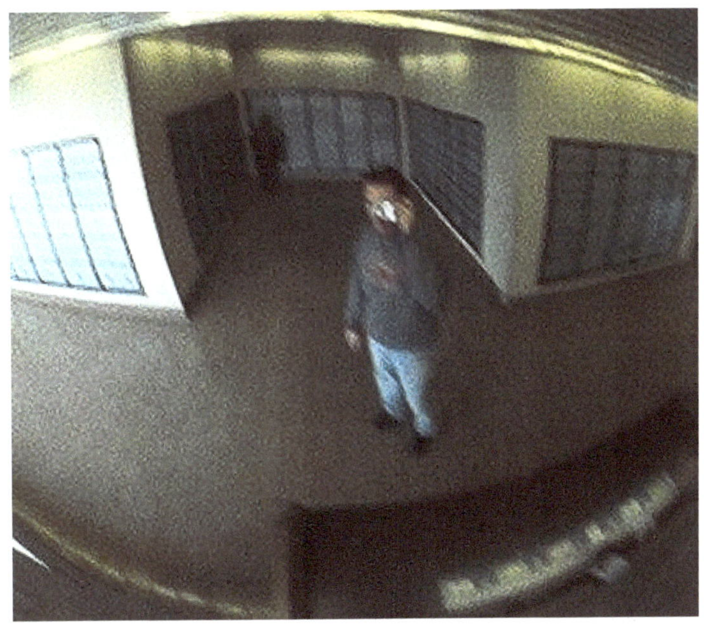

If what I write appears to be negative, I would counter that I am writing negative about the negative, and a negative times a negative equals a positive… right on!

Every time we edit our work, it becomes more watered down... eventually it means nothing whatsoever.

I'm not sure there's anything completely original within these pages… like anything else, others have arrived at similar conclusions based on their own experiences.

Editors, literary agents and publishers are censors, even more than they are marketers and promoters. If they don't like, agree with, or think they'll profit - they tell you to get lost!

When I was young I *wasted* my time daydreaming, now I waste it writing.

The only way I can avoid putting my foot in my mouth, is by keeping it permanently shut. Otherwise, everything I say *can and will* be used against me... but no one's prying my mouth open, this darn tongue just wags too much!

Read Kurt Vonnegut's obituary, enjoyed his wit and saved the newspaper for weeks, wanting to show the kids some of his quotes. I never found the "right time" to show it to them and like newspapers often do, it ended up a drop cloth.

If I complain, it's meant to encourage people to do something positive. Leaving *well enough alone*, leads to things falling apart, be they ideals or sky scrapers… it's a law of nature.

I write because it's one of the few things that doesn't feel like flipping burgers… not that I have anything against burgers.

If a guy can't get his point across in a hundred pages, then what's the use? That being said… I've exceeded the limit and will continue to as long as I possibly can!

About the Author

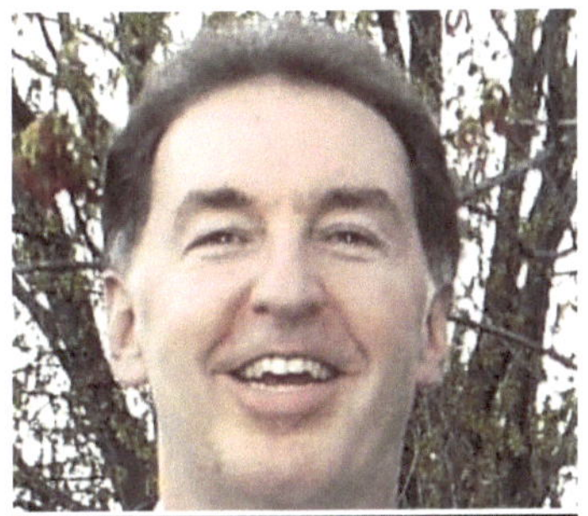

A New Jersey native, Ken Omar Eldib is a graduate of Oklahoma State University. In 1988, he started Global Trade Consulting, a company that provides market research to companies from around the world. He has seen much of America, as well as; Canada, Mexico, Europe, UK, Japan, Korea, Australia, the West Indies and Egypt several times. Ken has written numerous pieces for business magazines and has spoken publicly.

www.ingramcontent.com/pod-product-compliance
Lightning Source LLC
LaVergne TN
LVHW070117110826
845147LV00002B/141

9780966559835